AFFIRMATION and REALITY

Fundamentals of Humanistic Existential Therapy and Counseling

William V. Ofman, Ph.D.

Affirmation and Reality

Library of Congress Catalog Card Number: 76-46878
International Standard Book Number: 0-87424-304-1

FOREWORD

In humanistic existentialism Dr. William Ofman has found a radically free and open approach to psychotherapy and counseling. In it he has found the springboard for a bold reassessment of the problems of both the helper and the to-be-helped. Humanistic existentialism, as Ofman uses the term, refers first and most specifically to that view of human reality and of the individual's existential situation which may be found in the work of Jean-Paul Sartre. But while *Affirmation and Reality* adopts a Sartrean orientation, it is far more than an application or extension of Sartre's ideas. Ofman offers suggestions for a therapy which borrows richly from recent writings by humanistic psychologists; he finds much in R.D. Laing which is congenial, some in gestalt therapy, a little in the less doctrinaire writings of neo-Freudians. By the end of the book, humanistic existentialism refers to a synthesis of ideas which, along with many original insights from the author himself, constitutes Ofman's own unique approach to therapy.

Somewhat paradoxically, this humanistic existentialism seeks to find the individual *via* the universal. Like most humanistically oriented psychologists, the author recognizes that by definition all psychological study is reflexive since the human investigator has human being as his object. On the one hand, this leads him into that region where boundaries between psychology and philosophy tend to disappear. All existentialist psychologists insist that what is most significantly human will not be found in those areas where the person may be studied in the same way as any other animal or any scientific object. Ultimately the personal problems that are the most serious and the most difficult to solve may be those stemming directly from our existential situation. Ofman is thoroughly committed to the notion that the therapist's *Weltanschauung,* his overall philosophical beliefs—or over-beliefs as William James used to call them—will profoundly influence his attitude toward a patient or client. Therefore it is imperative that he should take the time to formulate and to examine these beliefs; he should not delude himself into feeling that in therapy a sophisticated scientific training is adequate protection against an infantile philosophical overview.

There is another aspect to Dr. Ofman's professional reflexivity. While recognizing that absolute impersonality is an illusion, that one's personal convictions are bound to affect any situation, he is acutely aware of the dangers of manipulating others. In building upon Sartre's declaration of the radical freedom of the human person, Dr. Ofman pledges himself to protect the freedom of those who seek his help. He envisions the therapeutic encounter neither as a teaching session nor as a confession hour in which the therapist himself stays uninvolved. Rather it is "a philosophical undertaking between two persons, each struggling to be real-beings." To attempt to change a person, he says, is to attempt to destroy his or her reality. It is to increase the violent affront to his or her sense of self which brought the person to the therapist in the first place. The counselor's task is to help another to perceive the nature of his basic orientation in the world. This is Sartre's "choice of being," which Ofman refers to as "the personal myth" by which each one of us lives. If the one who comes for counsel is troubled, this is because there are contradictions in the basic choice or because it involves disagreeable unforeseen consequences. The choice itself is the best one that he knew how to make, and he has made it for persuasive and excellent reasons. Ofman will not attack or even judge it. He will simply try to help the other to see it. The *other* may decide what to do about it.

In short, each one of us lives in a private world. There exists no one impersonal right world into which we might drag the mentally ill willy-nilly and force a cure upon them. Because Ofman, like Sartre, holds that the human being is a self-making process, he finds no given factors to render self-change impossible. Ofman has abandoned what I myself like to call the "acorn theory of the self," a controlling concept which, at least since Aristotle, has led individuals to lead their lives as if there were some absolute kernel of fixed potentialities determining both what one can and what one ought to do and be. For the ideal of "being oneself," existentialism has substituted that of "coming to the self" in a continuous search for new possibilities. It is only when the therapist believes that those who seek his help truly have this power of self-creation that he can effectively offer his services. But he must respect this capacity as well as recognize that it exists. He must not so exploit it as to turn it in the direction which the therapist has decided is good for his client. Ofman recognizes the danger that even too much trust in the therapist may become a device in bad faith for the client to escape the responsibility of a self-making.

Affirmation and Reality is a helpful introduction to current thought by psychologists with an existentialist orientation. It is a valuable development of possibilities inherent particularly in the philosophy of Sartre. Most of all, it is an illuminating and sensitive report on the reflections and self-questionings of a professor of psychology who is also a therapist, of one who finds the people who come to him for consultation worthy of the best that he or anyone else can help them discover for themselves.

Hazel E. Barnes
University of Colorado

PREFACE

You ought to know something about me at the outset. I hope you will know more about me at the end of this book. What can I tell you that will be meaningful? I can tell you that I want you to know what I have written; I know it has been important to me, and people tell me the ideas and ways that I have written about have been helpful and important to them. The people I speak about are students, persons who come for help (commonly called "clients"), and those intimates of mine who have dared themselves with me and with whom I have dared to be known.

I can tell you that my becoming a psychologist almost killed me, and though it has been 12 years since I earned my doctorate in psychology, I am still trying to get over my education. It wasn't that the work was difficult; it was more the constant violations of me as a person and the arrogance of the power of the academicians that was so very hard. It was not sufficient that I know what they wanted me to know. They wanted me. They wanted me to believe as they did. It is interesting to note that most of my confreres who were my graduated contemporaries and who now teach and/or are private practitioners as I am harbor a great deal of anger about their graduate education. Whenever we come together, we still speak of it. It is not so much that we look back in anger, but that we see so much of the same arrogant "education" happening. It took all we had to maintain our integrity, and when we spoke out, they questioned us.

It is interesting to me that Sartrean thought is relatively unknown in the counseling and psychology departments in the United States. Admittedly, it is difficult. Reading *Being and Nothingness* is an adventure in self-encounter with ignorance and trial. There is so much to know, so much to consider, so much to face in oneself.

What else can I tell you? I want you to know that writing does not come easily to me. I seem to do better speaking spontaneously to someone. I want you to know that often I feel like a stranger; the more in touch I am with myself and others—with my feelings—the more hurt there is. Often I feel that life was not made for humans, but it is the only life there is. I believe the only way to live one's death is to grasp at it with great clarity, to stand for oneself.

I want you to know that I am influenced by many and by none—that others have written importantly and beautifully, and that is one reason for my having quoted shamelessly. I want you to know what I have learned from my students, my children, my wife, my parents, and, importantly, from my clients who have had the courage to challenge every preconceived notion I held and hold. They are the courageous ones. They struggle to see and to maintain their presence and are willing to suffer their selfhood. I am often proud to share that vision with them. I often cry.

I believe that what I have written represents me now (1976). Who knows what I'll know tomorrow?

I know this:

אהיה אשר אהיה

(I am what I am).

I dedicate this book to Yoshka, Paula, Sheesh, Lisa, Josh, and Lana— and the Golden Peacock.

W.V.O.

Contents

Introduction

This is a book about the most serious of topics: the area of human endeavor that deals with helping relationships. It deals less with techniques, methods, strategies, or games, than with ways of looking at and thinking about the basic nature of human transactions. To attend to a summary of theories, approaches, or systems, or to a tissue of techniques seems to me to be indelicate. We are, after all, dealing with persons who are found in schools, colleges, universities, clinics, private offices and hospitals.

I believe that the helping person—a counselor or therapist—needs a fundamental, thorough grounding in how to think deeply about persons, the way they are, and the way they have become what they have become. That is not easy, but nothing less will do. The training of the various helping persons does not seem to include a sound grounding in philosophy, in the questions that relate to the basic nature of man—questions that transcend the issue of technique or of school. The result is the latching onto numerous psychotherapeutic fads.

My intent in this work is not to present yet another new system, but rather to describe a way of looking at persons and at the helping process that is foreign to the United States with its very strong pragmatic and empiricist tradition. Existentialism is a moist subject for most Americans, and it is rarely thought of as having relevance to academic psychology. Recently, it has been adopted in a glib and facile fashion by humanists who emphasize choice and responsibility in their work, but there has been no systematic presentation of a humanistic existentialist position, save in the work of Hazel Barnes (1959, 1967). There have been theistic existentialist writings based upon Heidegger's concepts, however, that have found their way into psychological and psychiatric literature (Tillich, 1952; Spiegelberg, 1972; Van den Berg, 1955, 1972; Colm, 1966; Sonnemann, 1954; Lyons, 1973; Keen, 1970; Frankl, 1963; Allers, 1961; and Boss, 1963).

What I have tried to do is to present a humanistic-existentialist (HE) view of persons and of the helping process. The effort addresses itself to any person who identifies himself with the helping process: the guidance worker in the school, the counselor, the counseling psychologist, the psychologist, the marriage counselor, the social worker, the pastoral counselor—in short, the therapist.

Chapter 1 lays the philosophical and theoretical foundations of the humanistic existentialist (HE). It attempts to bring together the difficult and scattered ideas in the literature and to present them in a cogent and unified fashion. Humanistic existentialism is contrasted with other existentialist positions to acquaint the reader with fundamental existentialist concepts.

Chapter 2 inspects the feeling or emotional aspects of man's existence. The major focus here is to contrast the HE view of man with the psychoanalytic and scientismic views. Here the concept of the unconcious is analyzed with all of its implications for counseling and psychotherapy, and alternative views are offered. There is also an exploration of dialectic science, and finally, a theory of feeling and emotion is offered that can account for human events as they are seen from the HE purview.

In Chapter 3, the HE conception of man is contrasted with that held by B.F. Skinner and the behaviorists.

The basic intent in Chapter 4 has been to compare the HE way of thinking about human *relationships* (and the therapeutic relationship specifically) with other conceptions. Finally, a radical nonchange approach to the helping process is presented—an approach that I believe is fully an outgrowth of the HE view of man, an approach that is fully homeoergic and committed to clarity, reality, and authenticity. The reader who is disinterested in theory but interested in the implications of the HE view on practice may want to skip from Chapter 1 to Chapter 4.

Two other points: I have quoted extensively because I believe that others have said things much better than I, and because they have understood and conceived of transactions better than I. Secondly, I have presented some transcribed tape-recordings of actual therapeutic transactions. They stand as they were tape-recorded save for changes in names and events, because people often speak about what they do in very different terms from what they actually do.

In closing, let me share an anecdote with you. A therapist (who was a client) came and reported that he had achieved a great triumph:

Pt: I believe that now I have withdrawn the judgmental process from others, they no longer control my behavior by their judgments. I now think only about my own good feelings about myself.

Th: What if you didn't even give that a thought?

Pt: You mean, not even thinking about feeling good about myself?

Th: Maybe.

Pt: Here, I thought I had fiddled with the introjected other, the judge.

Th: Maybe, just maybe Man, you and I, are not fit objects for judgment at all, either judgment by others, or by ourselves. Without judgment, reality exists.

1
The Humanistic Existentialist View of Man

An ontological approach in psychological theory can begin to straighten out this situation by seeing the essential similarity as our common ontological question (What does it mean that I am?) and by seeing the peripheral differences among men as our various answers, as expressed in our thought, feeling, and behavior. Men are born into a question. The answer is not thought or felt; it is lived. One's living is one's answer (Keen, 1972 p. 115).

In recent years, existentialist thought has been receiving increasingly greater attention from counselors, psychologists, and psychiatrists—in general, those persons called therapists, whose major concern is dealing with people who come to them for help with problems in their lives. The powerful influence of existentialist thought on educators and clinicians is evident in the proliferation of writing about and identification with the existentialist movement in journals and books and at professional meetings of counselors, professors of counseling, and psychotherapists of every theoretical persuasion. Bugental (1965) has aptly described the very good reasons for existentialism's appeal to the helping professions. We have, in our age, idolized technology and attempted to simplify the cause-and-effect relationships among events. General academic psychology has often mirrored this focus in its attempts to make man understandable in terms of animal urges or in terms of simple stimulus-response connections—connections that are, ultimately, rooted in a mechanical model of the "human machine." Humanistic existentialism (HE) stands firmly against the position that views man as a sophisticated computer, a complex rat, or an advanced naked ape; it stands against the notion redolent in current psychological theory that pushes the person into an ever more peripheral position; and it stands against the depersonalization inherent in behavioristic views of man such as those expressed in Skinner's work (1971).

In current social-psychological and educational literature, man is too often viewed as a commodity to be treated, influenced, taught, used, or manipulated in ways useful to the dominant social system. Neither the scientist nor the clinician remains neutral in this enterprise.

How does the psychiatrist confront the so-called mental patient or those in-criminated as mentally ill? How does he respond to their claims, and to the claims of those who, because of their relationship to the patient, have an interest in his condition? Ostensibly, the psychiatrist behaves as the medical scientist he claims to be is supposed to behave—by remaining "dispassionate" and "neutral" with respect to the "mental diseases" he diagnoses; and tries to "cure." But what if these "diseases" are, as I claim, largely human conflicts and the products of such conflicts? How can an expert help his fellow man in con-flict and remain aloof from the conflict? The answer is that he can't. Thus while ostensibly acting as neutral scientists, psychiatrists are actually *the partisan advocates of one party to a conflict* and the opponents of another [emphasis supplied]. As a rule, when the psychiatrist is faced with minor ethical and social conflicts, such as "neurotic patients" often present, he actually supports the patient's self-defined interests (and opposes the interests of those with whom the patient is in conflict), whereas, when the psychiatrist is faced with major ethical and social conflicts, such as "psychotic patients" often present, he actu-ally opposes the patient's self-defined interests (and supports the interests of those with whom the patient is in conflict). However—and this is the point I wish to emphasize here—in both instances psychiatrists habitually conceal and mystify their partnership behind a cloak of therapeutic neutrality, never ad-mitting to being either the patient's ally or his adversary. Instead of friend or foe, the psychiatrist claims to be doctor and scientist. Instead of defining his intervention as helping or harming, liberating or oppressing the "patient," the psychiatrist insists on defining it as "diagnosing" and "treating mental illness." Precisely herein, I submit, lie the contemporary psychiatrist's moral failure and technical incompetence (Szasz, 1970, pp. 6-7). *wow.*

In one context, man is drawn to one side of an equation that is weighted heavily on the side of a super-depersonalized nature in whose grip man inexorably remains and whose rules he must follow or suffer dire con-sequences. In another context, man is more or less a pawn of a transcendent deity whose laws he must follow or, again, pay heavy penalties. In a third view, man is seen as necessarily conforming to the demands of a transcendent state that owns him, shapes him, and makes him a part of its system, indeed digests and assimilates him.

Have traditional psychotherapeutic approaches left man out as the cen-tral figure? Man is viewed variously as a commodity, as one with his social role, as an intelligent rat, as a meaningless cipher in a brute universe, and as being in the grip of instinctual drives and emotions or of cyclical events in his life history. In traditional psychology, man possesses only a vague illusion of freedom of choice; if indeed psychology centers on man as an object of its study, it then avoids discussing his reality by creating lists of categories (diagnostic or otherwise) to define his essence. In all the tradi-tional ways in which man has been viewed, man, the person, is lost in a welter of ideal images and abstractions.

Humanistic existentialism is basically a movement of revolt. The hu-manistic existentialist refuses to see man as an object to be manipulated or controlled mechanically by positive or negative reinforcers. The HE refuses to accept the reduction of man to an object that is irrationally sick and in need of being cured or straightened out. Humanistic existentialism stands *for* the rediscovery of each person's quest for his own uniqueness as a dignified individual and for his responsible autonomy. The movement stands *against* the ubiquitous forces that, by design, negligence, or omission, strive to make the person feel that he is simply one with his social role or, in fact, nothing but his role. It is against the view that man can be fully explained by animal psychology or by ethological formulations, or that man is the victim of a phylogenetic continuum in which he is different only in degree from subhuman species. It opposes the assertion that man is a victim of mysterious forces hidden in the recesses of an unconscious that is, by definition, inaccessible to him.

We use the term *humanistic existentialism* to describe a nontheistic approach to human life (as contrasted with the religious approaches of Kierkegaard, Marcel, and Tillich). It is an approach that is holistic as opposed to reductionistic and one in which man has a central (homeoergic) as opposed to a peripheral position. (By peripheral, I mean the view that man is nothing more than a black box responding to stimuli in the environment, understandable only in terms of observable, measurable responses.) The humanistic existentialist chooses to place human reality at the center of his concern, departing, in this approach, from the orthodox views of man represented by most contemporary educational, psychological, and psychotherapeutic practices.

Despite the force of the essentialistic doctrines that underlie the work of many scientists and behavior researchers, the humanistic existentialist has come to recognize that man intuitively rails against categorization and classification and that he will, when encouraged and permitted, choose to focus on the central facts of his existence. The difficulty of this enterprise and the notion that its dynamics are not quantifiable in terms comfortable to standard behavior scientists ought not to limit its study. The humanistic existentialist does not limit himself to studying only that behavior which can be studied in the same manner as a chemical reaction. He does not stop at a reductionistic description of the human condition because the analysis of experience and the description of its component parts does not necessarily account for experience. Thus, the humanistic existentialist, incurably subjective, is most interested in how a person defines his own reality, the way he expresses his intentions about it, and the way in which he internalizes and perceives it. This internalization is a function of the person's intentions, of his way of being in the world, of his project in life, and of his personal myth. The particular way in which one man chooses freely to maintain and structure his reality forms the basis for his response to whatever conditions confront him. It is a mistake to hold that the stimulus—that thing out there upon which competent observers can agree—completely controls the manner in which the person will respond. Indeed, that thing

out there takes on meaning only as the person brings his free consciousness
and his awareness *to* it.

It is not sufficient, then, to merely offer a number of propositions or a
system of assertions about the relationship between the world "out there"
and the way in which a person responds to that world. The important goal
is neither a systematic set of relationships or categories nor a tight logical
system, but an analysis of the reality within which one man is an encoun-
tering participant and the way in which that man's life can be lived. In a
more profound sense, the HE focus is on the way life is, the way things are,
and the ways people live their lives, choosing either to pay attention to or
to deny the way things are for *them*.

A discussion of human reality—that reality with which the humanistic
existentialist is most intensely concerned (i.e., experience)—raises questions that transcend the individual and his personal struggle with life,
making the construction of ready textbook answers impossible. No manual
can tell man how to deal with the vicissitudes he must confront during his
life. We have only highly individual assumptions of responsibility about
the choices one elects to see and to make. In the larger sense, the humanistic existentialist is much less interested in solutions to problems than
in the assumption of responsibility for the way in which man chooses to
structure his existence in the world. Such a task has no text, and certainly
there is no recipe book by which to live. As one highly perceptive client
put it, "The way is that there is no 'way.' " To suggest, then, that a set of
techniques can be a way of life would be to suggest a lie.

Although a great variety of writers of widely divergent views have been
labeled existentialists, most share a core of identifiable approaches to the
central issues involved in man's existence. These ways of thinking do not
provide answers so much as they suggest an attitude toward the questions
that individuals ask about their lives. So let us turn now to the major premises of the HE approach. The reader might well be warned that the following discussion intertwines philosophy and psychology, presented in an
unstructured manner, to better convey the mood of existential thought.

EXISTENTIALISM AND ESSENTIALISM

> It is an indication that one has misunderstood Existentialism if one uses it
> without reference to its opposite. Philosophical ideas necessarily appear in
> pairs of contrasting concepts, like subject and object, ideal and real, rational
> and irrational. In this same way, existentialism refers to its opposite, essen-
> tialism, and I would be at a loss to say anything about the one without saying
> something about the other (Tillich, 1961, p.8).

Paul Tillich's terse statement points the way to the clarification of existentialism. When we are thinking of a concept as a *thing,* whether it is
Sartre's paper cutter (which we shall consider in a moment), a steady-state

universe constantly replenishing itself, man's instinctual nature, or the fact that man is constantly struggling between Eros and Thanatos, we are considering that concept in terms of an essence. Whenever we begin a question with, "What is the nature of...," we are usually asking for the defining characteristics of that thing. Those characteristics or attributes without which the object or event would be known as something different constitute its essence.

Now, an essence need not necessarily represent anything that exists in real life. We may use the analogy of a playwright creating a character and his role in a play. That role is then played by an actor who tries to understand and express what the author had in mind. Thus, we may think of some object, some figure, or some event, but it is unimportant whether anything with those defining characteristics in fact exists in the observable world; that is, it is unimportant whether something or someone actually plays out the "role" we have conjured up.

It is important to note, however, that the *idea* in question *precedes the object*. In the mind of the artisan, for example, the idea of a chair must precede cutting the wood to create it. In humanistic existential thought, this essentialistic doctrine is true of all things in the universe except man. Man develops in a way that is radically different in nature from the development of other objects within the universe. For him alone, existence precedes essence: by dint of man's unique consciousness, by his ability to use propositional speech, and by his ability to introduce a psychic distance between himself and the object of his thought.

> There are, however, only rare moments in this monumental development in which an almost pure existentialism has been reached. An example is Sartre's doctrine of man. I refer to a sentence in which the whole problem of essentialism and existentialism comes into the open, his famous statement that man's essence is his existence. The meaning of this sentence is that man is a being of whom no essence can be affirmed, for such an essence would introduce a permanent element, contradictory to man's power of transforming himself indefinitely (Tillich, 1961, p. 9).

No playwright has ever "thought up" man. Man exists first, what he is or will be does not preexist his reality as a schematic diagram or blueprint; on the contrary, the question of what is man is settled only in the course of his life, in the course of his actions, as a function of his intentions, and as a function of his choices. Man's choices, then, define him, but in a flexible and ephemeral way, for he is always free to choose anew and, thus, to radically redefine himself. By his every choice and by the activity subsequent to that choice, man forms and defines his own essence.

If man's existence precedes his essence, then, a definition of man is impossible, for his nature absolutely precludes his being cast into some permanent mold. Man appears imbedded in human possibility and *then*

conceives himself thus. Perhaps humanistic existentialism's most important contribution to a new and radically different view of human nature
will be the concept that, paradoxically, there is no "human nature." We
have only the nature that each human chooses to describe himself.

Kaplan's statement clarifies this central concept further:

> Everything else but man is subject to the law of identity: A is identical with A;
> A is A, was A, and will be A, nothing but A. Everything but man is just the
> thing that is and absolutely nothing else. Only man is not subject to the law of
> identity.... In the very act of becoming aware of the particular "this" that he
> is—whatever it may be—the human being has already transcended it. Man is
> the being whose existence is constituted by this fact: that he is continually be-
> coming what he was not (1961, p. 104).

We may also turn to the originator of these concepts, Sartre:

> What they [all existentialists] have in common is that they think that existence
> precedes essence, or, if you prefer, that subjectivity must be the starting point.
>
> Just what does that mean? Let us consider some object that is manufactured,
> for example a book or a paper-cutter: here is an object which has been made
> by an artisan whose inspiration came from a concept. He referred to the con-
> cept of what a paper-cutter is and likewise to a known method of production,
> which is part of this concept, something which is, by and large, a routine. Thus,
> the paper-cutter is at once an object produced in a certain way and, on the
> other hand, one having a specific use; and one cannot postulate a man who
> produces a paper-cutter but does not know what it is used for. Therefore, let
> us say that, for the paper-cutter, essence—that is, the ensemble of both the
> production routines and the properties which enable it to be both produced
> and defined—precedes existence. Thus, the presence of the paper-cutter or
> book in front of me is determined. Therefore, we have here a technical view
> of the world whereby it can be said that production precedes existence.
>
> When we conceive God as the Creator, He is generally thought of as a superior
> sort of artisan . . . and that when God creates, He knows exactly what He is
> creating. Thus, the concept of man in the mind of God is comparable to the
> concept of a paper-cutter in the mind of the manufacturer, and following
> certain techniques and a conception, God produces man.... Thus, the individ-
> ual man is the realization of a certain concept in the divine intelligence.
>
> [The idea of essence preceding existence] is found everywhere. Man has a
> human nature; this human nature, which is the concept of the human, is found
> in all men, which means that each man is a particular example of a universal
> concept, man. In Kant, the result of this universality is that the wild-man, the
> natural man, as well as the bourgeois, are circumscribed by the same definition
> and have the same basic qualities. Thus here too the essence of man precedes
> the historical existence that we find in nature....
>
> If God does not exist, there is at least one being in whom existence precedes
> essence, a being who exists before he can be defined by any concept, and . . . this
> being is man. This means that, first of all, man exists, turns up, appears on the
> scene, and, only afterwards, defines himself.... Thus, there is no human
> nature, since there is no God to conceive it. Not only is man what he conceives
> himself to be, but he is also only what he wills himself to be after this thrust
> toward existence.

Man is nothing else but what he makes of himself. Such is the first principle
of existentialism (1967, pp. 34-36).

The humanistic existentialist derives from Sartre's doctrine a notion
that most contemporary thinkers in the field of epistemology have come to
understand: that every truth and every action imply a uniquely human
commitment, a human setting, and a human subjectivity. Polanyi (1964)
echoes this view. He believes that personal knowledge manifests itself
everywhere—in the appreciation of statistical probability and in the order
of the exact sciences. In all science, the act of knowing inescapably includes
the act of appraisal; this act represents a personal coefficient that shapes all
factual knowledge and bridges the disjunction between subjectivity and
objectivity. Further, all knowing is, indeed, a passionate, committed *participation* that, at the root of things, may be subjective.

The notion that man is totally responsible for a constant process of self-
definition and redefinition, and that this definition and redefinition constitute his reality, has profound implications for the helping process and the
helper's view of what patterns of behavior or speech he will term sick or
healthy. Ultimately, it affects whether the helper believes a person needs
counseling, therapy, or help of any kind. Singer (1965) addresses himself
to this issue:

> It might be asked why so much space has been devoted here to the view that the
> focus of inquiry must be the values human beings harbor and the choices they
> make. The reason lies in the consequences of the proposition. If one accepts the
> position that the focus of inquiry must be the person's system of values, one
> is confronted with two difficult yet relatively well-defined issues: (1) what, if
> anything, may then be deemed the "essential" nature of man; what constitutes
> the aggregate of . . . "human universals"; and (2) should this aggregate, once
> determined, be the guide in deciding whether a person's system of values is
> "healthy" or "ill"; should one consider a system of values in harmony with
> such "human universals" as reflecting well-being or is a system of values which
> rejects "human universals" reflective of the good life? These considerations
> lead to the conclusion that the definition of psychopathology depends upon
> the psychotherapist's conception of the nature of man . . . and upon the psycho-
> therapist's philosophical position in relation to this conception . . . A therapist
> then deems nonpathological all those aspects of behavior which are in ac-
> cordance with his idealized image of man; all that is at variance with this image
> is pathological (pp. 12-13).

In opposing the various essentialistic doctrines that predominate in the
field of counseling and therapy, and in denying the existence of a fixed human nature that determines what each member of the species must be, the
humanistic existentialist asserts the emptiness of historicity and a strict
determinism. There is nothing at all to determine man; each man is free to
define his own life, even to end it, if he so chooses. This freedom is attested
to by the variety of lives men choose to live and by statistics on suicide. As
we shall see, the helper's image of the nature of man is critically important

in that divergent images—essential or existential—lead to widely varying and distinctly different options for response on the therapist's part.

MAN'S THROWN CONDITION

In the humanistic existentialist view of life and reality, there are no answers. For the humanistic existentialist, man is "thrown," or flung, into the world without a blueprint or map to guide him. Furthermore, he is forever lured by a siren song that suggests the possibility of discovering an exterior meaning in his being in the world, of discovering his identity, and of discovering certain objective regularities upon which to rely and base his hope.

In everyday human discourse, in the consulting room or outside it, we see evidence of the appeal of a search for a transcendent blueprint that can be accepted with a sigh of relief, signifying the discovery of something to work toward, some goal to fulfill. "If I could only know what it *really* is to be a woman or a wife or a mother, then I could live up to it and relax," states the client.[1] To discover her desired "real" identity, this person undertakes the study of anthropology and of the ethological foundations for the eternal feminine role, a pursuit that, unhappily, fails to clarify *her* situation as the mother of a teenage youth who wears his hair long and prefers smoking pot to going to classes. In the same vein, many clients come to their helpers in the quest of their "true calling" or vocation. This they hope to discover by means of their scores on an IBM answer sheet to a vocational-interest blank. This kind of quest for identity is doomed to frustration in the HE view, because resolutions of the major problems in human life seldom continue to be effective over long periods of time.

Many persons view their identity, or "calling," as lying "somewhere—if only I could discover it," and persist in the search for "somewhere" as some have persisted in the search for the fountain of youth. But in the humanistic existentialist view, there is no way to discover a person's identity or his true calling. There is no answer to the question, "What am I, really?" and it is not even possible to arrive in any permanent sense at a discovery of "what I want." Man cannot place these kinds of questions and quests outside himself, to be answered by the interpretation of tests or by the discovery of a genuine map to the "place" where identity awaits only the undertaking of the proper journey or the acquisition of the proper key. The most significant issues in life have not been settled beforehand. Man, for all his longing after them, cannot discover the answers to his questions about life, he cannot discover his meaning, and he cannot discover his goals. He is doomed to *invent* them for himself.

---

[1] And many modern writers provide such essentials, as in Ernest Becker's statement that man's search for the "heroic" is the essential force in his life (cf., Ernest Becker, 1971).

Interestingly enough, even the religious existentialists seem to concur in the concept of the absolute necessity for man's invention of his own way of life. These thinkers assert that, even if there is a God (and they believe there is), He has not defined the human condition in those aspects that are most critical to man. Thus, even in a theistic context we must make choices about the central issues of our relationships, our patterns of behavior, and our lifestyles.) *right.*

Humanistic existentialism is, then, a psychology of possibility. Words such as "doomed" and "thrown" seem to lend to this way of thinking an aura of pessimism and gloominess. But far from being pessimistic, humanistic existentialism engages a vital force of optimism and of commitment to seeing life as it really is, without illusion and without false hope, and to dealing with it on its terms. Sartre puts it well:

> When all is said and done what we are accused of, at bottom, is not our pessimism, but of an optimistic toughness. . . . You see that it cannot be taken for a philosophy of quietism, since man's destiny is within himself; nor for an attempt to discourage man from acting since it tells him that the only hope is in his acting and that action is the only thing that enables man to live (1967, pp. 49-50).

To describe man's thrown condition, Bugental allegorically places an ordinary urban professional and his family on an island, where, as castaways, they are able to stay alive indefinitely only through the father's own wits and his own will. As the years pass, this tight family comes to realize that help will not come, that the island is all there is:

> This is a picture of man's plight; of your plight and of mine. I am on a little island of the clearly known, which is in the sea of the generally known, which is in the ocean of the barely known or but guessed at, which itself swims in the midst of the immensity of the totally unknown. Yet from the farthest galaxy may stream, even at this moment, influences so potent that the whole course of my life can be altered (1965, p. 21).

The thrown condition of which the humanistic existentialist speaks represents the recognition that the world is as it presents itself to us, that these are our lives as we choose to live them, that our lives will end, and that we have no guarantees. We have no alternative but to deal with our lives without hope instilled by voices from the beyond and without hope for a reality that will appear to us from behind the scenes and illuminate the road of our lives. In this life, the humanistic existentialist recognizes that *wow* there is nothing to wait for. He must choose to act in accordance with the situation in which he finds himself and in accordance with the way he sees that situation. On this tight little island, within the limited span his life encompasses, man can choose to cling to whatever values he wants and to whatever lifestyles he wishes. He can choose to live as he has lived before his shipwreck or he can elect to make a *depass,* to make a radical departure, to make a "turning." He has freedom on his island, all the freedom he has ever had or will have, since freedom is not to be *had;* he is free. Man is limited only by what he does not really experience as limiting: the stature of his body, the strength of his muscles, the limits of his imagination.

The HE knows that he can make a radical choice to be different or to remain the same, whichever he wants, and he is willing to make this choice, knowing that there are negative aspects attached to *each* choice. Reality for the HE is the appreciation of freedom to make any human choice and the knowledge that any choice has both positive and negative consequences. He knows that he ultimately does what he wants and, moreover, that many, in bad faith, attribute choice and want only to positive aspects of their choices, excluding those aspects that are negative.

He knows that he alone infuses meaning into his world and that his world is closed to transcendental mysteries. He knows the limits of his knowing, but he does not make a mystery of this lack. He knows that, beyond man, there are no watchful and saving powers at work, no principles of compensation, but rather only meaningless, brute, and alien forces, and of these he makes no mystery either. This is not only true of him and for him, he knows, but others as well, and he knows that he cannot enter into the world of others or into their minds because they are separate; they, like he, must solve their problems of life for themselves.

As I write these lines, I notice a growing anxiety within me. Such thoughts are not comfortable. How nice and how comforting it would be to disbelieve them, to forsake what I know to be the truth, for some hopeful and salving transcendental faith. It is appealing to deny the ambiguity inherent in freedom, reducing the mysterious and unknown to forces that we can understand, and making the leap Kierkegaard finally made, to a faith that the world is open to the possibility of redeeming and saving grace. It is also tempting, perhaps, to think of a "God beyond God" as the source of this dreadful freedom I feel, a being to whom, somehow, I can turn. If such a being existed, my freedom would be constrained by the fact that freedom could then be actualized only when it constituted an offering to a something beyond, and I would owe my obedience to this something that transcended me—not the vulgar obedience of psychological or actual genuflection, but an obedience that would be rendered freely of me. But despite the attraction of these thoughts, my dignity and my vision demand the choice to see things as they are in this world, to believe what I see.[2]

---

[2]cf., John Wild (1963) for another example of man's thrown condition.

THE FREUDIAN VIEW OF EXISTENCE

Man's thrown condition is denied by the naturalist who fondly dreams of that time when the behavioral and social sciences will be as precise and as predictive of events as the physical sciences. Then man will at last be capable of predicting and controlling his own destiny. Inside this new, complete order, he will be free. In this golden age, "good" will be determinable by research findings, and it will be absolutely quantified.

Freud, of course, was this kind of man—a naturalist—as are his current followers. In Freud's thinking, as in the thinking of Freudians generally (Trilling, 1971; Singer, 1965), man is destined to struggle with an instinctually regressive, hostile, and destructive element that is inherent in his biological makeup. The Freudian holds to what can be labeled a tension-reduction or regressive hypothesis about the essential autonomous order that is the nature of man. Man's inherent tendency, a tendency common to all living matter, is to strive toward his own annihilation, toward quiet and entropy. In this position the child is inevitably born in anger, and the major thrust of human behavior and striving is toward a steady state in which pain and arousal are minimized. Thus, the pursuit of pleasure is the minimization of the impact of inner and outer stimulation. The aim of *status quo ante* both represents the basically conservative striving of man and defines him. Man longs for the diminution of stimulation; that is his basic nature. Life, for the Freudian, is an incessant struggle between the regressive, conservative pull that is part of the person's essence and the world, others, and civilization, that doggedly and spitefully proscribe man's basic urges toward self-elimination.

Freud's view takes a more structured form in the doctrine of the unconscious, a doctrine that remains strongly entrenched in modern psychoanalytic thinking (although the details of the self-destructive essential nature have recently been altered; cf., Masserman, 1968, pp. 189-224). In the Freudian scheme, there are two systems in the human mind: one conscious or manifest and the other subconscious (latent or covert) or unavailable to consciousness (in principle unknowable) but available of a dim knowing.

In the Freudian system, the new as well as the old, the conscious, aware, or manifest portion of the human psyche serves as a mask or expressive-deceptive cover for the wants and the intentions of the unconscious portion. The energy of the id intends, in the main, the immediate and blind gratification of instinctual and libidinal drives; while the ego, whose major effort is the person's survival, undertakes to control and direct the blind and primitive press of the id. In doing so it may go so far as to push that press completely out of awareness, to repress it. It is by this manuever of automatically repressing the impulses of the id that the ego facilitates the existence of civilization, of society, and of family, an accomplishment that, in turn, supports the possibility of the survival of the species.

The tragic view continues with the extrapolation of a hydraulic model to the human psyche. It asserts that, once pushed down, controlled, and repressed, the impulses of the id do not passively follow the ego's orders to lie quietly, or be still. In their unconscious chamber, they rest uneasily, ready to rise to the surface and show themselves with the cry of, "I want! Now!" Toward this end, they act as underground, subversive forces upon the conscious portion of the psyche, and they often triumph. But the ego will not permit raw expression, and a compromise is struck: the id impulses are permitted to express themselves only via a devious route, through slips, accidental eruptions, parapraxes, and, mainly in symbolic form, in dreams.

> This symbolic expression of the repressed instinctual drives typically involves some degree of pain and malfunction and is called a neurosis. As Freud put it, *"We are all ill"* . . . *neurosis is of the very nature of the mind.* Its intensity varies from individual to individual; in some the pain or malfunction caused by the symbolizing process is so considerable as to require clinical treatment. But the psychic dynamics of such persons are not different from those of the generality of mankind. *We are all neurotic* (Trilling, 1971, p. 42) [emphasis supplied].

As if "We are all neurotic" were not sufficient, the story continues in this manner: the ego is not entirely conscious either. There is a part of the conscious system that is also unavailable to awareness. This part acts just like that which was repressed, and thus it, too, induces a powerful struggle to be expressed without showing its true identity. The Freudian topology has then not only a top chamber (ego) and a bottom chamber (id), but yet another higher chamber that exerts its effects from the top. With this view of human nature there is no hope that human ills can be alleviated by modifying the contract between the ego and the social system. No amount of tinkering with society can cure man. Freud outlined this concept in *Civilization and Its Discontents,* a work whose major thesis is that civilization and society stand in a necessary but not sufficient relationship to human frustration and personal pain.

Man is, then, inevitably an adversary to himself. "The direct agent of man's unhappiness is an element of the unconscious itself" (Trilling, 1971, p. 44); this agent is the superego.[3] The superego goes far beyond any of

---

[3]Note the following:

Superego: that part of the EGO in which SELF-OBSERVATION, self-criticism, and other reflective activities develop. That part of the ego in which parental introjections are located. Since Freud maintained that self-observation is dependent on INTERNALIZATION of the parents, these two definitions tally. The superego differs from the CONSCIENCE in that (1) it belongs to a different frame of reference (i.e., METAPSYCHOLOGY not ethics; (2) it includes UNCONSCIOUS elements; and (3) injunctions and inhibitions emanative from it derive from the subject's past and may be in conflict with his present values. It is not maintained that the superego is an accurate replica of the parental figures who have been introjected, since the relevant internalizations are held to occur early in child-society's demands in directing against the ego an unrelenting barrage of its own demands. The evolution of Freudian theory has posited a secession of a part of the ego and the establishment of an autonomous "state"—the superego—that, as a colony now seceded, turns against its parent nation and becomes more committed to the ideals of the parent country than the parent was itself. The superego is not synonymous with conscience, however, though conscience is a part of its armamentarium. The major part of the superego is that which is concerned with the ego ideal. This part is engaged in a gratuitous striving for an ideal image—a process, largely beyond the reach of reasonableness—that it has instituted against the ego. The effects of this process on the Ego are felt as the pain of guilt. The sense of guilt, it must be made clear, is not the remorse that follows some real or imagined infraction of socially correct or ethical behavior. Guilt is divorced from actual behaviors, deriving instead from the *wish* to destroy that arises as a result of the conflict between the superego and infantile-sexual-aggressive wishes. Guilt is almost entirely interior in the adolescent and the adult. Further, guilt is strongly associated with the innate regressive nature of man: the destructive instinct and the person's awareness of his impulse to destroy what he loves and to defy that to which he submits (that is, his awareness of basic hostility—Thanatos, or the destructive instinct, as Freud called it).

Guilt is usually experienced as a general dulling of affect, as depression or anxiety, but it must be noted that this guilt is not rooted in the world, in time, or in space; it is solely an inner experience. Guilt may have had its origins in the evolutionary history of the species—man serving the needs of the tribe or the group, the child dealing with the family situation—but now it is totally autonomous from outer reality:

> Yet when we have given all possible recognition to the essential and bene-
> ficent part that the superego plays in the creation and maintenance of civilized
> society, we cannot ignore its deplorable irrationality and cruelty. These traits
> manifest themselves in an ultimate form in the terrible paradox that although
> the superego demands renunciation on the part of the ego, every renunciation
> which the ego makes at its behest, so far from appeasing it, actually increases
> its severity. The aggression which the ego surrenders is appropriated by the
> superego to intensify its own aggression against the ego, an aggression which
> has no motive save that of its own aggrandizement. The more the ego submits
> to the superego, the more the superego demands of it in the way of submission
> (Trilling, 1971, p. 44).

For the Freudian, that is the order of things. This tragic view is based

---

hood, when the infant endows his object with his own characteristics. As a result, the severity or intol-
erance of the superego derives (in part at least) from the violence of the subject's own feelings in in-
fancy. It is also assumed that the energies of the superego derive from the ID; i.e., that the self-attack-
ing tendency of the superego provides an outlet for the subject's own aggressive impulses. This is an
example of TURNING AGAINST THE SELF (Rycroft, 1968, pp. 160-61).

on a concept of the human mind discovered by "scientific investigation" that was rooted in an ethos of Freud's time.[4]

The Freudian understands that the superego acts now although it is necessarily tied to man's past. The superego is a fact, a given of man's biological makeup; it defines man's nature, and nothing can really be done about it. Man is doomed in the same sense in which the existentialist sees him as doomed, but he is entrapped—entrapped in a nature, in an essence, that is inherently and inexorably against itself. From the humanistic existentialist point of view, Freud clearly saw the tragic nature of man and of life, but he based his view of that nature on the wrong reasons. For the Freudian, man adjusting is man sublimating, and what is pathological or "sick" in the rationalist-Freudian context is man's refusal to recognize and to accept the basic paradox of human nature, of the order of things.

I include this brief excursion into Freudian theory to illustrate that in a way, the psychoanalyst also sees man's condition as being "thrown," but in a totally different manner than the humanistic existentialist. The important point for the therapeutic practitioner is once again underscored:

> Descriptions of man do not merely describe, they *prescribe*. A person acts in the world as a being with the limits, strengths, and weaknesses he believes are his "nature." Someone persuaded him that that is how he *is* (Jourard, 1974, p. 2).

The therapist's view of the basic nature of man inevitably influences the manner in which the therapist responds and "teaches" the patient what he can hope for himself. We will return to this important point repeatedly.

Simone de Beauvoir (1967) has placed man's thrown condition in the context of a constant dealing with the ambiguity life presents to man. She points out the long history of man's attempts to deny that condition.

> "The continuous work of our life . . . is to build death." Man knows and thinks this tragic ambivalence which the animal and the plant merely undergo. A new paradox is thereby introduced into his destiny. "Rational animal," "thinking reed," he escapes from his natural condition without, however, freeing himself from it. He is still part of this world of which he is a consciousness. He asserts himself as a pure internality against which no external power can take hold, and he also experiences himself as a thing crushed by the dark weight of other things. At every moment he can grasp the nontemporal truth of his existence. But between the past which no longer is and the future which is not yet, this moment when he exists is nothing. This privilege, which he alone possesses, of being a sovereign and unique subject amidst a universe of objects, is what he shares with all his fellow-men. In turn an object for others, he is nothing more than an individual in the collectivity on which he depends.
>
> As long as there have been men and they have lived, they have all felt this tragic ambiguity of their condition, but as long as there have been philosophers

---

[4]See van den Berg's (1961) analysis of this ethos and its effects on Freud's discoveries.

and they have thought, most of them have tried to mask it. They have striven to reduce mind to matter, or to reabsorb matter into mind, or to merge them within a single substance. Those who have accepted the dualism have established a hierarchy between body and soul which permits of considering as negligible the part of the self which cannot be saved. They have denied death, either by integrating it with life or by promising to man immortality. Or, again they have denied life, considering it as a veil of illusion beneath which is hidden the truth of Nirvana (pp. 7-8).

In direct opposition to all theistic systems, the humanistic existentialist recognizes the thrown condition, fully aware of the anguish that his vision brings. Man is thrown because his condition is not to be defined without him, without a constantly nagging ambiguity. Ambiguity exists because man cannot find any external justification for his life; there is no outside appeal. In rejecting the hope of the religious existentialist or the essentialistic Freudian, the humanistic existentialist chooses the one idea that seems to underlie all humanistic thought: the world in which man finds himself is not a world that has been "given" to him by some foreign entity, nor by biology, a world to whose nature or essence he must struggle to force himself to yield; the only world that is, is the world that is willed by man, by his intentions, and by his consciousness—a homeoergic world (cf., Lamont, 1967).

The humanistic existentialist, unlike the religious existentialist, asserts that the only possible authentic attitude is not to wait for and not to recognize any absolute that is foreign to him. Instead of being lured by the hope for an omen or sign from somewhere out there, he recognizes it for what it is and abandons hope of a transcendent, superhuman objectivity. For the humanistic existentialist, there is no right way to act other than to be right in his own eyes. And because he is thrown and has no one to rely on, his actions are definitive, engaged. There is no pardon or redemption or undoing of his actions in a later appeal; there is nothing to which to appeal. Thus, man carries the absolute, inexcusable responsibility for his actions and for a world that is not the work of a transcendent mystery, but of himself. "It is up to man to make it important to be man, and he alone can feel his success or failure" (de Beauvoir, 1967, p. 16).

This, then, is the thrown condition of which the humanistic existentialist speaks when he describes the ground in which he is a figure. It might also be added that it is this very ambiguous, thrown condition that emanates in the existentialist's optimistic toughness, and that is based on the will to see things as they are. This attitude is expressed in a statement often attributed to Dostoevsky: If there is no God, all things are possible.[5]

---

[5]The most appropriate quotation that I could find in Dostoevsky is: "If God exists, all is His will and from His will I cannot escape. If not, it's all my will and I am bound to show self-will" (*The Possessed.* 1948, p. 561).

CONSCIOUSNESS AND FREEDOM

A very important aspect of humanistic existentialist thought is existentialism's view of human consciousness and its major attribute, freedom. The humanistic existentialist conceives of reality as being cleaved into two dimensions: (1) *being-in-itself,* which includes all of nonconscious reality, and (2) *being-for-itself,* which is the being of man. The being of man is distinguished by his consciousness. Kaufmann put it well when he described being-in-itself as that being that rests in itself, that has an essence, a blueprint; this is the being of such things as tables, chairs, typewriters, and rocks. Being-for-itself is that being that is aware of itself: man (1956). Being-in-itself is simply a kind of fullness without form, without differentiation, and without any significance or meaning at all; the most it simply is, is.

Being-for-itself is the being of human reality. It is not precisely different because it is conscious, but it most certainly is that part of being that gives rise to and permits of consciousness. The major difference between the two types of being is that with being-for-itself or with consciousness, a "nothingness" comes into the world. Perhaps this is the clearest way in which to introduce some ideas from Sartre's major work, *Being and Nothingness* (1956), in which this concept is elucidated. Consciousness, or conscious self-awareness, is closely interwoven with the introduction of a film of nothingness or a distance—a kind of break, a psychic withdrawal, a rupture in the world. For the humanistic existentialist, consciousness is an event that, by its self-awareness, assumes a distance and thus an attitude, a point of view toward all of brute, nonconscious reality and toward other human beings. Consciousness is not simply a free-floating entity in man; rather, it is always a consciousness *of* something. Consciousness is the distinction between the object viewed and the *noticing* that the object is not "I"; and, to complicate the matter further, consciousness is the awareness of that very process. The process can be verbally diagrammed in this manner: the chair; the chair is there; there is a difference between the chair and me; the chair is not "I"; I am making the distinction between the chair and myself.

It is this kind of separation from brute being-in-itself, and the constantly accompanying reflection upon it and upon the aware self (which is noted as propositional or conceptual thought), that introduces nothingness, and thus meaning, into the world, or a universe that, without an observer, would be totally without significance. This is so because it takes conscious man to "see" the brute universe, reflect upon it, make a psychic withdrawal from it, and, by his awareness and self-awareness, infuse meaning into it.

This is the meaning of nothingness: consciousness effects a kind of psychic withdrawal from the world; it stands apart from its object; it creates a gulf between itself and its object of purview. Since consciousness exists only as consciousness *of* an object, consciousness grows out of nonbeing and is dependent upon it. Consciousness could not exist at all if there were not an outside world for it to be conscious of. Consciousness has no interiority; it is dependent upon the world, but it is not being of it. Basic to the idea of consciousness is the "standing-back," the stirring of a psychological mutiny in the universe. Out of this mutiny arises the ability to put the whole of life and the whole of nonlife into question. By this gulf of nothingness, by this process of consciousness, of awareness-in-distance, our awareness of objects *is* the assumption of a point of view on all of reality, on the valuing of it, and on the invention of a relationship between me and the table upon which I write. "Every conscious existence exists as consciousness of existing . . . at one stroke it determines itself as consciousness of perception as perception" (Sartre, 1956, p. liv).

The humanistic existentialist's view of consciousness is different from that of the Cartesian "cogito ergo sum." The first conscious event is *not* the awareness of an event (that is, "I am aware of *it*"). Instead, "It (the event) is there!" The "there" at once indicates my awareness of the object itself and my apprehension of the fact of this awareness; the object and I are not the same thing. The object of which I am aware is *not* my awareness; it is somehow separate from me. There is a gulf of nothingness between me and the object of my consciousness, the not-me.

Consciousness, therefore, is not a thing, but an intending, and consciousness is always a consciousness of something: it is *merely* that psychological withdrawal from the object of conscious attention. It is as if consciousness were a film of nothingness between itself and "outside" objects. To sum it up, for the humanistic existentialist, consciousness is nothing but the act of withdrawal implied in the statements, "That is there" and "It is not me."

This view of consciousness is not alien to contemporary humanistic psychology in general. Bonner (1965), not an existentialist, expresses an analogous view:

> But consciousness does not exist *uberhaupt:* it is always the property of an individual. Consciousness is but another term for *experience.* Experience is characterized by the fact that it is *my* experience. As experience, consciousness includes the capacity of being aware of our own consciousness—of self-consciousness (p. 192).

But Bonner falls into a quasi-essentialistic position when he compares consciousness and awareness to a process. The humanistic existentialist does not view the mind or consciousness as a process at all.

Ernest Keen (1970, 1972), a contemporary clinician, comes closest to the humanistic existentialist posture in his discussion of experience and consciousness. Keen points out that the major focus of contemporary psychoanalytic theory, for instance, is upon a person's character structure. And this structure (as we have previously indicated) consists largely of the manner in which the person deals with basic, inevitable conflicts between instinct and societal inhibitors to their expression, that is, in man's unique style of sublimating. It is basically a biologically oriented view. Keen admits that while character structure is a larger unit of study than that which interests the behaviorist (habit), it has still much in common with the behaviorist view of man: "The *Ego,* for example, is a concept that is imbedded in a theory of man that is highly mechanical in style, biological in rationale, and if not strictly measurable, hopes someday to be so" (1970, p. 4).

Keen comes very close to the HE position when he asserts that unlike behaviorism with its emphasis on behavior and unlike psychoanalysis with its emphasis on instinct, existential clinical psychology takes *experience* as its starting point. While habit is important for the behaviorist, for the HE, the importance is in how habit is experienced by the actor. Likewise, in terms of psychoanalytic character structure, that structure becomes important mainly in terms of how it is experienced by the person experiencing the conflict.

HE psychology does not look to the learned habit or character structure for basic explanations of psychological difficulties. Habits and structures are merely "containers" or guideposts to a mutual understanding of a person's experience in the world, of the manner in which a particular person uniquely relates to that world.

> Abnormality, the problem that is attacked, is in the person's *experience* rather than in his behavior or his character structure. This approach is perhaps the psychological ramification of the philosophical view which places consciousness in the center of the definition of man, rather than on the periphery as an epiphenomenon (Keen, p. 4).

Close to the HE position, Keen accepts the view of human consciousness (consciousness-as-nothingness) as a central notion and sees that this idea leads to a radical redefinition of man and of those aspects of man that psychologists have traditionally attempted to understand. But for Keen, consciousness is a different kind of intervening variable. While experience (or consciousness) stands between stimulus input and behavioral output, it is more than a mere connecting link between the two. Consciousness is central in that it informs the input as well as the output. In this schema, there is no raw stimulus that acts upon the passive organism. A stimulus is not a given, apart from consciousness's awareness *of* it. And that consciousness *of* it is, at once, an imparting of meaning *to* it. Similarly, the meaning of human responses is not self-evident without the inclusion of the person's experience of intentions.

With respect to the psychophysical correlation, the HE view of consciousness requires a shift in our way of thinking about events. For example, to construe the act of seeing a tree in terms of reflected light activating retinal and visual cortex events is *not* to take the HE view of consciousness seriously. This physicalistic way of thinking may explain what goes along with consciousness, but it is *not* a statement about conscious experience. The physical events may correlate with consciousness, but they are not consciousness.

Keen holds that the crucial problem for a psychology based on HE terms, where human consciousness is central (i.e., homeoergic) is the construction of a language that is quite different from a language of *things*. The creation of such a metaphor, of such a language, is one of the basic thrusts of this book.

KNOWING

The humanistic existentialist sees the whole area of knowledge (that which man knows) as arising from the "hole-in-being," or nothingness, position. It is man's unique consciousness-as-fissure that permits of knowing, and all of knowing begins with this knowing of nothingness. There appears to be a dualism between the knower and the known, like that between the person who speaks and one who analyzes the speech of others. Yet the one who analyzes others' language is himself the *user* of language. "For man, the concept of meaning can be fathomed only in relation to the self" (Stent, 1975, p. 1057). Because it is man who is capable of entering into an analysis of language, words, and concepts, we are fully capable of choosing to use words as they are, to modify them, or even, ultimately, to discard any or all of our constructions completely (Poole, 1972). Thus, we ourselves originate language and knowledge, and, because we are the agents and the cause, we are free—free because we constitute the causal agency of our conceptions.

In our ability both to use our language and to analyze it (to step back from language and become aware of it, and, further, to use language to analyze this process), we are able to see ourselves remarkably unfettered and free. It is the fundamental belief of the humanistic existentialist that the changes of mind are, at bottom, unconditioned or undetermined. Man's shifts in attitude, in project, and in wants must be unconditioned, these shifts must be self-generative, at least in the sense that man can take any attitude toward reality that he chooses freely. This is the unique connection between the nothingness that consciousness is and freedom: both are self-determined.

All that can be known is that man is free to change the shape of his project, his language, and his construction of reality. This is so because, in the first place, any attempt to account for man's freedom to change his constructions, upon whatever basis he will, is itself a construction that is adopted freely and so is available for further change. That is not to deny that certain basic projects bring consequences that man may not find desirable. Certainly, all choices carry their own duties with them. But if one has freely, and for the best of all possible reasons, chosen to go down a certain path and finds that path to be filled with mud that gets in the way of one's progress, crawls into the shoes and up the legs, and pulls one down, one cannot will not be pulled down; one must change paths. Yet, as will be seen later, most clients are very unwilling to change; they prefer to continue on the same path and somehow blame themselves: "How come I can't conquer this mud? I must be doing something wrong in my walking on this path." Or, the client might wish to deny the existence of the mud and his irritation with it. To change paths is to choose a different way of life, to become a different person, and this seems a difficult task. Perhaps that is why counseling or psychotherapy, in the traditional modes, is often so frustrating and why there seem to be so many reversions. Many people are willing to "dither" with their approach to the mud, but not with their choice of the path.

At this point something needs to be said about the role of insight as a special form of knowing, the changing of paths, and the different levels of knowing. It has been pointed out that the attainment of insight may not be sufficient as a condition of a conversion in one's way of being in the world. London (1964) and others have commented upon the fact that an alteration in a person's subjective experience of himself as he is in the world or as he is in his situation is not therapy if it does not change his overt behavior. The HE therapist thoroughly disagrees because this view assumes that behavior can and does occur independently of our consciousness or of our experience. It is as if behavior has a kind of autonomy vis-à-vis the total person. Of course, some behaviors (though not real acts) may occur in a manner that seems independent of our explicit awareness of that behavior. The important point, however, is that at the moment that we choose to become aware of (notice) our behavior, we have the options of behaving in that manner or not, or of stopping that behavior.

The concept of insight takes on various meanings, depending on the particular theory of human behavior involved. Insight in Freudian terms is quite different from insight in Jungian terms or Rankian terms. According to psychoanalytic theory, insight means to be informed about the causes of one's symptoms (conversions of instinctual energy). This is insight into oneself as an object of one's biology or of one's past. It is an awareness of the nature of the self that does not take the meaning of freedom and of consciousness seriously.

The HE therapist believes that insight plays a major role in the affirmation of the reality of a person's existence, although insight may not be sufficient if change is one's major goal (and we shall speak about change later). It is often heard in groups and individual therapy that "I understand up here (in the head) why I do that, but I don't *feel* any different." In the traditional psychodynamic mode, this might be interpreted to mean that a person's insight is not deep enough or that he has not yet "worked through" sufficiently. But in the HE mode, the essential insight is that such a statement illuminates that person's *commitment* to maintaining his way of being, his position—that, while he *understands* the connection between his suffering and his project and priorities in life, he is unwilling to tinker with his *commitment* to his hopes and his priorities. His commitment to his position is signaled by his feeling or lack of feeling for the connection between his cognitive understanding and his feeling-life. That is, he is unwilling to explicitly utter his basic commitment structure. *What about this unwillingness to speak?*

Pt: Doctor, I understand why I do this thing, it is fruitless, it seems, we have seen that it gets me nowhere. But I cannot change it. It feels like I must continue to do it.

Th: Well, that says that your lack of "emotional" understanding merely signals that you are committed to being the way you are or have been. Look at how important it is for you to stay exactly as you are. Is there anything wrong with that?

CONSCIOUSNESS AS PROCESS

As opposed to dualists and others who view consciousness as a process, the humanistic existentialist holds that man's knowledge must be adopted freely if it is to be considered knowledge at all. If man's construction about knowledge, about language, or about any event in his experience were *not* freely adopted but, rather, strictly "caused" in us, we would fall into a deterministic, essentialistic position, in which the person's mind would be like a kind of natural reflex, impulse, or instinct rooted in a kind of "process." This process conception of consciousness is not freedom. It is inimical to freedom because, when consciousness is viewed as *in* experiencing a process, it cannot at the same time be said to be free *of* that process that defines it.

The humanistic existentialist, then, views man's mind and man's consciousness uniquely as completely free and thus free of any process. Consciousness cannot be a process because if consciousness were not free *from* that process, then it would be unable to know and to be aware *of* its own process (and indeed it does seem to be aware; I can be aware of my awareness). If consciousness were viewed as a process, only limited, hazy self-consciousness would be possible, and this would be colored by the interposing filter of the operations of the process itself. Consciousness can only be a nothingness; anything more defines it and thus places it in parentheses, making it unfree.

To suppose that man can know anything at all is to suppose that he is free. Knowledge, then, also supports the humanistic existentialist notion of the absolute freedom that is consciousness. Man is his freedom, but, paradoxically, in being aware of this, in knowing this, he knows at first only his nothingness—that hole-in-being that separates him from the object of his awareness.

The humanistic existentialist is critical both of the Kantian and the Hegelian views of consciousness and of the modern behavior-theory-oriented psychologists in the following way: to define freedom, to make it into a "something," is to delimit freedom and thus to make it unfree. Those theorists who suppose that there is a "how" or a "why" to our consciousness, by supposing preconditions or processes, limit consciousness and therefore make it unfree and incapable of knowledge and, most significantly, make it incapable of self-knowledge. (A process is itself locked into that process and cannot rise above it.) This is crucial both to the counselor or therapist and to the person who comes to him. It is not necessarily the content of man's consciousness and his constructions that are important, but rather that these constructions have been made freely, that they have been caused by nothing other than man's own free consciousness.

The humanistic existentialist believes that human freedom is absolute. Since consciousness is "nothing," it has no content at all (i.e., no reflexes, no instincts, no tropisms); it is only the establishment of a relation, a point of view. Consciousness is, therefore, a free valuation of oneself toward the object of awareness. The person *is* that choice of attitude; that choice is also he, and that is all he is. Man is free to choose and rechoose and to question, at each moment in time, his view of his relationships with the persons around him, his past, and his future courses of action. Man is not a process; rather, he is self-making. Out of his own free consciousness, he gives birth to himself. Again, consciousness is freedom, in the sense that it forms a film of nothingness, a distance, between it and its object and is, thus, never totally determined by that object or by the past history of man's relationships with that object. It is always our free choice to view events, to evaluate them, and to internalize them by having an attitude toward them.

ANGUISH

It is through his consciousness that man is free to put everything into question, even his own awareness of consciousness, and it is this uniquely human ability to distance oneself from the material universe and to conceptualize it that constitutes man's freedom and his possibility for constantly choosing anew. It is this very freedom, this realization that he is nothing at all other than this choice and rechoice, that brings him to fear and anguish: "If *nothing* compels me to save my life, *nothing* prevents me from precipitating myself into the abyss. The decisive conduct will emanate from a self which I am not yet. . . . In terms of this moment, I play with my possibilities" (Sartre, 1956, p. 32).

It has been said that the apprehension of such a freedom is a dreadful thing and that man may not be up to dealing with it. Indeed, in working with persons, the denial of freedom and the establishment of ways of living that limit one's freedom of choice are central issues. The difficulty a person has in facing his freedom and in accepting it as his condition leads persons to dealings with the world and with themselves that are, in essence, conducted in bad faith—a concept that will be discussed later.

COSMOLOGIES, CHOICE, AND THE PERSONAL MYTH

I have spoken of consciousness as *being* freedom, and I have said that choices are made freely, that we are free at any time to choose differently. The question might be asked at this point, "Yes, but don't most people really act quite consistently, and don't most of us have an underlying pattern, a kind of basic lifestyle that does not seem to be freely chosen?" The humanistic existentialist would agree that most persons do indeed have a basic set of choices that make up what is called a "project" or basic cosmology to which all the lesser decisions and elections are intimately related. The question, then, is whether these basic projects have been chosen by the person, or whether they have in some manner been made for him by his nature, by the "way he is wired," or by his "blueprint." Do not our projects simply well up within us as overwhelming compulsions from which we cannot escape? I will not enter fully into the discussion of instincts and impulses at this point, but only comment briefly on these questions here.

The Freudian who believes, for example, that one of the basic projects of women is their desire to possess a male penis uses this "specific feminine factor" to explain feminine psychology. Note the intentions and the thinking of a deterministic essentialist:

I believe we have found this specific factor, and indeed where we expected to find it, even though in a surprising form. Where we expected to find it, I say, for it lies in the castration complex.... The castration complex of girls is also started by the sight of the genitals of the other sex. They at once notice the difference and, it must be admitted, its significance too. They feel seriously wronged, often declare that they want "to have something like it too," and fall a victim to "envy for the penis," which will leave ineradicable traces on their development and the formation of their character and which will not be surmounted in even the most favorable cases without a severe expenditure of energy.... The discovery that she is castrated is a turning-point in a girl's growth.... In the absence of fear of castration the chief motive is lacking which leads boys to surmount the Oedipus complex. Girls remain in it for an indeterminate length of time; they demolish it late and, even so, incompletely. In these circumstances the formation of the super-ego must suffer; it cannot attain the strength and independence which gives it its cultural significance, and feminists are not pleased when we point out to them the effects of this fact upon the average female character.... The determinants of women's choice of an object are ... often made in accordance with the narcissistic ideal of the man who the girl wished to become.... The fact that women must be regarded as having little sense of justice is no doubt related to the predominance of envy in their mental life.... We also regard women as weaker in their social interests and as having less capacity for sublimating their instincts than men (Freud, 1966, pp. 588-89).

The Adlerian who holds that man's most basic, essential, and unchanging drive is toward power and perfection believes, as does the drive-reduction theorist (whose major project for man is homeostasis), that man's overall projects are naturally determined: thus, man himself has no choice about them. Just as man's basic orientations in the Jungian system were made *for* man, man has neither choice nor freedom in his basic projects, his cosmologies. His projects were made for him by his nature, by his evolutionary history, by social forces that have impinged upon him, by inevitable epigenetic psychosexual events, or by immutable stages in his life history. If this is the case, of course, our choice of basic project would never change because it could not.

The client says, "Listen, man, sex grabs me. I can't help it. I see a groovy chick, and everything goes kaplooey in me. Man, that's my nature talkin'. No use denying it. Don't blame me for taking on the jail-bait chick. It's those juices talkin'." In different words, this young man could say that his very nature craves sexual gratification; if this were his fundamental choice even at the age of 15, where would he get the energy to choose another project? Here the Freudian would say that the solution for him—indeed, the only possible solution—would be to sublimate his sexual energy into socially useful activities. Or he would say that if he *understood* his need to copulate (if he gained insight) he would no longer *need* to do it; by explaining the client's project to him, the therapist would, hopefully, effectively *explain it away*. The humanistic existentialist holds that the young man's basic choice is to view himself as an impulse-ridden, determined creature, and that choice is seen in many areas of his life, not only in his sexual expression. Further, the basic choice he makes, because *he* makes it (it is not made *for* him), is his free assumption; nothing determines it. Thus, the person can constantly put himself in a position to alter his fundamental project.

One of the basic concepts of the HE is the concept of a basic project. While various theorists have postulated universal strivings in man—for power as in Adler; for the heroic as in Rank and Becker; towards self-actualization as in the Rogerians and Humanists—the HE holds that there is no collective, basic project that directs and accounts for human experience. Each person has invented and built and seems committed to a basic way of organizing his priorities in his world, and this may be either explicitly known to him or not. But he does seem to have such a basic engagement illuminated by his way of being and which we prefer to call his *personal myth*.

One of the major thrusts in therapy seems to be the awareness and the explicit articulation of the fundamental or personal myth to which much of what the person does is intricately connected. It has been my experience that coming to grips with the personal myth is a difficult process for most clients since describing it explicitly requires a responsible position in the world for that person. But such responsibility is what the HE values.

I would like to illustrate one such personal myth, evoked in therapy, that seemed to illuminate and affirm much of what the person involved was engaged in. The personal myth was given a name, and it was called the "Walled City":

> I see a Chinese scroll—painting, in tones of green and earth colors. There is a scene that is misty, a mountain gently sloping upward, and on the top of this mountain there is a castle—indeed, a small city. It is surrounded by a large, thick wall, like the Wall of China.
>
> Inside this Walled City, there is much to fascinate. There are all kinds of interesting things: books, animals, theatres, whole libraries, concubines, scientific equipment, music, art.
>
> I am the prince in that city; it is mine. I have the freedom to roam within it, within the walls, and can, when I choose, be completely entertained within it. All my "toys" are there.
>
> Now the walls of the city are gated, and the gate is in my command. The people are outside of it; they inhabit the principality that surrounds my Walled City. Me, I can enter and exit the city at will, and I choose very carefully those persons whom I invite into my Walled City. I can go down outside of the wall and interact with the people who live and play outside of the Walled City, but I am but dimly engaged with them. I retreat to my walled city often, whenever I choose. There are only three or four people whom I have invited to share my Walled City with. And our life together within the city is sometimes difficult. Occasionally, I have to ask these special intimates to leave. Or I leave.
>
> Outside, I give the appearance of being involved, but I am only dimly and occasionally deeply involved with them. I retreat to my Walled City often. I need it. I understand now why I do. It is all right. I see my commitment to it, to my way, and see the pain connected with living that way. I embrace the pain of it within the context of my basic commitment. Everything I do, all my relationships, my love, my sex, my work makes sense to me. I no longer feel guilt about it, I feel compassion for me and for my Walled City. I embrace it. It is mine. It is me.

The client's assumption of responsibility for his engagement in the world, born of explicit awareness and of careful attention to his life is the only change in therapy that the HE values (perhaps it is entirely enough of a change). The explicit awareness of the person's basic way of being-in-the-world and the assumption of affirming responsibility for that way of being is the only "stake" the HE therapist has. Any other goal is frankly manipulative and violates the integrity of that person's subjectivity. The honoring (there is no word in English that does not have a positive or negative ring to it), the taking, the embracing of the reality of one's life, and the explicit seeing of the price one pays for it, is entirely sufficient.

VALUES

Persons can see, if they choose, that their basic choices, their projects, and their cosmologies have been for them the basic and true source of values in their lives. The person has given value to his choices and to his acts merely by choosing them. But usually persons prefer to declare that the value existed "out there" in the world, and so fall into self-deception. The humanistic existentialist holds that values do not exist "out there," but rather that we give value to an act or event by choosing to do it or by choosing it. What gives value to anything is that we do it. *We* are the source of value in the world. As Greene says:

> If one looks for ... a standard in existentialism ... the first thing one finds is, as we have seen, that freedom itself ... appears as the source of ultimate value. Values are generated by our free decisions: they start up, Sartre declares, like partridges before our acts. Yet the *only* value, it seems, that can stand against the charge of bad faith, the only self-justifying value, is the value of that very free decision itself. Acts done and lives lived in bad faith are those in which we cloak from ourselves the nature of our freedom, in which, to escape dread, we try to make our subjectivity into an object and so, though, of course, we *do* act freely even in such self-deception, we betray our freedom by disguising it.
>
> To be sure ... the ultimate value is honesty rather than freedom. We are free in any case; from that fact, both glorious and fearful, there is no escape as long as we live at all. But it is a fact that we may or may not face honestly. Good for the individual resides in the integrity with which he recognizes his freedom and acts while so recognizing it. Evil, conversely, is the life of fraudulent objectivity, the denial of freedom (1948, p. 143).

The only source of value, then, and an ultimate value in its own right, is the person's freedom to choose. Indeed, in choosing sexual gratification as a prime way of life, the 15-year-old boy mentioned earlier infuses that behavior with value.

If we see that we are the source of value and that this source of all value is actually our freedom to choose, we can also see what in fact is the most valuable: our freedom to rechoose our basic project, to make a radical choice in life. In making our own freedom the most fundamental value of all, we set ourselves on the road toward making all our choices, and toward allowing the choices of others, in the context of a respect for and further-ance of freedom. The choice of freedom may be a new project, then. The young man referred to earlier once he understands the freedom that he *has* (and has denied), may be free to choose to value other lifestyles or other projects. Conversely, he may choose to remain with his project and to suffer the consequences since any new project will also have its positive and negative aspects.

Further, in the understanding that life and our projects have no value or meaning or significance in themselves, that they gain significance *only* because *we* choose them, we can also understand that we are free to give significance to life and so make our life meaningful by the way we live it.

The humanistic existentialist helper would want the person who comes to him to see that his choice of valuing a certain mode of existence or a certain construction of reality is his free choice, that he may own his choice, and that he is responsible. In his responsibility, nothing outside him *made* him choose his cosmology or his lifestyle; he is free to rechoose at any time. He would also see that such radical choices are not easy or rapidly made, but they are *possible*. This is in opposition to the view that persons characteristically hold as they come to counselors—seeing themselves as determined entities in a determined and locked-in universe. For the HE helper, the ultimate project that the person might consider to value *is* the project or fundamental choice of his own freedom and that of others, his decision to choose and rechoose the way in which he lives his life—to reclaim ownership over his existence.

> [Existentialism] can demand only that each of us seek his *own* freedom. Such a demand is, in fact, it seems to me, a legitimate moral claim. Therein lies the genuine strength of the philosophy that expresses it, with its telling revelations, on the social as well as the individual level, of the infinite varieties of bad faith by which most of us allow ourselves to pretend to live (Greene, 1948, p. 145).

2
Man as Feeling and Feeling Man

I believe that one cannot understand psychological disturbances from the
outside, *on the basis of a positivistic determinism, or reconstruct them with a
combination of concepts that remain outside the illness as lived and experienced. I also believe that one cannot study, let alone cure, a neurosis without a
fundamental respect for the person of the patient, without a constant effort to
grasp the basic situation and to relive it, without an attempt to rediscover the
response of the person to that situation, and . . I regard mental illness as the
"way out" that the free organism, in its total unity, invents in order to be able to
live through an intolerable situation (Sartre, 1971).* Dostoevsky's Underground Man.

Classically, psychologists and counselors have dealt with persons who
have come to them because they have been troubled in some way about
some aspect of their lives. Characteristically, these clients speak of feeling
that something is not right with them, and they say that they do not know
why they feel the way they do. Persons come to helpers because they are
anxious, depressed, confused, or hostile or because they "feel bad" about
themselves. They are experiencing emotions and feelings that seem to be
separated from a cause or a reason, as though they had a functional
autonomy all their own.

Such persons see themselves as irrationally "sick"—in the grip of some
emotional disorder of which they must be cured. They see their emotional
lives as divorced from themselves, from the rest of their lives, and from
their intentions, and, consequently, they see themselves as bedevilled or
emotionally disturbed. Celia, in T. S. Eliot's *The Cocktail Party* (1950, p.
130), puts the case well:

But first I must tell you
That I should really like to think there's something
Wrong with me—
Because if there isn't then there's something wrong
Or at least, very different from what it seems to be with the world itself—and
     that's much more
Frightening! That would be terrible. So I'd rather believe
There is something wrong with me, that could be put right.
I'd do anything you told me, to get back to normality.

Celia here expresses her faith in an essentialistic, ideal view of the world. When she sees that the world in not as she had thought it should be, she prefers to call herself sick, rather than change her view.

The humanistic existentialist psychologist is interested in emotion as a total human experience. He believes that the facts of man's emotions cannot be explained by a mechanistic or reductionistic approach. A mechanistic or reductionistic approach attempts to explain man through smaller and smaller quanta, finally ending up with physics—the physics of the neural response. This approach is based upon the belief that if one gets down to the basics, the smallest element, the simplest building block (*à la* physics), then understanding will be complete.

REDUCTIONISM AND INTENTIONALITY

In keeping with my intention to describe an HE view of human reality and emotions, it seems appropriate here to comment on reductionism since it is still a dominant way of thinking about understanding persons. It is the view that in order to truly understand, one must reduce things to ever smaller and simpler elements. A reductionist approach (and its corollary, historical/evolutionary explanation) suggests that causal explanations alone are valid and that intentional, proactive, or purposive explanations are unscientific. This view, a remnant of the thinking of Newton, Descartes, and Comte, denies a way of appreciating connections or of explaining goal-directed behavior by referring to goals. In referring to a goal or end or purpose, we can now see that one does *not* fall prey to teleology (as was once thought) or to giving to the future a causal efficiency in the now. In point of fact, the purposive explanation provides the present moment with the causal agency of an intention to attain a certain position, state, or event in the future.

The distinction between mechanistic or reductionistic and purposive explanations of human behavior is logically spurious. Both are equally admissible. However, understanding human reality within a mechanistic-reductionistic explanatory scheme leads in a totally divergent direction from a purposive or intentional scheme. Both ways of explaining seem plausible, but each leads to entirely differing ways of thinking about man and understanding human reality. Ways of understanding persons in terms other than intentions or purposes are often referred to as *structural* explanations. But the HE chooses to understand a person as a function of the way in which he intends, the ways he projects himself into the world and, therefore, the ways in which he chooses his projects. These projects (overarching goals and aims in life—the way a person wishes his biography written and his epitaph composed) are most often structured in terms of how one sees oneself in the world and how he wills to *be*. We shall return to the question of intentionality after a brief discussion about the reductionistic mode, which is pertinent both to the ways in which persons have thought about their emotional lives and to the ways in which HE thinks about man.

In our quest for explanation and understanding, we seem to be seduced by a misleading analogy to a highly successful scientific discipline—physics. In a discipline like physics, a complex event may be understood better if it is taken apart and reduced to its simplest processes. Similarly, a complex behavior pattern like thinking, then, should also be better understood if it is reduced to its simplest processes—processes that might be at the level of neurochemistry. This is the stand of the mechanistic psychologist.

There is yet another form of reductionism that should be mentioned here—the hierarchical approach that places man at the top of the evolutionary ladder and organizes other animals at progressively simpler levels beneath him. The one reductionist holds that man is nothing more than genes, hormones, and so forth, and, consequently, to be understood he must be explained in physicalistic terms (i.e., man did so-and-so *because* adrenalin was released into his bloodstream). The other reductionist states: "Man did so-and-so because his evolutionary predecessor had a particular predisposition that was evolutionarily determined in this way." The central question to be considered about this approach is whether it is true, in fact, that physiological or evolutionary-historical constructs are more basic than psychological constructs. The answer depends entirely on the view, the intentions, and interests of the theorist, and it depends on his commitments. Each of us interprets and, indeed, generates data according to the logical net of a theoretical structure we have chosen for fulfilling our intentions and purposes as persons, scientists, and theoreticians. If we are committed to a reductionistic view because we are more successful or more comfortable with it, then we shall choose our data, our experiments, and our "masters" in terms of a very basic, single system of connections for all meanings; we will thus have to discover the *one* fundamental substratum that explains a phenomenon. In each case, we shall find answers in terms of the questions we choose to ask (Langer, 1942; Zimbardo, 1969 a and b; Wheelis, 1971).

It is important to note that although complex thoughts or emotional behaviors are closely associated with neural and hormonal processes, they are not identical to them. Fear is not simply the constriction of blood vessels; heat is not simply the movement of molecules. The temptation to reduce two correlated processes, one to the other, leads to such sentences as "Thinking is nothing but subvocal speech," and "Colors are nothing but waves of differing wavelengths." Such statements fall prey to what is called the reductive fallacy (Hospers, 1967, pp. 387-91).

Interestingly, both B. F. Skinner (1953, pp. 27-29) and Julian Rotter recognize the inutility of reductionistic thinking and of the reductive fallacy:

The psychological and physiological represent points of view regarding an event, but they are only two of many such points of view that might be used to understand or describe human behavior. There are also biological, biochemical, and sociological, and economic points of view, and many others as well. Of course, it is possible to find correlations between descriptions of human behavior made from a sociological and a psychological point of view and also find correlations made from a physiological and psychological point of view. These correlations imply neither causality nor dependency of one mode of description upon another. The emphasis in the past on integrating psychology and physiology or on trying to explain psychology by physiology may well be an historical accident rather than necessarily the most useful approach. . . It would seem for the present . . . that it should be most profitable to attempt to develop psychological concepts that will predict behavior without recourse to physiological descriptions. Although constructs in all scientific areas should be consistent, they need not be considered to exist in some heirarchy with each system dependent upon another, more basic system (Rotter, 1954, pp. 40-44).

To take the argument further, it is entirely possible that we shall be able to know the exact neurological events that immediately precede a particular behavior, and these particular events will be preceded by yet other neurological events, and so on. The whole series of events that lead, let us say, to a handshake, will eventually lead us to an event that is an interaction between the person's view of things and another event outside him in time and space.

In direct opposition to the reductionistic approach, the HE believes that there is no valid argument demonstrating that merely because one event temporally antedates another, the two events are causally connected. Yet forms of this argument are used to try to explain complex human behavior by drawing upon prior, lower, or simpler animal forms—a kind of evolutionary reductionism that is untenable. The HE holds that physicalistic reduction leads to a fallacy and explains little.

From the HE point of view, all analyses that attempt to reduce human behavior have the same limitation, whether the reductions are framed in the vocabulary of atomic physics, chemistry, biochemistry, neurology, physiology, behavior, or learning theory or, for that matter, in the language of psychoanalytic theory. In every case, by reason of the reduction, the reality of the person and personal reality itself is lost. Each of these reductive operations ends in very specific but related conglomerates of *inert* totalities. These inert, passive-in-themselves totalities are then considered to be irreducible building blocks that are, then, constituents of personal reality. To the HE such an operation is irrelevant to his concern with human reality, and it is a point about something entirely different.

Reductive analyses consist of statements about the way in which a personal entity is constituted by means of factors that are exterior to it (even when the factors are forces within the person's body, they are exterior in the sense of being within his body as an object for another and not the body in which he exists) [in this connection one might call attention to Sartre's chapter on the body, 1956, pp. 303-360]. Personal life, however, is not only constituted from the exterior but *constitutes itself* on the basis of this exterior constitution of it. Put another way, the person chooses himself on the basis of (against, in the face of, or in compliance with) the totality of factors that condition him (Cooper, 1967, p. 13).

The HE believes that such complex human attributes as consciousness, integrity, and freedom may not be reduced to simpler constituent forms without being destroyed. He denies the necessity for temporal or physicalistic reductions. Instead, the HE wants to help grasp man's meaning as man creates it through his own unique consciousness and his unique stance: intentionality, a concept to which we now turn.

INTENTIONALITY AND CONSCIOUSNESS

Since the HE view of man's unique self-reflexive consciousness-as-nothingness is central to an understanding of man, let me again point out that to be conscious means to be conscious *of* something. Consciousness is always a pointing toward something outside itself—an object or event—and always implies an attitude, a project, or an *intention*. It is in this way that intentionality gives meaningful content to consciousness. Consciousness cannot exist in a vacuum; it has no interiority; it is always a consciousness of something. Thus it is integrally connected with the world. Consciousness is determined both by itself and by the term to which it is related. Intentionality is a dialectic relationship within which meaning originates—it is an interaction through which a person transforms the brute material of his surroundings into his "situation." Man, then, is always in a situation. To extend the analogy further, it seems to me that there is an incurable "us-ness" (cf., Laing, 1971, Part I).

In experiencing consciousness in a reflexive way, we are in a continuous process of shaping and reshaping the human world. Man creates his own meaning, and every meaning involves a commitment to act. The act of inattention or repression is a knowledge of something toward which a person will *not* take action. Consequently, he has chosen not to "know" it. To attend to something, to take it seriously, implies a readiness to make some decision about the situation. When a person decides not to decide, he wills not to attend to what faces him in life. If a person takes a look at the shape of his life, he is then ready to become aware and to act. In each case, he has power over and is fully responsible for his attitude or his situation.

The intentional view sees consciousness as inseparable from its object, and this view is antithetical to a reductionistic/mechanical view of knowledge and man. Consciousness is intentional in that it is never wrapped up in itself alone, ready to be analyzed. Intentionality implies that consciousness is not merely passive and acted upon; rather, consciousness is intercourse with reality, and knowledge always has an object that is codetermined by one person and his intentions. This concept implies that by means of knowledge and self-knowledge, man overcomes the determinism of brute nature and of natural processes, for it is through man's consciousness that brute nature and its processes are-for-man. This is not to say that nature, things of nature, and natural processes are not reality; they are the facticity, the density with which consciousness deals, and this dealing is important. The concept of intentionality means that man encounters nature and himself in a mutually determining process. The knower and the known are born together.

> We are always beyond ourselves in the venture, the task of finding and giving, as best we can, significance to our world, the world which is always beyond us at the horizon, but whose concrescence, whose interpretation, whose meaning we are (Greene, 1966, p. 91).

The recognition of commitment as a part of knowing or intending anything at all is becoming a part of our epistemology. Polanyi (1963) restores the knower and his known to their proper functioning by stressing the very commitment of the knower and the tacit element in knowledge:

> This view entails a decisive change in our ideal of knowledge. The participations of the knower in shaping his knowledge, which had hitherto been tolerated only as a flaw—a shortcoming to be eliminated from perfect knowledge—is now recognized as the true guide and master of our cognitive power. . . . The ideal of a knowledge embodied in strictly impersonal statements now appears self-contradictory, meaningless, a fit subject for ridicule. We must learn to accept as our ideal a knowledge that is manifestly personal (pp. 26-27).

Rollo May (1969) takes the same position when he says that one of the serious errors of psychology has been to rend asunder the knower and the known, to bracket out part of experience and never put it back again; that is, to follow the analytical-reductionistic mode. In his discussion of intentionality, May concludes that every meaning has within it a commitment, but he makes the important clarification:

> And this does *not* refer to the use of my muscles *after* I get an idea in order to accomplish the idea. And most of all it does *not* refer to what a behaviorist might say on reading these paragraphs, "Just as we've always said—the consciousness is only in the act anyway, and we might as well study only the muscular action" (p. 230).

It should be clear here that I am making a rather explicit statement about the nature of man. I am positing that the concept of intentionality-which-is-consciousness means that in addition to brute reality, man tends to invent meaning and that this is his very nature. Man *is* intentional; he *is* orientation and directedness to the world. To confront and to encounter and thus to impart meaning to whatever he meets is his task in life. It is this concept that has led Sartre to say, "The world is human."

> We can see the very particular position of consciousness: being is everywhere, opposite me, around me; it weighs down on me, it besieges me, and I am perpetually referred from being to being; that table which is there is being and *nothing* more; that rock, that tree, that landscape—being and *nothing* else. I want to grasp this being and I no longer find anything but *myself.* This is because knowledge, intermediate between being and non-being, refers me to absolute being if I want to make knowledge subjective and refers me to myself when I think to grasp the absolute (Sartre, 1956, p. 218).

Another important phenomenologist, Maurice Merleau-Ponty, also makes the uniqueness of consciousness dependent on the central fact of intentionality. Though Merleau-Ponty (1962) differs somewhat from Sartre in that he softens Sartrean subjectivity, he nevertheless sees intentionality as being at the heart of understanding man's actions. For Merleau-Ponty, intentionality is essentially identical to the act of perception:

> Consciousness, through which from the outset a world forms itself around me and begins to exist for me. To return to the things themselves is to return to that world which precedes knowledge, of which knowledge always *speaks* (1962, p. ix).

The reductionistic, mechanomorphic attempts to understand man differ from the HE approach, which takes as its basis man's consciousness, his totality, his perception—in short, the multiply determined nature of his reality. The world is human, and the proper focus for study of man is man.

The HE chooses to understand a person in light of his projects in life, in light of his freely chosen personal myth—his intentions. It is intentionality that gives meaning to experience because it is our imagined participation in the present and in the future that molds our awareness of our capacity to change, to shape, to structure, and, through commitment, to restructure our being-in-the-world. For the HE, then, man is to be understood by his intentions, by his motives, and by his proactive goals (Bonner, 1965).

This way of thinking about man is radically different from the mechanistic view that the person is a subject or, an essence that is in some way a self-enclosed system and that human consciousness can only be understood by the postulation of the presence of ever smaller units of experience. While the HE believes that consciousness begins with mental activity, he holds that such activities are intimately related to their objects. In this way, there can be no ideal desire and no ideal fear. Each desire is a desire *for* something; each fear is a fear *of* something; and each act of understanding is an understanding of something. Further, to understand one pole of this relation, it is absolutely necessary to understand the other dialectical pole. We cannot, for instance, understand the fear of something unless we also understand the *intentional* act of fearing that brings the emotion fear into a person's world.

If a person accepts a meager salary for his work, that acceptance might be based on the fact that he is afraid (afraid of starving, for example), but fear is the way *that* person intends and makes his world meaningful. But note that fear does not come from that person's past or from the operant sequences to which the person was subjected[1]; the person's fear is intended toward the nonexistent future. The fear might say (as we have indicated), "I don't want to starve to death; I don't want my family to suffer," but the fear of starvation has meaning only as it projects itself toward an end that that person ideally creates. He wants to preserve his life, which he sees as possibly being in jeopardy. Further, this fear can only be meaningfully understood in relation to the values that person has given to his life in his situation,[2] under the circumstances in which he lives. Obviously, there have

---

[1]Even if this were so, that person would still have chosen to believe his experience, his past, or the operant sequences. There is ample evidence for this in experimental social psychology. While the use of schedules of reinforcement, and the newer fashions of behavior therapies, have seemed to enable behavior scientists and therapists to manipulate the responses of a wide variety of subjects, one must face the fact that in the real, pedestrian world of daily living and choosing, persons more often than not show a great deal of tolerance for and unresponsiveness to states of "drive," deprivation, or arousal that they meet in their lives. The belief that man is at the mercy of environmental stimuli and physiological demand has been shown to be largely "unreal" in the human domain by such researchers as Philip Zimbardo and his associates (1966), by Schachter and Singer (1962), and by Schachter (1967).

While no one denies the *facts* of laboratory studies of motivation, behavior shaping, conditioning, and that central concern of current psychology, behavior control, it must be remembered that the *conditions* of such experimentation have typically been designed to place persons and other organisms into relatively passive positions, in which the only task is to simply convert stimuli into expected responses. Zimbardo (1969a) aptly points out that the typical laboratory approach neglects attention to the central processes that characterize the behavior of persons in their ordinary lives, as opposed to the laboratory:

> People have cognitions about the conditions associated with their entrance into, and acceptance of, deprivation and aversive states. When man exercises his volition, chooses to commit himself to a course of action, and accepts personal responsiblity for its consequences, he distinguishes himself as unique among living creatures and calls into question our laws of behavioral control (p. 238).

[2]Zimbardo and his colleagues have found that the impact on behavior of what is called a drive stimulus (for example, pain) can be greatly mitigated and changed by the creation of a set of circumstances that help the subject become an *active* agent in the act of making a cognitive appraisal of the relationships between himself and his commitment or the situation in which he finds himself.

> This occurs where subjects are made aware of their volition in choosing to enter or to avoid a state known to be unpleasant and where their commitment is supported by only minimal extrinsic justifications. When a person must directly confront the environment which his choice has created for him, then cognitive intervention destroys the isomorphic correspondence between stimulus level and reactivity. In the process of having to generate *intrinsic* justifications... man shifts the locus of control of his behavior from external stimuli to internal cognitive controls (1969b, p. 238).

The studies of Zimbardo and his coworkers indicate that such a degree of cognitive control

been persons who have so structured their experiences that they have been willing to starve to death, to take their own lives, or to become martyrs because their values or their intentions were different. Again, the person who fears says, "No matter what, I intend to live." And only in terms of his intentions, only in terms of that system of hierarchies of ideal objects he values, may the fear refer and become understood. This person has chosen the meager salary, then, for the best of all possible reasons, reasons that are based on the way in which he chooses to live, on the way in which he has perceived and structured his reality. He has only to weigh the negative and positive consequences of his basic intentional choice in each circumstance where those consequences of his choice arise.

> Thus the motive makes itself understood as what it is by means of the ensemble of being which "are not," by ideal existences, and by the future. Just as the future turns back upon the present and the past is ordered to elucidate them, so it is the ensemble of my projects which turns back in order to confer upon the *motive* its structure as a motive. It is only because I escape the in-itself by nihilating myself towards my possibilities that this in-itself can take on value as a cause or motive. Causes and motives have meaning only inside a projected ensemble which is precisely an ensemble of non-existents [or more precisely, an ensemble of *not-yet* existents]. And this ensemble is ultimately *myself* as transcendence; it is Me in so far as I have to be myself outside of myself (Sartre, 1956, p. 437).

My major point has been that the concept of intentionality refers to a person's wholeness, to his state of being, to his basic way of approaching life, to his basic project, and to the totality of the person's orientation to the world in the situation of a particular time in his life.[3] In a very real sense, the person's way of being is expressed in the situation in which he finds himself, and everything about him speaks *of* him: his posture, his speech, his dress, his work, and the way in which he approaches his counseling—as client or therapist.

---

over motivation encompasses a great many "drives" formerly thought absolute such as hunger, thirst, pain, and social needs such as achievement, approval, and aggression. Zimbardo summarizes and conceptualizes his important research in terms of human freedom:

> Through utilizing cognitive controls (of virtually limitless potential) man gains freedom from the behaviorial proscriptions—imposed by his history, physiology, and ecology. Indeed, thinking and believing can make it so! (Zimbardo, 1969b, p. 240)

[3]Perhaps something more needs to be said about this central concept in existential thought: intentionality. Basically, the notion of intentionality is intimately related to the concept of transcendence; it is a reference to what is possible, to what man's ontological quest aims toward: to surpass his ontic level towards the ontological, to reach for his aim, his basic, fundamental engagement or project in a perpetual, ongoing, open encounter with the world and with man himself-in-the-world. In theological terms, that ultimate transcendence is conceived in terms of God. In HE terms, that ultimate transcendence is conceived in terms of being a free agent, a self-cause, a system of energy that aims at passing beyond all determining limits.

AND IN THERAPY . . .

Counseling and general therapeutic work in an HE frame are based on the fundamental fact of human existence; in "human existence" we include all the meanings that have already been given to man's consciousness, to his freedom, to his intentionality: the "here" of his being in existence in the world, the given and historically developed structure of meaning he *gives* to the world and that constitutes the meaning of his behavior. If one wants to know what man is like, then one must study man's dialog with objects and with his fellow man. It is impossible to know a person without taking *that* person (i.e., his personal reality) into account. In HE therapeutic work, no general theory of man can help in the task of knowing a person. The foremost task is the development of an understanding of the meaning-structures of the particular person's world, of *that* person-sitting-opposite-me-as-a-unique-free-consciousness, of *that* person's intentions toward which all his activities are directed. To be able to accomplish that, the therapist must abandon theory for the reality of that person "there."

Arthur Miller, in his play *The Price,* has his heroine, Esther, say at various times, "I can never believe what I see." As the play proceeds and she sees the crumbling of her hope that things are not what she has wished them to be, she repeats, "I can never believe anything I see. But I'm going to. That's all I'm going to do. What I see."

We have alluded to the aspect of human reality represented by a mutual, codetermined intercourse or encounter with the world and to the twin of this encounter—the fact that every meaning we intend into reality carries imbedded within it a certain commitment, a certain position, stand, or attitude that we are willing to take toward our situation. Each intentional act contains in its fabric a push toward an action. We cannot understand behavior reductively; we must understand it as a being-in-relation-to and as an expression of its intention, of its basic project. Perception, intention, and action, then, are firmly interwoven. To paraphrase Merleau-Ponty, the intention comes to know itself and *to be* by an incarnation of itself in action (1962, 183ff.).

The concept of attention is integral here. In the HE view, a person will be unwilling to attend to an object, fact, or situation until he is willing to experience some potency, some action, regarding it.[4] Thus we see clients who are unwilling to take a different stand toward their world view, toward their cosmology, or to look at and inspect their intentions, and, still staying with their old systems, they expect things to be different for them. Consider, for example, a 23-year old woman who is locked into indecision about a divorce from her husband of three years. She cannot decide to finally initiate

---

[4]That action may be nothing more than an affirmation, an embracing, or the simple statement, "Yes, that is what I want; that is what I am." The "now" is, of course, implied.

divorce proceedings and go to her lover, nor can she decide to relinquish her lover and reestablish her marriage. This woman's indecision *is her intention*. It is an expression of her world view:

> Somewhere inside me there is the true answer to my happiness, to what I should do—divorce my husband and go to X or give X up and stay with my husband. So, Doctor, put me under hypnosis to discover the locked-up bubble inside me that contains my decision, where the answer lies to what will be a happier choice for me.

At the same time that she is telling her dream and seeing the "right" decision elicited, she is also saying that she knows there is no secret place where the right decision lies and that it is silly to look for omens of this correct choice. But she does not really believe it. She is not ready to take a position on (and thus to see) what she later comes to see:

> If I really believed that I make my own truth by acting, then I would decide. I can't know what the future will bring, but I am not ready to take a position of action. I still hope for and wait for an omen to reveal the right decision for me; I still read the horoscopes in the paper, as if the truth is "there" somewhere. I see that I am committed to this view.

This person's basic meaning is her way of seeing the world—a view in which truth and "good decisions" are known and exist and we match our decisions with that ideal world. Her commitment is to seek omens in dreams and astrology in hope that the truth, the right decision, will "come to her." Her basic intention is expressed in her inaction, in her deliberation. Her committed choice is to hope and to wait. In understanding this woman or in explaining her behavior, we do not resort to analyzing or to reducing her behavior to ever smaller units. On the contrary, we "expand" the case to a statement that speaks of her basic intentionality, of her intimate relationship with the world via her basic project, which is to deny that she is free to invent her decisions, and to wait for decisions to befall her. Rollo May speaks to this point:

> We sense we shall be fired from our job, someone we love will die imminently. But what goes on is a curious inner conversation with ourselves, "I know I *will* be able to see this later on, but I cannot see it now," which is simply a way of saying, "I know it is true, but I cannot permit myself to see it." The patient, like all of us, cannot permit himself to perceive until he is ready to take some stand toward the event (1969b, p. 83).

Most often persons are unwilling to see something because to take a look means that a different position is already in effect, that a change in one's intentions, in one's cosmology,[5] has taken place. And most persons are

---

[5]By cosmology, I mean that system of basic perceptions and the hierarchical organization of assumptions, assertions, and conceptions which culminate in a person's belief system, his view of how the world is, and of how he must be in that world in order to accomplish his major projects.

unwilling to do that—to inspect or to dither with their intentions merely by seeing clearly. They prefer to hold on to their hopes in the face of massive disconfirmations of reality, and their suffering is the negative aspect of their commitment.

Another example of this idea is the instance of insight following a different course of action rather than leading it (Hobbs, 1962). Allen Wheelis puts it brilliantly:

> The most common delusion of patients, and strangely, even of experienced therapists, is that insight produces change; and the most common disappointment of therapy is that is does not. Insight is instrumental to change, often an essential component of the process, but does not directly achieve it. The most comprehensive and penetrating interpretation—true, relevant, well expressed, perfectly timed—may lie inert in the patient's mind; for he may always, if he be so inclined, say, "Yes, but it doesn't help."[6] If a therapist takes the position, as many do, that a correct interpretation is one that gets results, that the getting of results is an essential criterion for the correctness of an interpretation, then he will be driven to more and more remote constructions of childhood events, will move further and further from present reality, responding always to the patient's "Yes, but why?" with further reachings for more distant antecedents. The patient will be saying in effect, "Yes, but what are you going to do about it?" and the therapist instead of saying as he should, "What are *you* going to do about it?" responds according to his professional overestimate of the efficacy of insight by struggling toward some ever more basic formulation (1969, p. 59).

It is a mistake to believe that the particular lifestyle that brings difficulty to the person is somehow an affliction. The symptom does not afflict the person. The symptom *is* the person. This is so because the person continues to lead his life according to his belief-system, meanings, and intentions. The pain and the pleasure in his life follow these intentions, and when he is ready to take some different position toward his system (take some action, make some change) it will already have changed.

As yet another example, consider an anguished woman who has twice attempted suicide because she cannot make decisions about what color to paint her furnishings or whether to purchase a new house. She says that if she buys a new house and it turns out to be a mistake, she will not be able to live. Consequently, she cannot make a decision. She is in a constant state of worry, distress, and indecision because a decision is irrevocable and will mark her inferiority as a person if it does not turn out perfectly; then she will have to take her own life. This person's cosmology is based on an "adult world" where decisions are always correct. "Adults know what they want, and they get it without indecision. And these adults always decide correctly." This woman cannot face the fact that the future is in principle unknowable and that there is no serious adult world "out there" that is

---

[6]This would be but another example of that person's strong commitment to his position.

always correct. Instead, she prefers to maintain the safety of believing in an ideal adult world against which she always compares herself. Since her comparisons always leave her wanting, she lives in a great deal of pain. She wants to get rid of the pain, but she is not ready to lead her life on a different basis. She knows intellectually that there is no adult world out there, but she is not willing to risk a life without essentialistic premises and assertions.

"After what shall I model myself then?" the woman asks when her assertion about the adult world is queried. "Without that, what do I have? It would be unbearable." The seminal issue is that life as she has structured it *is* unbearable *now*. There is no use waiting for change to happen as a function of insight. Insight is finely interwoven with action. What needs to be illuminated is the "cosmology," the intentionality, of the person, and what it brings him or her in terms of happiness and pain. Thus, in most persons the bargain is struck:

> I must be willing to tolerate the pain in my life brought about by my meanings, to which I hold for the best of all possible reasons. I believe in them; I hope for them; I am committed to them. But when the pain becomes too great, I want to relieve it, without tinkering with my commitments. I prophesy that a life of different meanings where there is no authority other than the authority I create in the way I freely choose to live my life is too much for me to bear.

But that is only a hunch. It remains untested, and the person is unwilling to strike out in a new direction to confront it, to test it, to "check it out" with new behavior, new meanings. One is the other; I am my actions; I influence them, and they influence me.

In the broadest sense of the word, then, the endeavor to help persons to be in reality is to help them see and own their cosmologies, their intentions, their myths. I might add here that, beyond that recognition, it may be none of the therapist's business what the person *does* about them. As we shall see later, our prime concern is not to change behavior as such, not to strive for solutions to problems, but to help the person assume responsibility for his life. The HE feels that any other position is clearly manipulative and makes the counselor-therapist an arm of the administrative agencies of society or its institutions in subtly "helping" the person to conform to the behavioral styles, personality theory, mores, and values of the particular subculture or historical period in which he happens to exist.[7] The only way to avoid the error of what Silvan Tomkins calls a "systematic training in indecision"—the search for that which "drives them from their unconscious minds" or for the infantile or even preneonatal source of their behavioral patterns—or to avoid the therapist's playing psychological policeman is to broaden the person's base of thinking about himself in terms of his basic humanness, his free intentionality, and his commitments.

---

[7]In this connection, see Halleck (1971).

At the beginning of this section we noted Celia's unwillingness to accept her view of the world and her preference for calling herself sick. It is very difficult for persons to accept the fact that they are fully responsible for their intentions, for their basic projects, and for their interactions with the world. In her speech to Riley, Celia said that she would rather be sick than see the world as it appeared to her. That basic magical conversion is what we shall address when we consider the emotional life of man.

THE PSYCHOANALYTIC VIEW AND THE CONCEPT OF THE UNCONSCIOUS

The concept of the unconscious is basic to the Freudian view and emotion has an important related position in that system. Freud's great spokesman, Fenichel, conveys this:

> The portion of the conscious that is best known is the "repressed"—that which is unconscious because strong dynamic forces hinder its becoming conscious. The repressed pushes toward consciousness and motility; it consists of impulses seeking outlets. In this seeking activity, it tends to produce "derivatives," that is, to displace its cathexes into associatively connected ideas that are less objectionable to the conscious ego.... The repressed consists, first of all, of the ideas and conceptions connected with the aim of the warded-off impulses which, by being warded off, have lost their connection with verbal expression; by regaining verbalization, unconscious ideas become preconscious. But it is also meaningful to talk about unconscious sensation, feelings, or emotions.... They are unconscious "dispositions" toward these qualities, unconscious "longing for affects" striving towards development of affects that are held in check by opposing forces, while the individual does not know that he has such readiness toward rage or sexual excitement or anxiety or guilt feeling or whatever it may be...such unconscious dispositions toward affect...develop derivatives, betray themselves in dreams, in symptoms, and in other substitute formulation, or through the rigidity of the opposing behavior, or, finally, merely in general weariness (1945, p. 17).

Further on,

> Emotional spells occur without the consent or even against the will of the individual; persons who undergo emotional spells have "lost control."...In general the organism tends towards emotional regressions if it is in a state of tension. This is why an unduly intense emotional reaction generally can be regarded as a "derivative" of something that was previously suppressed (p. 21).

While more recent developments in ego psychology have added an important dimension to a psychoanalytic understanding of persons, they have taken nothing from the basic psychodynamic formulations of the role of unconscious processes. About the unconscious, Rappaport (1959) writes:

> The observations that in hypnosis and in the course of free association, the patient became aware of past experiences, or of relations between them, led to the assumption of the "nonconscious" survival of such experiences and the "nonconscious" existence of such relationships. But only the discovery that

such nonconscious experiences and relationships are subject to rules (e.g., the pleasure principle and the mechanisms of the primary process) different from those of our conscious behavior and thinking made the above mentioned phenomena . . . into evidence for the assumption of unconscious psychological processes. The essence of this assumption is that it conceptualizes these observations in psychological terms, though the processes inferred from them are subject to rules different from those of the familiar, conscious psychological processes. . . . It rejects both consciousness and logical relations as necessary criteria of psychological processes, and thus arrives at the concept of unconscious psychological processes *abiding by rules other than those of conscious processes* (1959, p. 112) [emphasis supplied].

Emotional spells and emotion generally are defined as a discharge of affect through channels other than those that exist for conscious volition. In a later formulation, emotional responses are a signal for help to the ego in order that the ego may deal with a mounting drive-press, but again, in nonconscious, automatic terms. We see then how such terms as "undergoing an emotion" or "emotions that surprise one" or "emotion as an irresistible force that develops according to laws peculiar to itself and whose course we are powerless to change" can come into being. The psychoanalytic structure sees man as being unaware of what he is doing when he feels whatever he feels in a particular situation. Sometimes he is even struggling against being inundated in spite of himself—the emotion occurs "against the will of the individual" (Fenichel, 1945, p. 17).

There are two important points to be made clear about the Freudian view of emotion. First, psychoanalytic theory *does* accept emotion as signifying something (as opposed to Skinner, who defines emotions as "a particular state of strength or weakness in one or more responses induced by any one class of operations" (1953, p. 166). That is, analytic theory seems to point out that every state of consciousness is a derivative *only*, and the equivalent of something other than itself. Consciousness then is the symbolic representation of the desire that resided in the unconscious and has been repressed therein by censorship. Emotion is not a thing in itself, but an echo, a compromise, so to speak, in a struggle between irresistible instinctual desires and the counterforces of the ego that have to repress them.

Second, it is crucial to note that there *is no* implication, no hint, no idea, in consciousness of what the "real" unconscious desire is. The woman who wants to become pregnant has no idea that behind her wish is the desire to have a male infant who, in turn, will supply her with her missing (castrated) penis—the part that will then complete her.

But *all* of them [girls] make the mother responsible: she deprived them of something or took something away from them . . . the aim is now to get from the father the "supplies" that the mother had denied them. In the girl's fantasy, the idea "penis" is replaced by the idea "child" . . . (Fenichel, 1945, p. 90).

Indeed, in this case, though the female does not have any hint of the reality of it, all of feminine psychology is totally dependent upon her unknown lack and desire for a penis: "Her whole development may be said to take place under the influence of her envy for the penis" (Freud, 1949, p. 97).

The central aspect here is that to the woman, her cognitive wish is "pure": to become a mother. If it were not pure, if she had some hint of her unconscious desire to have a penis, then she would be simply dishonest, and that is precisely *not* what the analyst means. What the analyst means is that the symbol (pregnancy) is cut off from the thing for which the symbol stands. Pregnancy is only an "external sign," then, a trace, even a symptom of the real, unknown meaning.

To the humanistic existentialist, the Freudian state of consciousness stands in direct opposition to the very meaning of consciousness—a consciousness that contains no hidden clauses at all. The HE view, which contrasts with the self-obliviousness of the psychoanalytic view, has special significance to the person who deals with others in a helping capacity because, depending upon his view of consciousness, he can aid and abet the fiction of the "patient" or can help him on the road toward autonomy, clarity, and responsibility. The counselor or therapist, by his stand, can help the person who comes to him to view his life in terms of unconsciously determined impulses, or he can help him see his life in terms of commitments, projects, and freedom. By the nature of his responses (based on his conception of reality) the therapist lets the person know what his values are and helps the person to view reality in terms of those values. If a therapist believes in the concept of the Freudian unconscious, then, when a person says to him, "I don't know," the therapist will think and respond in terms of "Well, yes, of course you don't know; it is unconscious," and so will understand (support) the client's view of himself as "having an area of understanding that is oblivious to him." On the other hand, if the therapist views human reality as essentially lucid, with no unknowable areas, he might respond to an "I don't know" on the client's part with, "When you say, 'I don't know,' it means to me that you don't wish to look or to attend; it is not so deeply hidden that you can't discover the reason for it quite soon, in this hour." Whatever the therapist does, he informs the person of his values and so teaches the person how he might think about himself and in what terms human beings are to be defined or not to be defined at all.

The salient features of the Freudian unconscious can be summarized as follows:

1. The unconscious is a world unto itself—outside conscious awareness, inaccessible to inspection. One can only know derivatives of it, never the unconscious itself.
2. The unconscious is governed by the primary process.
3. The unconscious is the reservoir of repressed material. There are two

kinds of repression: primal repression and repression proper. Both occur automatically and without awareness. Primal repression refers to the automatic activity that prevents an instinctual object-choice—a choice that has never been conscious—from becoming conscious. Primal repressions are somewhat like the Jungian collective unconscious in that they are innately determined barriers designed to keep a large and significant part of the contents of the id permanently out of the person's awareness.

As Hall says:

> These primal repressions have been built into the person as a result of racial experiences with painful situations. For example, the taboo against incest is said to be based on a strong desire for sexual relations with one's father or mother. The expression of this desire is punished by the parents. When this happens over and over again during the racial history of mankind, the repression of the incestuous desire is built into man and becomes a primal repression. This means that each new generation does not have to learn to repress the desire since the repression itself is inherited (1954, p. 87).[7]

4. The unconscious determines that there is a link and a direct causal chain between the psychosexual epigenesis of the growing person and the behavior of the adult.

5. The unconscious influences conscious life at all times, albeit unknowingly, in veiled or symbolic fashion.

6. There is an inherent determinism between the child and the adult; between the conscious and the unconscious, between the impulse life of the person and the ego:

> Analytic experience has convinced us of the complete truth of the common assertion that the child is psychologically the father of the man and that the events of his first years are of paramount importance for his whole subsequent life... it is easy to observe the extent to which a child's susceptibility [to sexual stimulation and seduction] is aroused by such experiences and how his own sexual impulses are thus forced into certain channels which they can never leave again (Freud, 1949, p. 87).

7. Basically, it is the unconscious, and mostly sexual drives—wishes, ideas, and impulses—that cause *all* behavior.

> As regards another point—the specific instinctual factor—we come upon an interesting discrepancy between theory and experience. Theoretically there is no objection to supposing that any sort of instinctual demand whatever could occasion these same repressions and their consequences; but our observation shows us invariably, so far as we can judge, that the excitations that play this pathogenic part arise from the component instincts of sexual life. The symtoms of neuroses are exclusively, it might be said, either a substitutive satisfaction of some sexual impulse or measures to prevent such satisfaction, and are as a rule compromises between the two, of the kind that arises according to the laws operating between contraries in the unconscious (Freud, 1949, p. 85).

8. The unconscious *resists* becoming conscious. Even though the repression is automatic and immediate, the repressed impulses strain toward expression, but the resistance they meet causes them to be expressed in highly veiled, symbolic forms or as symptoms that are seen as compromises between the need for unconscious expression of impulses and resistance against their expression.

9. "The unconscious is really unconscious": I may know my ego, but I cannot know my id.

10. Most of the psychic energy in personality is contained in the unconscious.

11. Man is doomed to have to repress his impulses, and civilization and mental health are essentially functions of adequate repression and sublimation. As Freud writes:

> It may be difficult, too, for many of us to abandon the belief that there is an instinct towards perfection at work in human beings, which has brought them to their present high level of intellectual achievement and *ethical sublimation* and which may be expected to watch over their development into supermen. I have no faith, however, in the existence of any such internal instinct and I cannot see how this benevolent illusion is to be preserved. The present development of human beings requires, as it seems to me, no different explanation from that of animals. What appears in a minority of human individuals as an untiring compulsion toward further perfection can easily be understood as a result of *the instinctual repression upon which is based all that is most precious in human civilization* (1961, p. 36) [emphasis supplied].

With this description of the principles of the unconscious as laid out by Freud and his followers (according to Freud's last statements) we can proceed to the HE position regarding the unconscious. The HE challenges the concepts of the unconscious on three grounds: the evidence for a *unity* in psychological life, the assertion that there can not be censorship without a knowing censor, and the assertion that consciousness cannot be blind to itself because consciousness is a being the nature of which is to be conscious of itself.

THE CONCEPT OF BAD FAITH AS AN ALTERNATIVE TO THE UNCONSCIOUS

Instead of resorting to the concept of the unconscious in explaining human behavior, the HE utilizes instead the concept of bad faith. By bad faith I do not merely mean lying to others, because lying implies that the liar is in fact in complete possession of the truth, which he chooses to hide from others. While the person's intention is to deceive, he might even be willing to admit the truth to a chosen few when it suits his purpose.

Bad faith, on the other hand, is a lie to oneself: it is from me, from myself, that I intend to hide the truth. There is no duality here, no distinction between the lie and the one to whom one is lying. Significantly, bad faith is founded on the notion of the unity of a single consciousness.

Consciousness seems to be as essential to selfhood as is unity. There is no self without a mind and no mind without awareness. Animals have personality, no doubt, but no animal can say "I," and to say so with meaning implies awareness of who is saying it. To have a self is to be self-conscious.... An "unconscious idea" in the strict sense is thus a contradiction in terms. To have an idea is to think of something, and this in turn presupposed being aware of oneself as having that thought.... Every thought is, so to say, conceived in awareness: its being is its being known for what it is.... An unconscious idea need not always have been unconscious but may have become so as a result of censorship and repression. But even this is puzzling. For who is it that excludes the content from *my* consciousness? I as censor must be other than the I who am unaware of what the censor has repressed. But I am not other than myself. As Sartre has argued, "The very essence of the reflexive idea of hiding from oneself implies the unity of one and the same psychic mechanism" (Kaplan, 1970, p. 6A).

We see, then, that bad faith does not come from the outside, nor does it come from others. One does not *undergo* bad faith, just as one does not undergo an emotion. Bad faith is not a state. It is a commitment to a way of being, just as emotion is a choice and the consequence of that choice. We might ask the question, "Why is it that I find myself so often unaware of the source of my feelings, or conflicts, or emotions? Why do I sense the inadequacy of my conception of myself concerning this whole issue?"

Two answers seem to recur in my work with clients. The events that lead by progression to a certain act, feeling, or emotion are not sufficiently attended to; and, secondly, when they are attended to, they are not believed. The reason they are not believed is that people have been taught, through obscurantist and incorrect assumptions that may go something like the following: "The reason for my hostility to my supervisor cannot be as simple as the fact that he is a bastard; I must have some other 'deeper reason' in my unconscious. I do not exist in an interpersonal world. You see, Doctor, I do need therapy." Or, "I must endure this bad marriage or relationship because 'healthy people' do. My feelings must not be right; they must signify some pathology."

Bad faith is the converse of authentic existence. Essentialistic strivings, socially accepted norms, normative-statistical thinking, living for others, and "oughts" in general are often used to deny the validity of a person's vision and help him not to trust what he actually feels.

One patient had a sister who had been severely ill and was anxious about the illness. During a discussion with the sister about her illness, the patient, in a burst of concern and good feeling for the ill sister, offered her therapy hour to the sister. The sister came to see the therapist, and after a few minutes stated that she must be paranoid or crazy. When queried as to what led her to think so, she reported that she had a dream that the patient who had given up her therapy hour for her had actually stabbed her and tried to kill her. She saw the patient as a hostile creature. "Now, there must be something wrong with me. She did, after all, give me her hour. She must have good feelings about me. Yet I had this dream and this feeling that she *was* hostile to me. That can't be. I must be paranoid."

When asked to look at the good reasons for these feelings, it was found that the woman thought any decision that a person made had to be a *pure* decision. If her sister (the regular patient) had offered her the hour, the offer could not be tainted with mixed feelings or with some resentment. As she spoke about it, she revealed the attitude that mixed feelings are "sick," that only sick people have conflicts, and, as a former therapist had told her, that "ambivalence is the hallmark of neurosis." She was asked to examine the truth about her own decisions. Were they ever pure? Was she ever 100-percent certain about anything she had to decide about? She said that her decisions were always based on "the weight of the evidence, as I know it," but rarely with any 100-percent sureness. She then wondered whether this was a normal state of affairs and asked the therapist:

Pt: Listen, how do you feel about your decisions? Do you ever have mixed-up feelings about them?

Th: Whenever I am asked a question like that, I feel in danger.[8] I think that you are doing what you seem to have talked about before, gauging your own thoughts and actions according to some statistical norm. I'm not trying to avoid answering merely to avoid it—I'll answer it, but we have to talk later about what that kind of question means, and what that kind of position leads you to. Anyway, the truth about my decisions seems to be that they are rarely zero or 100-percent. I find that in *my* life there is rarely a moment of absolute purity of choice. That most of my choices are made on the *weight* of my feeling or preferences—40:60 maybe at best, but rarely zero or 100. But the other side of the choice, the other alternative, somehow continues to live in me. I decided to buy X car as opposed to Y car. I bought the X car, and I too somehow expected the Y car to disappear as a function of my decision. But it seems to me now that only computers can make a "yes" choice without any regrets about the "no" part of it. Maybe your sister wanted to give up her hour, oh, let's say 60 percent, but she also regretted doing it. The 40 percent still lives in her, and you sensed that. But your belief in the purity of the decision-making process did not permit you to see the whole of that reality. You called yourself sick instead.

This proved to be a provocative confrontation because the sister went on to describe her own ambivalence about many things, and how she continually put herself down for not being "certain" or sure of many things and

---

[8]The danger here is that with persons who search for agreement, the therapist might agree and so support the patient's own feelings: "Hey, Doc, you ever do that?" If the answer is affirmative, the patient feels supported, but what if the answer is negative?

many of the decisions that she made. Her former therapist had taught her that ambivalence was sick or neurotic. This had perpetuated her feelings of unreality about herself and her denial of the truth of her own vision. This is but one example of how people deny the truth about themselves on the basis of some "system" of what should be, on the basis of a serious world (Sartre, 1956; Barnes, 1959). When the sister came to grips with the reality of things for her—that she is often unsure of her decisions (and that indeed is the place where a *decision*[9] is required) and often thinks about the alternative—and when she recognized how she had devaluated and "put down" that reality, she seemed to feel more whole.

Another example of this wish for purity might be helpful. A woman who was divorcing her husband was constantly worried because even after she had decided to proceed with the divorce, she still thought about her former husband and was not absolutely certain about her decision:

Th: I wonder what you expected about your decisions?

Pt: Well, I expected that once I decided, that would be the end of it, and I wouldn't think about it anymore. I wonder whether the fact that I still think about Steve means that I shouldn't divorce him.

Th: I don't know about that. But I certainly see how you think about decisions and yourself in general.

The idea of man-as-computer who can make difficult decisions with ease and without ever thinking back to the other alternative, and the idea of "health" associated with that kind of purity often replaces the reality of what *is* for the individual person.

Huxley seems to hit on the idea in a similar way:

Nobody needs to go anywhere else. We are all, if we only knew it, already there.

If I only knew who in fact I am, I should cease to behave as what I think I am; and if I stopped behaving as what I think I am, I should know who I am.

What in fact I am, if only the Manichee I think I am would allow me to know it, is the reconciliation of yes and no lived out in total acceptance and the blessed experience of Not-Two.

Because his aspiration to perpetuate only the "yes" in every pair of opposites can never, in the nature of things, be realized, the insulated Manichee I think I am condemns himself to endlessly repeated frustration, endlessly repeated conflicts with other aspiring and frustrated Manichees.

Knowing who in fact we are results in Good Being, and Good Being results in the most appropriate kind of good doing. But good doing does not of itself result in Good Being. We can be virtuous without knowing who in fact we are. The beings who are merely good are not Good Beings; they are just pillars of society....

Good Being is knowing who in fact we are; and in order to know who in fact we are, we must first know, moment by moment, who we think we are and what

---

[9]A *decision* is required when the two sides of an issue are relatively equally weighted; when one side clearly outweighs the other, no decision is required; it is a foregone conclusion.

the bad habit of thought compels us to feel and do. A moment of clear and complete knowledge of what we think we are, but in fact are not, puts a stop, for the moment, to the Manichean charade. If we renew, until they become a continuity, these moments of the knowledge of what we are not, we may find ourselves, all of a sudden, knowing who in fact we are (1962, pp. 36-36).

Significantly, in the HE view, the lie and the liar are *of* the same person; we must, at every level, sense the truth (albeit often in a prereflective fashion) in our capacity as the deceiver:

Better yet I must know the truth exactly *in order* to conceal it more carefully— and that is not two different moments, which in a pinch would allow us to reestablish a semblance of duality—but in the unitary structure of a single project (Sartre, 1956, p. 49).

Since, for the HE, consciousness can hold no secrets from itself (it is totally one and translucent), then when we affect ourselves to bad faith, we must be conscious of our bad faith. It is in this manner that bad faith is always a very precarious project; nevertheless it has, for a great many people, a very durable aspect, even to becoming a lifestyle. I find in working with people that such a lifestyle costs the person something, usually a sense of self-betrayal and a profound sense of disquiet, anxiety, and "lostness."

To avoid the total, inescapable responsibility that translucency (even potential translucency) imposes on man, people more than gladly look for recourse in the existence of an unconscious, in the presence of structures that are unknown and for which one cannot be held responsible. In the standard psychoanalytic formulation this unconscious is defined as "repression proper":

By being kept out of awareness, [note here that who is being kept out of awareness is not named], dangerous instinctual object-choices are unable to evoke anxiety on the principle that what we don't know can't hurt us. However, these object-choices may affect behavior in various indirect ways or associate themselves with material which does become conscious, thereby arousing anxiety. The Ego may then deal with the disguised penetration of threatening Id-cathexes into consciousness or behavior by instituting repression proper.... Repression proper... forces a dangerous memory, idea, or perception out of consciousness and sets up a barrier against any form of motor discharge (Hall, 1954, p. 88).

This statement describes a construct of a kind of censor that is like a border, with customs and various controls all necessary to reestablish the duality of the deceiver and the deceived.

Since Freud defined the original psychic reality as constituted by the Id[10], we see that the instincts in the Id make up reality, but a reality that by

---

[10]According to Hall:

Freud speaks of the Id as being the true psychic reality. By this he means that the Id is the primary subjective reality, the inner world that exists before the individual has had experience of the external world. Not only are the instincts and reflexes inborn, but also the images that are produced by tension states may also be innate. This means that a hungry baby can have an image of food without having had to associate food with hunger (Hall, 1954, p. 20).

virtue of the distinction between the Ego and the Id, has been cut into two pieces. Psychic reality is divided: "I am the Ego, but I am not the Id." Further, "I myself can never know the truth." The truth of man's reality then, is, totally dependent upon another—the psychoanalyst! The analyst must serve as mediator between the forever unconscious drives and impulses and their conscious derivatives.

The psychoanalyst uses the notion of unconscious dynamics in this manner: unconscious instincts exert a press; automatic censorship via repression occurs, resulting in symptoms that are veiled compromises between the unknowable unconscious and the demands of reality. All this is in service of establishing the concept of censorship without a censor, theft without thieves, and automatic psychological functions without functionaries.

The same issue applies to resistance, which becomes manifest when the analyst, via interpretation, makes attempts at making conscious a repressed wish. What part of the self does the actual resisting? How can one resist what one does not know? Clearly, if there is to be censorship, there must also be knowledge of what it is that needs to be censored, and the censor must be the only part of the personality that can understand what the analyst is driving at in his attempts at interpretation. The censor must, then, know what it is repressing so that it can be discriminating and not repress everything in sight; thus, it permits "lawful" impulses such as hunger and thirst to emerge into consciousness:

> The censor must also apprehend them *as to be repressed* which implies in it at the very least an awareness of its activity. In a word, how could the censor discern the impulses needing to be repressed without being conscious of discerning them? How can we conceive of a knowledge which is ignorant of itself? To know is to know that one knows.... All knowing is consciousness of knowing. Thus the resistance of the patient implies on the level of the censor an awareness of the thing repressed as such, a comprehension of the end towards which the questions of the psychoanalyst are leading, and an act of synthetic connection by which it compares the *truth* of the repressed complex to the psychoanalytic hypotheses which aims at it (Sartre, 1956, pp. 52-53).

When we examine the concept of an unconscious impulse disguising itself in the slips and symbols, the parapraxes of behavior, we encounter similar difficulties. How can the repressed drive disguise itself if it is not conscious of being repressed, if it is not conscious of having been pushed back because of what it is, and if it is not conscious of the project of disguise?

To add to the confusion, Laing (1971) points out that further verbal structures are needed to square the unconscious, censorship, resistance, and interpretation. Such verbal incongruities add greatly to the therapist's confusion and, importantly, to the patient's. The lay person has learned of these ideas (unconscious, repression, resistance), that have been popularized and takes them to be a truth against which to compare his own experience, and he often comes up wanting. To extricate itself from a logically untenable situation, psychoanalysis has had to establish a censor in bad faith, and an autonomous censor at that. Often this structure is used to punish the patient subtly: since man has no freedom in this system, he has no choice but to be sick; external forces in combination with his structural dynamics have pinned him to the wall. The patient has little choice but to become neurotic or psychotic, but he does have a choice of cooperating or not cooperating with the treatment. His lack of cooperation is called resistance, a choice on the part of the patient "not to see, not to get well" (cf., Laing, 1971, pp. 67-75).

In therapeutic situations the concept of the Freudian unconscious leads to practical difficulties. The theme is the same: the patient is not free to be conscious, yet he is held free and responsible for his resistance to treatment. As we have seen, these positions are clearly contradictory, both logically and in terms of our own awareness. Further, in analytic terms, if the analyst is able to overcome the resistance to his interpretation, the patient must accept the interpretation as the truth. If he does not, then the interpretation was given "too soon" or, again, the patient is resisting. In any event, the patient is unable to interpret his own feelings and needs the analyst as a mediator. The analyst takes the patient's acceptance of the truth of the much-resisted interpretation as self-fulfilling evidence of two kinds: (1) evidence of the existence of the unconscious and (2) evidence that the aim of psychoanalytic therapy is closer in view. The patient can go on, then, to the "proper cure." Note, here, Sartre's view of the uses of the patient's testimony as evidence of a self-fulfilling prophecy on the analyst's part:

Precisely because the goal of the inquiry must be to discover a *choice* and not a *state,* the investigator must recall on every occasion that his object is not a datum buried in the darkness of the unconscious but a free, conscious determination—which is not even resident in consciousness, but which is one with this consciousness itself. Empirical psychoanalysis is often in sight of an existential discovery, but it always stops part way. When it thus approaches the fundamental choice the resistance of the subject collapses suddenly and he *recognizes* the image of himself which is presented to him as if he were seeing himself in a mirror. This involuntary testimony of the subject is precious for the psychoanalyst; he sees there the sign that he has reached his goal; he can pass on from the investigation proper to the cure. But nothing in his principles or in his initial postulates permits him to understand or to utilize this testimony. Where could he gain any such right? If the complex is really unconscious... how could the subject *recognize* it? Does the unconscious complex recognize itself?... Shall we say on the other hand that it is the subject as conscious who recognizes the image presented [to him by the analyst as an interpretation]? But how could he compare it with his true state since that is out of reach and since he has never had any knowledge of it? At most he will be able to judge that the psychoanalytic explanation of this case is a *probable* hypothesis, which derives its probability from the number of behavior patterns which it explains. His relation to this interpretation is that of a third party, that of the psychoanalyst himself; he has no privileged position. And if he *believes* in the probability of the psychoanalytic hypothesis, is this simple belief, which lives in the limits of his consciousness, able to effect the breakdown of the barriers which dam up the unconscious tendencies? The psychoanalyst doubtless has some obscure picture of an abrupt coincidence of conscious and unconscious. But he has removed all methods of conceiving of this coincidence in any positive sense. . . . In this case, as we have seen, the traditional psychoanalytic interpretation does not cause him to attain *consciousness* of what he is; it causes him to attain *knowledge* of what he is (1956, pp. 573-74).

Despite the psychoanalyst's injunction against advice and giving information, these processes are imbedded in working with an analysand who is considered to suffer mainly from ignorance. The analyst must teach, and the analysand must accept. Freud (1910) originally viewed neurosis as an ignorance of the facts of one's life and considered the analyst's role to be the "removal of ignorance" by giving the patient information about the causal connection between his illness and his life. Later his position changed: "The pathological factor is not his ignorance in itself, but the root of this ignorance in his *inner resistances;* it was they that first called this ignorance into being, and they still maintain it now" (1910, p. 225).

Freud recognized that this was merely a shift relative to the *content* of interpretations. He never abandoned teaching procedures that led to the conquest of passion by reason:

Since, however, psycho-analysis cannot dispense with giving this information, it lays down that this shall not be done before two conditions have been fulfilled. First, the patient must, through preparation, himself have reached the neighborhood of what he has repressed, and secondly, he must have formed a sufficient attachment (transference) to the physician for his emotional relationship to make a fresh flight impossible.

Only when these conditions have been fulfilled is it possible to recognize and to master the resistances which have led to the repression and the ignorance (pp. 225-226).

The standard psychoanalytic formulation seems to give rise to a paradox. The process of recognizing and accepting or rejecting the analyst's interpretation implies a comparative process on the part of the patient, a comparison of the analyst's interpretation with the patient's "inner truth." To be capable of this comparison, the patient must be conscious, aware of his own unconscious processes.

In psychoanalytic terms, then, there is no way in which resistance, symbolization, censorship, or repression can be coherently or logically understood. There cannot be censorship without a censor, and there is no way that any person cannot know (1) what needs to be repressed, (2) that what needs to be repressed has been repressed, and (3) what the content of the repression was. Experiences cannot be hidden or denied if one does not know what needs to be hidden.

Only one recourse is left: the presumption of a concept wherein the person is possessed or inhabited by forces of which he has no awareness—forces that, in a hydraulic-like mode, manipulate the expression, fluidity, and transformation of energy. This mode is one wherein solipsism prevails: unconscious impulses are not permitted conscious awareness and are *therefore* repressed. This is a construct that has no logical or syntactical meaning. Compare it, for the sake of clarity, to an analogous statement: I do not know the time because time is unknowable—*therefore* time is repressed. Conkling has put the case well:

> We do not know the unconscious. We do not know the impulse. We do not know that we have repressed. But we know the painful impulse and recognize it when it has been pointed out in analysis. It is curious that this "knowledge" would be trusted as evidence by the therapist because in terms of meaning Freud could have just as easily talked of "forces of evil" or some other such vacuous notion. Given the constitution of the censor, he could not perform the function Freud assigns to him and still remain consistent with the theory in which he is couched. Metaphors notwithstanding, the process itself is not consistent. It would be hard to conceive of a meaningful foundation of repression which was not inordinately mechanistic and relied on viewing man as a peculiar kind of robot (1968, pp. 98-99).

This would be a robot who has no choice about becoming sick since he is completely unconscious of his impulses, but who is given the choice by the analyst of cooperating or not cooperating with the treatment, and the choice of accepting or not accepting the analyst's interpretations. These interpretations, in turn, are based on the analyst's theory and the analyst's world-view.[11] In the final analysis, the analyst teaches the patient what life is all about, what man is all about, what his cosmology should be. When the patient accepts the cosmology with all its subordinate corollaries, he is pronounced cured, even though, as one analyst pointed out to me, "he commits suicide or murder the next day."

The self-fulfilling prophecy finds its place in psychoanalytic thought in this manner: "If you deny that you are not ruled by unconscious forces, then you are simply further unaware of the reality of absolute necessity and

---

[11]In discussing interpretation and whole concept of imposing preconceived notions on the patient, Sullivan has warned that the therapist may all too often interpret the material presented by the patient to fit the therapist's notions of what constitutes a person and ignore the reality of the patient:

> Some people have great difficulty in developing alternative hypotheses for any given set of facts. The first thing that comes to mind seems to them to be self-evident. Anything else is self-evidently erroneous. They can scarcely listen to a presentation of contradictory data; they may be polite and hear one out, only to renew the presentation of their previous views.... This sort of person and the one whose security depends on creating an impression of omniscience are alike unsuited to the role of psychiatrist (1941, p. 187).

determinism of sexual impulses. You cannot 'admit' that you are not the creator of your self (and therefore free) because you are infected with narcissism." Freud (1925) made this point strongly:

> We learn that, when we come to try to comprehend neurotic disorders, by far the most significance attaches to the sexual instincts; in fact neuroses are the specific disorders, so to speak, of the sexual function (p. 348).
>
> The whole process, however, only becomes possible through the single circumstance that you are mistaken in another important point as well. You believe that you are informed of all that goes on in your mind if it is of any importance at all, because your consciousness then gives you news of it.... In all cases, however, the news that reaches your consciousness is incomplete and often not to be relied on.... You conduct yourself like an absolute sovereign. It is thus that psycho-analysis wishes to educate the ego. But these two discoveries—that the life of the sexual instincts cannot be totally restrained, and that mental processes are in themselves unconscious and only reach the ego and come under its control through incomplete and untrustworthy perception—amount to a statement that THE EGO IS NOT MASTER IN ITS OWN HOUSE. Together they represent the third wound inflicted on man's self-love, that which I call the PSYCHOLOGICAL one. No wonder therefore, that the ego shows no favour to psycho-analysis and persistently refuses to believe in it (p. 355).

It is in this manner, by rejecting the conscious unity of the psychological nature of man, that Freud and the Freudians are forced to imply everywhere a "magic unity" linking distant phenomena across obstacles.

> The unconscious drive (Trieb) through magic is endowed with the character "repressed" or "condemned," which completely pervades it, colors it, and magically provides its symbolism. Similarly the conscious phenomenon is entirely colored by its symbolic meaning although it cannot apprehend this meaning by itself in clear consciousness.... Aside from its inferiority in principle, the explanation by magic does not avoid the coexistence—on the level of the unconscious, on that of the censor, and on that of consciousness—of two contradictory, complementary structures which reciprocally imply and destroy each other. Proponents of the theory have hypostasized and "reified" bad faith; they have not escaped it (Sartre, 1956, pp. 53-54).

Before carrying our discussion further, let us summarize: on the one hand, because it splinters psychological unity, the explanation of human behavior by means of the unconscious cannot account for the facts of those behaviors that come to the psychologist's attention, even though it might appear at first sight to have explained them. On the other hand, we see a wide variety of behaviors in bad faith that explicitly reject this kind of explanation precisely because their essence implies that they can appear only in the translucency of consciousness. Such thinking about unity and translucency, gives true hope and dignity to man's endeavors; it helps man to understand his phenomenal world and to affirm it, and it leads to the possibility of man's assumption of responsibility in his life. This position truly makes man's universe among others a hominocentric one. Further, and importantly, this kind of thinking tends to eliminate the "teaching," "expert" role that helpers seem to assume with the client, a role that is based on the arrogance of superior knowledge, a greater knowledge of the person than the person has himself. That arrogant position, I believe, further reinforces the person's problem of being unknowable to himself, of being driven by forces he can only hazily understand, and of being intrinsically, essentially divided, a "man against himself."

In summary, to the HE the concept of the Freudian unconscious is contradictory to the facts of human behavior. Consciousness cannot have in it an element of unconsciousness. There is no black box, no topographic place that is in principle unknown and unknowable to us. The whole logical structure of human reality, human consciousness, human unity, and human freedom leads to the firm conclusion that there can be nothing opaque, no "territories in hiding" cut off from our proximal consciousness and awareness if we do not wish to have it so.

Such statements about a superior position and a superior knowledge make a critical difference in how we shall think about and respond to our clients.

> Recently, an orthodox Freudian analyst described to the writer why patients come for therapy. He stated that the patient "is not potent." I commented, "The patient *feels* that he is not potent. His hope is often minimal." The analyst again said, "He *is* not potent." The orthodox analyst's comment embodies his perception of the patient. When asked why patients would be encouraged to return for therapy after they have completed analysis, the orthodox analyst replied, "Because I know more and am more expert. I am a physician and I read and study." There you have it. This intelligent and sensitive man, who also practices group therapy, believes that he continues to be the doctor, and he does not accept that therapy finally moves to a peer relationship. He believes that when the chips are down his knowledge makes him more expert. This internationally known and very experienced analyst confuses an essential point—to be an expert about living does not mean that one is expert in living (Rosenbaum, 1969, p. 68).

And again, the way in which the therapist responds *teaches* the client not only about the therapist and the client, but also makes a value statement about the way things really are. The client's progress in orthodox therapeutic formats inevitably is measured by his movement in relation to the therapist's conception of the nature of man.

REFLECTIVE AND PREREFLECTIVE MODES

What about our awareness of the fact that we are not always attending to all that goes on within us? When I look at myself at any given moment, it does seem that I am not aware of all that is going on within me. Clearly, the HE must be able to account for different types of consciousness. Just as clearly as I, at any given moment, do not know why I have responded thus and so to a specific situation, many clients say, "O.K., I see that I am free to choose this or that—just so long as I am *aware* of my situation, just so long as I am reflecting on it. But what about those things that I do without full awareness, without attention? They seem to trap me!"

For the HE, the danger here is that he will bring back the unconscious, "through the back door" as it were. The HE distinguishes between nonreflective consciousness and reflective consciousness. The difference between nonreflective or passive consciousness and reflective or active consciousness is that in the reflective mode we choose to pay close attention to our own responses, to the object of our awareness. We look at ourselves, we pay attention to our own inner process. This is, indeed, what happens in counseling and in therapy. The helper *participates* in the person's choice to look at himself. The nonreflective mode, on the other hand, is the choice to direct our awareness solely outward. In this mode we are aware of others, of objects, of events, but we choose not to attend to our own awareness of them.

To recall an earlier discussion, clients often say "I don't know" about their behaviors when they speak to the therapist. The orthodox analyst tends to think about an "I don't know" on the patient's part in this manner: "Of course he doesn't know." But the HE says, perhaps, "When you say 'I don't know,' might you not mean, 'I just don't want to look'? Let's take a look at [so and so]. It might not be so opaque that we can't come to understand it quite soon."

Surprisingly enough, most clients seem able to come to understand the possibilities of seeing and comprehending their so-called "unconscious" motives, if they choose to believe what they see about themselves instead of "buying" some other system that tells them that the "true" reasons are murky, deep, in the past, really hidden deep in the unconscious, and buried in symbolism. In fact, many persons choose (for good reasons) not to believe what indeed they see; they want to attribute their motives, attitudes, and behaviors to a realm of murky understanding and inevitable opacity. People have been taught to be oblivious to themselves for the good reason that such clarity of vision leads to a frightening responsibility and self-knowledge:

> Why will not the patient (child) let what *is* be *true?* The patient (child) will not let what *is* be true because when he perceives what *is,* he perceives directly the nature of the self and its relationship to reality. This he does not choose to tolerate. He perceives that he is not omnipotent; that he has need of and is dependent upon an outside world (mother and "life") for gratification and fulfillment, but that he does not control that source of gratification. The world may answer his pleas for help with a yes or no, but the principles that determine whether he gets a yes or no answer are largely independent of the system of energy he calls himself (Corey, 1966, p. 109).

To place it squarely within the framework of HE, the person will not only see but experience his ultimate freedom, his inescapable responsibility, his independence and lack of control over others, and the possibility that he can control his behavior on the road of life but not what *meets* him on that road. The HE believes that the person can come to understand clearly his basic projects in life, as well as the priorities he has chosen that lead to his actions. For example, a young man of 19 went to the university counseling center disturbed about the fact that he could not seem to form a lasting relationship with a girl. Every time it appeared, just as soon as his deep feeling would emerge, where love was discussed, his feeling would "suddenly disappear," and he could no longer care for the girl. It became inconsequential to him whether he saw her again or not. Associated with this phenomenon was a vexing and intermittent sexual impotency that this young man had experienced with a number of different girls, on a number of seemingly disparate occasions.

Pt: I tell you, it's just bugging the hell out of me. I don't know why this thing happens to me, but the feeling just goes away, vanishes. It really must be something very deep, something deeply wrong with me. Maybe I just can't love anyone. I seem to have had a very stormy childhood, and my parents fought a lot. Maybe that has something to do with it? I don't know. The only thing that I know is that the feeling just goes away like smoke disappears. I can't do anything about it. Wow, there sure must be something kinky in my mind.

Th: You seem to talk about it as if it happens to you, instead of you *making* it happen. Let's look at the good reasons why it might be important for you to shut your feeling down. You must have a good reason for...

Pt: I sure don't know what it might be. It's sick.

Th: You prefer to call it "sick," as if something is wrong with you. You call it names, instead of taking a good look at the reasons you might have for turning off.

Pt: Well, I guess [waits a long time], I think that I must be afraid to get involved. It scares me. I don't know whether I can live up to a relationship, of a real relationship with someone.

Th: You seem to see a deep relationship as demanding a lot of you—like work or something, and that scares you. Sure, that makes sense, if you see it that way, it *would* make sense that it would be scary.

Pt: Why should it scare me? That's not right, that's kinda weird.

Th: To be scared seems weird to you?

Pt: Yeah, I don't see anything to be scared of. I learned in my adjustment class that to be able to enter into deep relationships is a sign of health.

Th: You seem to take the attitude that your feelings are irrational. You say, "I'm scared," but there is really nothing to be scared of, as if your feelings had a life of their own.

Pt: Well, damn it, getting close to someone is dangerous. [forcefully] You begin to depend on them, and they on you, and it's all obligations and stuff like that.

The counselee went on to describe how he chose to see a deep relationship and how he wanted to maintain just a modicum of relatedness with persons—just the amount he could tolerate, not more. But he did not wish to authentically state that he could not tolerate, or was not willing, at this time in his life, to tolerate the anxiety feelings that accompanied his view of relationships in general. He saw relationships much as he did his feelings: as something to which one succumbs, rather than something that one works out and has freedom within. Another important point here is that the counselee did not take himself and his feeling seriously. His fears were unacceptable; he should not be afraid. He would rather call himself sick than affirm his own position by admitting how he structured his thinking about relationships and by accepting that these were good reasons, that his feelings followed his structure and "indicated" that structure rather than the other way around.

In HE therapeutic work the helper repeatedly points out the client's attempts to make a thing of himself and others by denying responsibility, choice, and good reasons and by accepting a serious world inhabited with a priori prerogatives and "shoulds" against which he compares and evaluates his own inner phenomenological reality. Feelings are a thing "out there," phenomena that "come over me from out there." Feelings represent something strange and weird, a price we must pay for our not always being fully human, for having an animal past. And the person himself is therefore an object, controlled by other things. Indeed, a relationship becomes not a viable being-in-relation to another, but rather enslavement. Again, there is some comfort in thinking about oneself as a machine. And the discipline of psychology has fostered this approach probably more than any other:

> A basically stimulus-response-oriented psychology has sold the belief that man is essentially a machine and that like any machine, he is capable of being simply "fixed up"—tuned up like a car, or, as the prevalent term has it, helped to "adjust." ... There is little doubt that in an era which has witnessed spectacular advances in technology, men (therapists and patients) look with hope to a machine model of man. If machines are perfectible, why should not people be equally maleable? So the patient, by definition terrified of being human, finds some false comfort in an image of non-humanness and the unrealistic, irrational hope of being a more effective machine. In this hope he of course reveals the depth of his pathology, for in effect he states that he looks toward the perpetuation of passivity, expects that he may remain basically passive, a machine activated by an outside source of energy, hopes that he may remain creature without becoming a creator—and do so without discomfort (Singer, 1965, pp. 107-8). It is to this issue that the concept of bad faith addresses itself: Despite other serious consequences, it is exquisitely tempting for man to abandon his humanness, his authentic being, and his freedom, because that abandonment *seems* to absolve man of his responsibility.

The major point to be made here is that the therapist, whoever he may be, cannot help but make his own position known by the nature, quality, and content of his interventions. He can aid and abet bad faith or point it out, together with the price that the patient must pay for his charade. The position of the therapist is critical here:

> When in therapy a life story of drift and constraint is reworked to expose alternatives for crucial courses of action, asking always, "Why did you do that?", attaching doubt to every explanation which is cast in the form of necessary reaction to antecedent cause, always reminding the patient that "Even so . . . it was possible to have acted otherwise,"—in all this one is rewriting the past, is taking the story of a life which was experienced as shaped by circumstance and which was recounted as such, and retelling it in terms of choice and responsibility. . . . And insofar as it may come to seem credible to rewrite one's life in terms of ignored choice, to assume responsibility retroactively for what one has done and so has become, it will become possible likewise to see alternatives in the present, to become aware that one is free now in this moment to choose how to live, and that what one will become will follow upon what he now does. . . .
>
> When, however, in therapy a life story is reworked to expose the forces which "drove" one to do as he did, emphasizing traumas which twisted him and shaped defenses, hidden constraints, situational and libidinal, which required that he react in the way he did and in no other—in all this, too, one is rewriting the past, is taking a story which must have contained some elements of freedom and responsibility and retelling it in terms of causes lying outside one's control, *so teaching the patient* to see himself as the product of inner and outer forces. Where he feels himself to be the author of actions, his analysis will reveal him as an object being acted upon. He then comes to regard himself as being lived by unknown and largely unknowable forces. As consolation prize, he may acquire the capacity to guess at the nature of those obscure forces that move him. But only guess. He must not attempt seriously to bear witness to that which, by definition, he cannot know. He must remain forever the dilettante, making modest conjecture at the gusts which blow him this way and that. He becomes not only an object but opaque, most necessarily to himself (Wheelis, 1969, pp. 56-66) [emphasis supplied].

The nadir of this kind of thinking was displayed by a psychiatrist who told me of treating a lonely and withdrawn young man—a schizophrenic. He told his patient that he did not need to feel bad or guilty about the things he did because he was being pushed by his schizophrenia, that he was sick and not in control but that when he was cured then he could feel guilty about the things he did.

The HE view of consciousness stands in direct contrast to this. *We* ourselves decide which things we will allow ourselves to look at (i.e., be explicitly aware of) and which things we will choose to ignore and by denying them attention, insist that they are outside of consciousness and therefore phenomena for which we are not and cannot be responsible. Bad faith is a way of organizing our reality. By pretending not to be aware of what we actually see or by acting prereflectively, we lie to ourselves. The primary mode of this kind of self-deception provides additional evidence for the power a free consciousness has to conceive of the being-in-itself, of nonexistence.

Bad faith accomplishes its task by turning a human reality into a non-human reality—an essentialistic, unfree, limited, determined *thing*. Man seems to have great difficulty in accepting the thought that his consciousness is nothing but a possibility for him to shape, mold, and invent, or that the essence of freedom is to make himself what he wills. Man seems all too willing to *be* anything so long as he can be it absolutely and irrevocably, whether it is a homosexual, a "hero," a paranoiac, sick, an "injustice collector," or an introversive personality. It seems to me one of man's reasons for choosing to do things that inevitably bring about guilt and self-punishment is the hidden (rather, hiding) self-perception that waits just behind awareness, nagging the person to become aware of the fraud he is perpetrating on himself and on the world.

Bad faith is ubiquitous; if humans were not capable of conceiving what is not true, there would be no such concept as bad faith. But bad faith exists; therefore people are capable of knowing what is true and of inventing the opposite. The necessary condition of bad faith is the grasping of our essential freedom and our possibilities. Bad faith, then, is man's attempt to avoid the anguish he feels when he is confronted with his freedom. (The word, confrontation, is used deliberately here, because the basis of confrontation in counseling and therapy within the HE mode is the confrontation of the person with (1) the freedom that he is, (2) the freedom that he has denied and is denying, and (3) the fact *that* he has and may still be denying his freedom.) Celia (see page 28), refused to believe what in fact she saw, as did Miller's heroine in *The Price*. Rather, she preferred to hope that what she saw was not true and called herself sick and available of cure. In effect, as do many who come for help, she rejects authentic suffering, the negative aspects of life, and elects instead the negative aspects of calling herself sick. In fact, people ensicken themselves by schizophren-*ing* or homosexual*izing,* and they suffer the negative aspects of those maneuvers. That, it seems to them, is more bearable, because if they "wait" long enough they can be "cured." But there is no cure for life!

THE SELF AND IDENTITY

The problem of self-deception is, more fundamentally, the problem of honesty and clarity. As Kaplan (1970) points out, what is to be explained is not so much how one can deceive himself in any respect as how one can know himself in every respect. Basically, self-deception is making oneself ignorant of what is in the self; knowledge, not ignorance, is the acquisition that needs to be explained. The HE view of the self is somewhat different from the common view and from the conglomerate of corporate entities that Abraham Kaplan posits. To the HE the person deceives himself because he does not wish to acknowledge to himself and to others *what is in fact true for him at that moment of his existence,* (e.g., confusion or nothingness), because he has in his mind the belief or hope that there must be something different from what he sees. He buys an essentialistic, serious system that runs counter to the truth of his own vision, a system based on the hope that if he believes the system rather than himself, he will somehow be cured of life. The person denies the truth of his vision on the basis of the "ought." Let me give an example that relates to the whole concept of identity, the concept of "Who am I really?"—a question that so very often comes up in therapeutic work:

Pt: Look, I came here to find out the real me. I know there is the whole problem of alienation, but I feel it more personally. I don't know which part of me is the real, the authentic, me.

Th: You sound as if you are speaking as if there is a real, authentic part of you, hidden somewhere, and you can't recognize it—which part of you it is.

Pt: Yeah, that's it! Everyone is always talking about being "real." Now, I know a lot about me. Heck, I'm in this training program here, and I've had a lot of therapy back in New York, but I'm confused—there must be a "realer" me there somewhere.

How the therapist conceives of this encounter will, to a large extent, depend on how he thinks about the problem of identity. The question of "who I am" can be taken two ways:

1. There is a hidden "real" me that needs to be uncovered. My identity is an entity to be discovered much as the fountain of youth needs to be discovered because it has a place, a form, a residence somewhere in Central America. The concept of a homunculus comes to mind. The "real" me is conceived of as a thing, with a topography and geography, that lies in waiting to be discovered (i.e., "The ultimate reality is my id," or "my search for the heroic," see Becker, 1971.)

2. Opposed to this essentialistic view is the HE view that conceives of identity as an emptiness to be *invented,* not discovered. It is never definable at a given moment but is always in the process of invention. I see the question of identity as it is raised by persons as being based on a frightening glimpse of possibility. The question "What am I?" carries with it its counterpart. We might diagram it this way:

> What I (in fact) am now
> and
> I am what? What can I become?

It seems that behind every person who takes seriously the question "Who am I?" is the glimpse of possibility, of becoming, of freedom. The glimpse of my freedom does not simply mean that I am free to choose, not only that I *choose,* but that *I* choose to be.

One of the basic problems in counseling and psychotherapy is that in the final analysis one has to deal with the cosmology of the person who comes to therapy: his basic way of structuring his universe, his engagements, his personal myth. Hobbs seems clear on this point:

> All approaches to psychotherapy seem to have a more or less elaborated conception of the nature of man which they, in essence, teach to the client. In doing so, they tie in with an ongoing process which is a unique and most exciting and engaging characteristic of man. Man constantly engages in building and repairing and extending and modifying cognitive structures that help him make personal sense of the world (1962, p. 746).

I believe that this is the meaning and end goal of counseling and therapy with another: touching upon, clarifying, and appreciating the result of a person's basic project in the world, his way of engaging the world. The positive and negative aspects *to him* are a function of his belief-system. As Fromm (1965) points out, the therapist must "get wet" in what is said to him by his patient, and this immersion is accomplished by deep attention, by feeling the patient's situation, and then by responding with therapeutic skill. By responding Fromm does not mean telling the patient what to do, but rather the therapist tells the patient what he hears—by telling the patient "so this is you." To be responsible, for Eric Fromm, means that the therapist is spontaneous, and truthful, stating what he or she feels, thinks, and sees, and then leaving the other person free, "free even to do what's bad for him" (p. 132).

In relation to the concept of identity, we find that there are two things, perhaps more, denied in the client's usual way of thinking:

1. A denial of what one, in fact, is *now* in favor of a structure that others have identified as a prerogative: "By this time you should have your impulses under control, you should be 'mature,' " etc.

2. A denial of the true glimpse and the anxiety accompanying the question of "what I really am": that it is anxiety-provoking *because* the mere question expresses in it the glimpse of the possibilities of becoming anything, many things; that it is nowhere written what one is or what one is to be where, as in a dictionary, you look up your name and find your vocation or your destiny; that there is no essential nature that defines one's identity at all, aside from the fact of birth and death and the limitations of one's body.

In working with people, I find that this glimpse of freedom and its denial constitute the reasons that the question "Who am I?" is accompanied by so much distress. To put it differently, "What am I?" seems to include "What am I to be? To what shall I commit myself?"

One of the major stumbling blocks to a clear recognition of the reality of one's identity as it exists now, and the freedom that such recognition entails, is that, as previously pointed out, the person accepts certain philosophies about the nature of man that identify the "real" self only with certain kinds of actions, choices, or admissions (ones denoting genital primacy, or striving for power, for example). What is so pernicious in these essentialistic philosophies is that embodied in them is a certain kind of presumptive definition. What purports to be a definition or analysis of basic human nature is, at bottom, a prescription or *caveat* to become or admit to being a certain kind of person.[12]

As the HE sees it, man becomes a self and achieves identity, in the act of choosing what self to become. Nothing is gained by the claim that there must have already been a basic self or a basic identity in order for a choice to be made. Quite the contrary, not only is nothing gained, but all is lost in such a belief, for when we tell a person that *he* has not chosen, then we are telling him that it is impossible for him to choose at all, that he is enslaved, that there is a mythical hidden agent such as "animal nature," instinct, or archetype, that controls his actions from behind the scenes.[13] In terms of freedom, necessity and causality, a free choice is not necessarily one that is somehow *uncaused.* The crux of the matter is *who* caused it. A free choice involves the causation of knowledge, reason, intelligence, perception, intuition, thought, or any power of the consciousness of the *person;* it is fruitless to wonder whether or not a particular act has a cause. It *is* caused, but it is *I* who have determined the motive behind it. I am the psychological laws. They do not determine me; they *are* me. And this is why freedom is absolutely inseparable from ultimate responsibility. It is never someone else who is acting. No one else moves my arm for me to stroke my lover. I am free to continue or to stop, and I am free and responsible for all that I do, for all my acts, for all my commitments. Freedom and responsibility are one. And only then is it *I* who do it. A free man is responsible, and my freedom lies in the assumption of that responsibility. Again, responsibility resolves to the fact that "I did it," that I am held and hold myself *response-able.*

---

[12]A variant on this type of answer is the assertion that a man needs food, which is very much like saying that a man *must* eat. For, at a common-sense level, the term "need" is mainly normative. It prescribes one of a set of standard goals. It usually functions as a diagnostic term with remedial implications. It implies that something is wrong with a person if certain conditions are absent. We say things like, "The trouble with Jones is that he needs a wife," or "Every child needs at least 10 hours of sleep." The implication is that there is a state of affairs the absence of which is or is likely to be damaging to the individual in question. The individual, like the patient, may well be unaware of what this state of affairs is. Indeed, when we say that a person needs something, we are often indicating a discrepancy between what he actually does and what he ought to be doing. In other words, the notion of "need" in ordinary language is seldom *explanatory.* It is used to point out what a person ought to be doing rather than to explain what he is doing. ... Reference to needs implies a standard pattern of prescribed goals; but it does not explain actions by reference to them. (Peters, 1958, pp. 17-18).

[13]cf. Stent, 1975.

The opposite of bad faith is authenticity: I have acted as I have chosen. An authentic response is cast in terms of "I want," and in appreciating that wanting and doing are the same: "I am free to choose, not only to *act* according to my choice but to structure my world 'in outlines' and headings that I order according to my priorities. And I see that there is a price to pay for each of my choices." I must add at this point, that part and parcel of authenticity is the seeing and the experiencing of the negative as well as the positive aspects of every choice one makes. The core of psychological difficulty, it seems to me, is the attempt to escape, via bad faith, from the negative aspects of life. In this conception, counseling or psychotherapy is not a process that "cures" a person; the therapist is not a healer since, as we have stated before, there is no cure for life. The therapeutic process is more a philosophic undertaking between two persons, each struggling to be real-beings. Psychotherapy is not the treatment of a disease, life is! People are absolutely perfect! It is our *conception* of life and people that is imperfect.

Therapy, then, is an act of courage in which two people (or more, in the case of a group) become intensely aware of their thrown condition, of their ultimate responsibility or freedom, dare to confront the self and the world in its absurd condition, and find that they are the centers, that there is no road map, no guru, and no blueprint for *their* lives. Therapy is not a teaching for adjustment; it is rather the facing up to reality—subjective and hard—and to the notion that life may not be made for people. Psychotherapy is the facing up to the fact of ultimate nonadjustability.

For the HE, the only thing that a person is not free to do is deny freedom. I am free, further, to accept things as they are or to build imaginary images of how things should be; I am free to conform to my past or to break with it; I am free to choose any goals or ends I desire; I am even free to adopt magical notions about my "feelings"; I am free to try to make a thing out of myself—even that is my choice.

It is this realization that man is totally responsible and totally without excuse not only for his acts but for his emotions and strong feelings, for the way he sees the world and the people in it, that may be too much for man to bear, causing him to resort to bad faith. He says, "I cannot," instead of "I will not."

THE TEACHING OF IRRESPONSIBILITY

I have repeatedly emphasized that the psychoanalytic view teaches the client irresponsibility. The basic difference between the psychoanalyst and the HE therapist is that while the analyst accounts for self-deception via a nonchoice, determined grammar of the unconscious (defense mechanisms, topological systems, and transfers of energy, loci, and states), the HE casts self-deception within the framework of commitments, goals, projects, and engagements and insists on the reality of choice, responsibility, and personal integrity.

In traditional psychoanalytic therapy the person is helped to trade freedom and integrity for security via sublimation. Frankel (1970) points out that almost everything in the traditional therapy contributes to this teaching. While the troubled person usually comes to the analyst as a desperate last resort, feeling himself to be a victim of circumstances beyond his control, the very fact that he is seeking help speaks of his ability to decide and his perception of some responsibility. "He is uncertain about what is properly within and beyond his control. But does the analyst utilize and build on this remaining nodule of responsibility? No." (p. 82) In being asked to free associate, the person is asked to abandon or suspend his judgment and his critical faculties, to stop discriminating between what is reality and what is fantasy. In interpreting dreams, there is emphasis on the fact that they are known only to the analyst, that they come from regions within the person where there is no control or consent. In fact, the patient is instructed that his volitions, his communications, his whole conscious mental life, are merely echoes of things and energies unknown to him now, and perhaps unknowable forever.

In psychoanalysis, he [the patient] is instructed that he best can understand his predicament through exhaustive examination of behavior generally regarded as outside his control.

Not only that, but the patient is invited to detail his woes while lying on a couch. Thus supine, with the analyst out of sight so that the patient will not be able to intuit approval or disapproval as indicated by facial expressions, he may "freely" associate. He will be free, that is, from noting the consequences of his behavior. Psychoanalysis is, of course, a private affair. And if the individual is having trouble coping with his life, what better place than the quiet, reflective atmosphere of the analyst's office? The patient immediately is instructed to postpone all major decisions. He gains the respectability of a prescription for what may be his trouble in the first place—inability to make a decision and to accept the consequences. And he is cut off from the significant people in his life—for him, probably a big relief....

While methodology today may be different, there still remains the basic assumption that the behavior of the neurotic is not motivated responsibly but instead is the result of unconscious processes. When the patient leaves psychoanalysis, he is firmly assured that in all or almost all he personally is blameless.... The psychoanalysed neurotic has purchased an anesthesia called peace of mind, which allows him to act out his life while at crucial moments refusing all responsibility for his actions and their consequences. Such a man is not free. But his situation brings us to a universal problem and to a question for the future of psychotherapy: Can a man live with the knowledge that he and he alone is responsible for his decisions? (Frankel, 1970, pp. 83, 85).

THE VIOLATION, SELF-DECEPTION AND EXPLICIT AWARENESS

What, then, can be the therapist's attitude—a point of view from which the therapist can at once see the person who comes for help as a responsible being and at the same time avoid fostering the growth of further essentialistic structures within the person? And, at base, how is self-deception to be understood in psychological terms? I propose that it can be clearly understood in just those linguistic terms to which I have alluded. In therapy, self-deception can be examined in terms of a person's willingness and courage to look at his priorities and commitments in the world in an explicitly aware fashion, to try to spell out the way he operates in the world, to try to utter the basic commitments in his existence and their consequences in everyday living—in a word, to lay out his personal myth clearly by focused, explicit attending.

Clearly, there are good reasons for a person *not* to spell out what is going on with him, to assume an "I don't know," inattentive attitude toward himself, his immediate goals, and his engagements.[14] If a person does not deny (that is, if he chooses to face, look at, spell out, *attend*), he may have to see how he deals with the violations and violence that have been done to him by important others in his life (i.e., to demystify others and see how they really were and are), how he has responded to the existential crisis in his life, how he might have sold out by not declaring himself fully and openly as he *has been*. He may have to recognize how he has responded to a violation of his own vision when others have questioned its validity. He may have to accept that he questioned his own vision, thus weakening his self-confidence and growing alienated from himself, and subsequently initiating the withdrawal and building of a complete insular intrapsychic reality. These are *alchemical operations* that change the nature of the outside world ("the sour grapes *are* sweet") or change the nature of the self ("they are right, my own perceptions cannot be right"). By denying the independent existence of others (through identification), they seem to remain under some measure of his control. The person who as a young child *is* dependent on others, at times for his very survival, participates in the violation process in this retroflexive manner:

> My mother cannot dislike me because of her own reasons independent of me. It must somehow be *my* fault. I was bad. I was not good enough. I

---

[14]It must be pointed out that there is a general commitment with persons *not* to be aware at most levels of their existence, for to become fully aware of any one engagement (project) in their lives will put them immediately in jeopardy of becoming aware of a more overarching engagement, thereby placing them in a responsible position in life. That is why, with people who are far removed from their responsible awareness, Gestalt techniques may be so effective, and at once so threatening (Perls, 1969; Fagan and Shepherd, 1970; Pursglove, 1969; Yontef, 1971; Perls, Hefferline, and Goodman, 1951).

deny that her response to me rests on both our shoulders. I must be able to "win her over." Therefore, if it is indeed *my* fault alone, then there is something I can do. I will change myself in order to change her. Then she will love me. Her love of me is *entirely* in my own hands. Thus I retain my illusion of omnipotence. She (eventually, "they") is *not* independent. I will not look at the facts as I see them, I will pay attention to another, manipulative structure that is in service of a controlling omnipotence.

In denying an independent existence to others, the person must also not attend to his own freedom but must deny his own independent, autonomous will as well. To notice explicitly that *he* does what he does because he freely chooses it, in terms of the other, and that he sees what he in fact sees in the world, would grant that same freedom to others, and this would endanger the totality of the illusory system of retroflexive omnipotence and control. In either case, the person refuses to look at and spell out clearly and explicitly what he sees of the other person, and what he, himself, is.

In another paradigm, one I believe is basic to what is commonly called psychopathology, the person chooses not to look at or spell out the facts as he sees them, and thus participates in the initial violation. By choosing not to declare himself as he *is,* as he sees things, or to declare what is true for him, he furthers the process of self-deception and self-obliviousness with a consequent loosening of confident action. Thus he becomes more and more unaware and lives more and more in an uncertain limbo in anxious confusion where, because of the refusal to spell out, be aware, or be explicit, there seems to be no connection between events, actions, the person's responses, and the person's feelings (c.f., in this connection, Kaiser, 1965). In many instances this "disordered," disconnected world cannot be tolerated and is ordered by means of a purely intrapsychic delusional system where everything gains supernatural or magical significance. In this system, everything is internal, and a mutual process is denied. Bateson, et al. (1956) and Watzlawick, et al. (1967) call this essential, pathogenic paradigm the double-bind; Laing (1971) calls it invalidation, and I call it violation. For example:

Child: Mother, you don't like me! [The child sees the annoyance on the mother's face, in her actions, and in her tone of voice. It is a *correct* perception of the mother's attitude.]

Mother: [She cannot face that fact: her cosmology demands that she must not have differing, changeable, ambivalent, or negative feelings toward her offspring. To her, to dislike her son denotes her not being "a good mother."] No, son, I don't dislike you. You know I love you. I *am* your mother!

But the child *knows* or senses the truth of the mother's feelings, even though she may deceive herself while attempting to deceive him about them. Further, she may be acting sincerely; she may believe that she is doing the best thing by protecting the son against her negative feelings.

The critical question here is *what shall the son do with his knowledge?*

If he is strong enough or if he has lived in a nonviolating environment, he may declare, "I don't care, I think you dislike me now. You are denying that for your own reasons," and maintain the integrity (sanity) of his self even though it may be at the expense of irritating and threatening the mother further and seeing the truth—that mothers, even his, sometimes dislike, even hate their children, and that *is* the way things seem to be.

Or, he may initiate and abet the basic pathogenic process by violating and loosening his integrity, thinking:

> I cannot be right. She is right. I am wrong. She has the ultimate truth. There is something wrong with me, with my vision, my mind, my self. I cannot, and must not, therefore, believe nor even attend to, seriously, what I see. I must not spell out the good reasons for what I see and sense. I must not see who she really is. *I cannot trust myself.* I (we) break the engaged encounter.[15] I must, therefore, be very careful and listen very carefully, because everything is meaningful in some way that I don't or can't know.

This way leads to a great dependence on others and a listening attitude: a looking outward carefully and a great leaning on others and external cues for one's identity. If that fails, one may turn totally inward and, again by breaking the encounter, attend only to an intrapsychic, retroflexive, schizophrening world.

Another way is to ignore or distract oneself from the situation by attending to other things peripheral to the situation; such as the past, the future, activities, actions, bodily movement, omens of the body (slight pains, tensions, one's stomach), memories, irrelevant happenings or events that exist in the phenomenal field, or a self-created world of perpetual crisis. Each response to the violating situation except the first leads to a break of the encounter—a refusal to be aware of the truth of the situation, and a capitulation to another by ignoring and not spelling out what is, in fact, happening with "them." Once begun, that process of self-obliviousness seems to have its own positively accelerating characteristics. That may be the basis for Laing's statement that eventually "no one in the situation may know what the situation is" (1971, p. 33). For reasons stemming from his own commitment, each person in the situation has refused to spell out the situation as it is and has ignored the truth; it is there, if he wishes to look at it and declare himself, but he chooses to maintain ambiguity and self-deception. He refuses to look at his engagements in the world. He refuses to take both his life and himself seriously and build another intrapsychic, retroflexive world. I believe that the violation paradigm may most parsimoniously account for much of what is called psychopathology.

---

[15] I shall deal with the concept of an engaged and broken encounter later in discussing the relationship.

EXPLICIT AWARENESS

We have seen that self-deception begins with a capitulating response to a violating situation. We may define a violating situation as any situation in which the person's vision is disconfirmed, where the person's integrity is placed in jeopardy or not accepted, where his interiority is ruptured, his subjectivity is violated, and where he is forced to submit to another's will. The submission to the other usually results from the other's *not* declaring his perspectival truth, by devious manipulating attitudes wherein the other refuses to declare his objection ("I don't like it!"), but rather tries to change the person ("You are wrong," implying: "You must change!"). The response to such a violating situation is to not attend to the truth of one's own vision. The situation in effect teaches the person the value of ambiguity, distraction, and self-obliviousness. Singer (1965), in one of the most important and penetrating books on psychotherapy, aptly points out that the major issue in psychopathology is a person's lack of awareness and avoidance of self-knowledge:

> [Humanistic] theorists consequently propose that psychopathology represents man's attempts to avoid the knowledge of his finiteness, his helplessness, and his dependence upon the world around him. They furthermore propose that psychopathology is failure to confront those forces which interfere with self-actualization, whether biological or social. Mental illness is seen as a refusal to acknowledge one's reaction in the face of such restricting and limiting circumstances. These latter theorists see man horrified by his awareness that fulfillment is so difficult and so limited, while Freud proposed that man is horrified by the awareness that living in harmony with one's regressive and destructive instincts is dangerous and can never be complete. While both groups assert, "You have the capacity to do what you must do" and "It's better to know than not to know, for to hear and see and know is health" they differ—and this difference is crucial—on what is to be seen and heard, and known. One group exclaims, "Be aware of your inherent regressive tendencies but renounce them." The other group insists "Be aware of your inherent power and constructive potentials and accept them—with the satisfactions they can bring and the pain and burdens they impose." (pp. 25-26)

The HE says, instead;

> You have no essential nature, you are multicapable; therefore be aware and take responsibility for how you freely, and for the best reasons, choose and have chosen to live. It is in your hands. The safest position of all is to see things clearly, to stand with your eyes open in explicit awareness. Spell out your commitments, and do not deny any part of them, neither the negative nor the positive.

For good interpersonal reasons, a person initially chooses not to be aware and then continues to practice and build an unaware, un-spelled-out, inexplicit lifestyle. This has a very close analogy in linguistic activity. In choosing an authentic life, one has to have the courage to make explicit, to utter clearly and in a fully articulated way, what he wants (who he is), specifically and generally in life and in a particular situation. I believe that the essence of reality is specificity; this, after all, is central to most psychotherapy and counseling, for the person is invited to talk, to explore himself deeply. In our terms, exploring oneself deeply (Truax and Carkhuff, 1967; Carkhuff and Berenson, 1967; Carkhuff, 1969) means a conscious effort to spell out those specific features of a person's being in the world that have heretofore not been spelled out. This spelling out establishes the crucial connection between one's wants in an overall sense and the outcomes of those wants and choices in a particular situation as the person lives that situation.[16] To put it another way, the spelling-out process provides an opportunity for a person to see deeply the good reasons for the things he does and feels, and how his wants "cast" him. In a deeper sense, it reacquaints him with his own ownership over his existence. Of course, that ownership brings with it both a positive and a negative aspect. Although it brings about a feeling of self-confident identity, of knowing who one is, it is nonetheless accompanied by the burden of responsibility.

As has already been pointed out, the therapist's attitude about the spelling-out is crucial. It is a common HE observation that although the person typically, comes to therapy suffering from the negative aspects of his choices, his suffering is somehow torn away and disconnected from his life. The important distinction between the HE view and others is that such connections between the way one has chosen to live and his suffering *are* considered to be available to the person if he wishes to spell out his engagements.

> We feel our suffering as alien, desperately unwanted, yet nothing imposes it. We eat, often exceedingly well; the roof over our head is timber and tile; deep carpets, thin china, great music, rare wine; a woman looks at us with love; we have friends, families; our needs are met. In some way, unnoticed, unknown, we must select our suffering, create it. It may be quite intense.... Yet no such feeling can be independent of behavior; and if only we find the connections we may begin to see how a change in the way we live will make for a change in the way we feel (Wheelis, 1970, pp. 13-14, 139).

For reasons previously mentioned, the person may say and even feel that he wants to spell out his engagements and look at his life, but he is, in fact, *unwilling* to do so, and he denies that he is unwilling. The HE will readily admit that he has good reasons for that denial and that there is no a priori ideal reason for the person to examine his life explicitly. It is wholly up to the person, and he will be willing to examine his projects only when he takes seriously the fact that his choice to deny is intimately connected with the negative aspects of his life, aspects that

---

[16]For an analogous view based upon perceptual psychology, see Murphy, 1975.

he experiences as painful. That is one of the basic reasons for the HE insistence upon helping the person to constantly look at what he *in fact* says about his life.

Pt: Doctor, you know, I have this very important job. I work at it very hard. It eats me up alive. Half my stomach is gone now. I hate this ulcer machine! It's so demanding, so taxing. All those decisions, so many people. It's a constant pressure.

Th: Sounds like you're responding correctly to the job as you see it. It's taxing, it taxes you. It's almost too much.

Pt: No. The job's a great job. It pays so damn well, 70 thou a year, and I'm a vice president. It's a great job. It's me, not the job.

Th: Yes, you like one part of what the job brings you—money, prestige, you told me about the Bentley, and you tell me about your home. It also seems to bring you a negative aspect. For you it's very demanding. It eats up your insides.

Pt: I want the damn job.

Th: I hear you.

Pt: I don't want the pressure!

Th: I see. [laughs]

Pt: Yeah, yeah, [laughs] I want a difficult situation to be easy for me. But I tell you, the goodies are great.

Th: And the other side is sour, acid.

Pt: I guess I want one more than the other. I mean, I've been sticking with it for 12 years now. It's so important for me, I don't know why.

Th: Well, look at it, try to spell out what you want, why you make it so important.

Pt: Well, it's so important to me to live in... and to be able to tell my friends where I live... and to drive the Rolls. And you know, it can all go down the drain if I mess up... even a little.

Th: Sounds like you made a good choice, and you're paying the price for that, for what you've made important in your life.

Pt: I wonder what it was that made me so ambitious. You know Doctor——[a former therapist whom the patient saw for 6 years] told me it was my desire to accumulate money in order to buy my mother's love. Is that what it's all about?

Th: I don't know what it's all about, but you do, or can look at what you want to be.

Pt: Happy, that's what.

Th: C'mon, let's be concrete.

Pt: I don't know. I'm not happy now, I'll tell you that!

Here the person wants to deny that *for him*, in terms of his basic projects in life, this job is difficult. It is important to him for what it brings him. He has placed value upon the things that great wealth and prestige bring him, but he is unwilling to look at the fact that they do not make him happy. He is unwilling to look at his basic ideals, his basic commitments, and to examine whether those things he has decided *should* make him happy, *do* in fact make him happy. The therapist is after a clear and explicit exploration of his wants and priorities and the prices he is paying for them. But like most people, he wants to deny that his suffering is connected with his own priorities: "Could it be my mother?"

It is important to emphasize that the person who deceives himself by not articulating his projects and priorities is not avoiding doing that capriciously. His avoidance of clarity is itself a commitment, an important choice made for good reasons (albeit one that is tacitly adopted) *not* to spell out, *not* to be aware. If this person began to spell out his situation, he would eventually have to confront his basic belief-system and his pervading and overarching engagements, and he knows this. He must know this in order to better keep away from spelling out his life. Thus his distal engagement in various situations stems from and is intimately connected with his basic project. Most persons are committed not to spell out their basic projects, for to do so would bring them into a position of responsibility where their lives, their feelings, and their actions would be identified with themselves, that is, with who they have committed themselves to be.

For the person who has been violated during his development, whose engagements in the past have proven unacceptable to significant others in his life to whom he has capitulated, it is perfectly sensible to adopt a policy of nonresponsibility or not declaring and owning who one is. Helmuth Kaiser (1965) has termed duplicity or self-deception the "universal symptom." I totally agree, but the HE sees the germ of self-deception to be sown during a basically violating situation in which the growing person's integrity was challenged. He faced an existential crisis of critical proportions: shall he (for the good reason of his requirements for personal survival) invalidate himself, or shall he declare himself as he sees himself and the situation? Both are difficult. The authentic choice has its positive aspects (personal authority, a sense of selfhood, a sense of knowing who one is, a sense of integrity) and its negative aspects (the giving up of control and omnipotence; awareness of ontological anxiety, of finiteness; a painful appreciation of the limits of human contacts; a sensation of aloneness; and, importantly, the burden of absolute, inexcusable personal responsibility).

How to conduct the therapeutic enterprise without further violation of the person is the most difficult and delicate of all human relationships (it is equalled in difficulty only by a long-lasting authentic love relationship) because it requires an authentic (and thereby authenticating) real-being-therapist.

In summary, the HE rejects the existence of an unconscious and its corollary trinity of ego, id, and superego. For the HE, human consciousness is unique in that it is a nihilation, an emptiness of possibilities, a withdrawal from the rest of being. Thus it cannot be opaque; it cannot have any interiority or any "hidden basements," as Fromm (1965) has put it.

The fact that man's consciousness *is* freedom (man may choose to deny it, but he cannot escape it) is inimical to the idea of an unconscious mind. A man cannot be both free and determined by those impulses and instincts that *on principle he cannot know.* The HE believes that the unconscious—a self-contradictory construct—was introduced because of a misunderstanding of the ubiquitous mechanisms of self-deception. The introduction of a separate and distinct trinity allows the possibility of having a lie without a liar. Thus the problem of people deceiving themselves is not dealt with adequately by calling upon an unconscious as an explanatory construct (cf., MacIntyre, 1958).

We have discussed the concept of repression and resistance and found that it too was faulty, much as Freud's revisionists have:

> As to the power of the "super-ego" which enables it to engender repression, Freud ascribes it mainly to the self-destructive instinct. . . . Freud believes that it is instinctual drives which, because of their antisocial character, succumb to repression by the superego. If for the sake of clarity I may express it in naive moral terms, it is in Freud's opinion the bad, the evil in man that is repressed. This doctrine undoubtedly contains one of Freud's striking discoveries. But I should like to suggest a more flexible formulation: what is repressed depends on the kind of facade an individual feels forced to present; everything is repressed which does not fit the facade. A person, for instance, may feel free to indulge in obscene thought and actions or to have death wishes against many people, but may repress any wish for personal gain. (Horney, 1939, p. 228).

We have inquired where resistance to the analyst's intervention arises. The patient is at once determined by the past and by his unconscious dynamisms, and yet is free to resist. Resistance cannot be the work of the ego, for persons *indicate* that they wish to feel better, to change, and these kinds of utterances are ego functions. Resistance cannot originate in the id, because by Freud's own definition id impulses are major energizers of human behavior, "the ultimate reality." Even though the id is constantly striving to make its contents known, it is unknown and largely unknowable to the person. We have seen that it is the censor that controls the passage of the real reasons for behavior from the id to the ego. But the censor must know *what* to censor in order to censor it. The censor must be aware (conscious) in order to know what to suppress or repress.

Yet another paradox was alluded to: the fact that psychoanalytic theory permits of the *symbolic* satisfaction of unconscious impulses. That is, if the raw material cannot pass border inspection, then a disguise is offered that the censor permits to pass to the ego. Again, there must be some awareness that these impulses will be censored *in order* for them to be disguised. Further, if the symbol can stand as a substitute for the object-choice and evoke nearly the same gratifications as the original id-impulse-wish, then consciousness must be at least partially aware of the meaning of the symbol. If, in fact, the ego and id are separate from each other as countries are separated from each other, then the connection between the symbolic manifestation of the unconscious impulse or "Trieb" is a magical one. The HE finds this an inferior concept on purely preferential ground. We conclude, as did Sartre, that:

> Thus, on the one hand the explanation by means of the unconscious, due to the fact that it breaks the psychic unity, cannot account for the facts which at first sight it appeared to explain [indeed it raises even more complex logical and philosophical questions]. And on the other hand, there exists an infinity of types of behavior in bad faith which explicitly rejects this kind of explanation because their essence implies that they can appear only in the translucency of consciousness (1956, p. 54).

THE HE VIEW OF EMOTIONS

HE psychologists are concerned with the fact of man's emotional life as a total human experience. We are interested in the phenomenology of emotion, grounded on the belief that *the fact* of emotions has to be seen for what it is, as opposed to what seems to be *behind* it or underneath it. We focus on the phenomenon of emotion as man experiences it.

In his much-neglected book *The Emotions: An Outline of a Theory* (1948), Sartre evaluates the attitudes reflected in the approach of contemporary psychology to human situations. The book also gives the framework from which the HE chooses to look at and think about persons in general. Sartre begins by suggesting that most orthodox psychology is interested in the acquisition of facts, and he defines facts as those events that, ideally, one should meet while investigating psychological events. Moreover, in the investigation, one must be prepared for the surprises that might enrich and illuminate facts gathered beforehand. The important point is that facts alone cannot be counted on to organize themselves in a synthetic totality that by itself might yield its meaning. Psychology as a science, Sartre continues, can furnish only a number of miscellaneous facts that may or may not have any connections with each other. This view is clearly in opposition to the modern behaviorists who place the study of man on the same basis as the study of physical properties. Hitt summarizes the behaviorist view and its implications for studying man:

> The behaviorist views man as a passive organism governed by external stimuli. Man can be manipulated through proper control of these stimuli. Moreover, the laws that govern man are essentially the same laws that govern all natural phenomena of the world; hence it is assumed that the scientific method used by the physical scientist is equally appropriate to the study of man (1969, p. 652).

In contrast, the HE considers man as that being who is the *source* of his own actions, a being free to choose in each situation how he will act. The essence of man is his own freedom; that exists inside him, not in the objects around him. Man is governed by his own unique consciousness. Thus, the appropriate methodology for the study of man is man's own experience, his phenomenology.

As has been said more recently, I believe by Erich Fromm, psychology as a science is currently interested in becoming more and more precise about fewer and fewer important things. Robert Oppenheimer (1956), addressing a group of psychologists, made an analogous statement:

> It is not always tactful to try to quantify; it is not always clear that by measuring one has found something very much worth measuring. It is true that for the Babylonians it was worth measuring—noting—the first appearance of the moon because it had a practical value. Their predictions, their prophecies, and the magic would not work without it; and I know that many psychologists have the same kind of reason for wanting to measure (p. 135).

The great hope that mere gathering and mensuration of facts will yield greatly in the explanation of man carries with it the consequence of expelling the essential in favor of the accidental. As Sartre emphasizes, it is impossible to formulate over all generalizing statements based on the accumulation of accidental facts. Polanyi (1963) seems to agree: to "take a watch to pieces and examine it, however carefully, its separate parts in turn, will never help one come across the principle by which a watch keeps time" (p. 47). In this connection, James Deese says:

> Behavior as the goal in the study of thought is wrong, and the characteristic emphasis of the psychological laboratory on the measurable response and the controlling independent variable is responsible for the sterility of the study of thought.... The model of experimenting taken from the physical sciences is useful as an aid in psychological research, but I have reached the conclusion that it no longer belongs in the center of psychology (1969, p. 522).

The contemporary psychologist wants to take emotion and make an objective thing out of it because he believes that he can study it only by objectifying it. His hope is that his disconnected facts will organize themselves into something that has overall relevance to man. Instead of studying human reality, such a psychologist studies the antecedent condition of which certain phenomena are functions (in isolation, as if phenomena such as memory, emotion, volition, drive, ambition, and love were insulated events residing in some loosely or disconnected whole). In this way, then, learning becomes divorced from the learner and from the learner's intentions and becomes an event that is a function merely of the presentation of certain other events such as the repetition of nonsense syllables, an event measured in terms of the probability of a change in behavior.

> And then, as logical consequences of this [the inseparability of what we are studying and the means that are used to study it], there is the idea of to-

tality of wholeness. Newtonian physics, classical science, was differential; anything that went on could be broken up into finer and finer elements and analyzed so. If one looks at an atomic phenomenon between the beginning and the end, the end will not be there; it will be a different phenomenon. Every pair of observations taking the form "we know this, we can predict that" is a global thing; it cannot be broken down (Oppenheimer, 1956, p. 134).

To the orthodox occidental psychologist, emotion must be viewed as an objective accident, a fact, and so it is studied in an encapsulated manner as are physical phenomena. Following the principles laid down in positivistic scientific approaches, the psychologist studying emotion is most interested in isolating the antecedent condition, the adequate stimulus (I shall leave the hoary argument of what stimulus *is* to others), the quantifiable behavior of the organism, his bodily state, and perhaps his subjective appraisal of the incident. The orthodox psychologist will not be interested in the emotion as an expression of human reality or of what man can be, but in the fragmented and isolated process of the emotion itself, bracketed from human reality.

> As a result, even when it has been duly described and explained it will never be anything but one fact among others, a fact closed in on itself which will never permit either of understanding a thing other than itself or of grasping by means of it the essential reality of man (Sartre, 1948, p. 9).

In opposition to the reductionistic psychologist, who from isolated bits of man's experience wants "sometime in the future" to build an anthropological psychology, the HE understands the incongruity between facts and totalities and follows the dictum that Husserl, the great phenomenologist, held: investigators who initiate their inquiry with facts will never arrive at the essential nature of human reality. The HE holds that only an understanding of the whole permits one to classify, organize, understand, or even *recognize* facts. If we did not have an overall understanding of emotion as a construct used to distinguish a special organization of events from the mass of other psychological events available to us, we should not even know how to think about it or how to study it at all.

There is a basic principle involved here. One must begin with man as a totality, with what man is, and with human reality in order to understand and formulate generalizations about what is of interest. A second basic principle is that psychological *facts* are secondary. They are secondary because the psychological facts we discover are the result of the *manner* in which man reacts in the world. The HE is interested, then, in a psychological anthropology that goes beyond what results from man's experience (bits and facts) to the very basic: to what man *is*—to consciousness, and to the fact that what gives value to man's actions is that these actions are *his*.

In terms of emotion, the HE is not so interested in the many faces or different kinds of emotion as separate events but rather in emotions as an organized consciousness. Just as we are less interested in the various intentions of man but want to lead man ever back to the idea of his intentionality, so we are less interested in cataloging emotions than in the fact that emotionality is an organized type of consciousness that intends or that illuminates that person's engagements, and commitments.

In terms of scientific investigation of human reality, the starting point must be man, for, as Bugental has aptly stated, "I mean, very literally, that any statement we make about the world (the 'out there') is inevitably, inescapably, a statement about our theory of ourselves (the 'in here')" (1967, p. 6). To put it another way, there is an absolute proximity of man the investigator and the thing (man) being investigated. This is essentially, radically, and critically different from man's investigations of other beings-in-themselves. The human reality that is being scrutinized is *our* reality. And human reality (as opposed to chairs or stoves, which "receive" their reality from the outside) is defined (seemingly paradoxically, since definition implies an essence) as that reality that assumes and undertakes its being, that reality that is responsible for its own reality.

As we have stated before, since consciousness is always a self-consciousness, human reality implies, at least at some level, an understanding of itself. To put this into more practical terms, persons who act most compulsively usually recognize that they *can* act otherwise. In effect, it is the understanding of one's condition that *is* human reality. I shall have more to say about unconsciousness later, but I must point out that the HE believes that an anthropology of man that can serve as the basis for noticing, discovering, and organizing the "facts" of human behavior is essential. This is precisely the reverse of the orthodox psychologist's work. The psychologist *begins* with isolated facts and tries to reduce these as much as possible into quantifiable bits, or with the relation of certain facts to outside forces, and sets up functional relations between external stimuli and measurable behaviors. The HE investigator begins with the synthetic whole of man, elects to establish the nature of man, and *then* elects to discover the facts or elements of human reality. This is the phenomenological approach.

The existential psychologist concerns himself with the whole phenomenon of man as an emotional being, not as a creature who occasionally *has* emotions that can be studied in piecemeal fashion. Man cannot be cut into parts for study. I recall that Dewey pointed out that even the reflex arc cannot be studied in isolation. So the HE studies those events that manifest themselves *as* themselves, not as appearances of something else that is more "real." The way in which the emotion appears is the way that it is; in the manner in which it presents itself (as itself), it will reveal the nature of humanity; it is consciousness with all that the concept of consciousness implies.

For the HE, an emotion is not *merely* an accidental appearance or an isolated fact. It is not an accident because human consciousness is not merely a conglomerate of facts. Rather, it is an expression of the totality of human reality in the intending form of emotion. Emotion is *not* a disordered state of consciousness, nor is it visceral action; it *is* consciousness. Emotion does not sweep over man from the outside or from his glands. Man himself, by his intentions, by his undertakings, underwrites and assumes his emotions, generates them and keeps the machinery of emotion going by staying on the road whose end he wishes. To the HE, emotion is an organized form of human reality. We are not driven by our emotions; we generate and drive our emotions in accordance with our commitments.

A word more on physiologizing seems necessary here. Phenomenology and HE psychology are interested in human events insofar as they illuminate and reveal human consciousness. Emotion, drive, impulse, and tropism do not exist as physiological events alone, since a stomach, a nervous system, a brain, or a body cannot be affected in itself, as a body somehow removed from what it means to be a person: the power to confer a meaning to "body's" manifestations. A more correct statement of the HE position would sound more arcane because of the difficulties of our language, but it would go something like this: a body cannot exist alone, I *am* my body, and I *am* means the conferring of meaning. For the HE, conciousness is the overarching fact that confers meaning, and from which meaning is gained:

> The mind is a comprehensive feature of man. It is the focus in terms of which we are subsidiarily aware of the play of man's features, utterance, and whole behavior. A man's mind is the meaning of these workings of his mind.... A comprehensive entity is something else than its particulars known focally, in themselves. Behaviorism, which suggests that these particulars should be studied in themselves, is totally impracticable. First, because the particulars, if observed in themselves, would be *meaningless;* second, because they cannot be so observed at all, since they form parts of a physiognomy and are therefore unspecifiable in the stronger sense of being *largely unknown*; and third, because it is impossible to keep track, even roughly, of a man's mental manifestations, *except by reading them as pointers to the mind from which* they originate. It is always the mind itself that we know primarily; any knowledge of its workings is derivative, vague, and uncertain (Polanyi, 1963, p. 65).

In summary, the HE basically sees emotions as ways in which man intends. Emotions are intentional organizations of human consciousness; they are not disordered states. It is important to recognize that persons do, in fact, deliberately focus upon an object, and if they wish to, they can recognize what it is they want to *accomplish* in initiating, generating, and keeping the machinery of their emotions going. The basic insight here is that if we but reflect and are willing to know, we all can know what the feeling or emotion means or signifies; this is so because at some level of awareness we *adopt* or *undertake* an emotional attitude. And we do so for good reasons—reasons that have to do with our intention-ality—as means to the accomplishment of a goal we wish to attain, but have difficulty in reaching directly. So, *emotions are special ways of getting what we want,* of confirming and illustrating who we are.

This kind of potential transparency is the unique contribution that logically follows from an HE view of human reality, and stands as a clear denial of unconscious processes claimed by psychoanalytic theory.

For the HE, emotional responsiveness involves the prereflective mode of consciousness and intentionality. In opposition to the classical views of emotions, feelings are not believed to be merely the consciousness *of* a bodily state. Anger, for example, is not primarily an awareness of being angry and wanting to strike out at somebody. In the HE view, emotions are neither primary instincts nor the sensing or awareness of "being in a state" of emotion.

"Emotional consciousness is, at first, consciousness *of* the world" (Sartre, 1948, p. 51); the world as it presents itself through our construc-tions of it and as a function of our projects in it (our intentions and our priorities) basically, of our engagement with it. Our unique, individual way of construing reality, via our intentions and projects, brings about the unique emotionality of which we are capable. We are not "just afraid"; we are afraid *of* something in the world, of which we are conscious. The statement made by many clients—"I can't do that, I am afraid of the *unknown*"—is untrue. Upon inspection, one always finds that what we fear is that with which we inhabit the "unknown"; but we choose not to pay attention to our inhabitations.

Emotions, then, are not self-sustaining nor are they self-generating; they are always intentional, purposive responses to those objects to which *we* give value in the world. Note what May says in this regard:

> What is omitted in my patient's (and society's) view is that emotions are not just a push from the rear but a *pointing toward* something, an impetus for forming something, a call to mold the situation. Feelings are not just a chance state of the moment, but a pointing toward the future, a way I *want* something to be.... That is to say, feelings are *intentional* (1969a, p. 91).

While May closely approximates the HE view, he does not make one point clear: our feelings are the very process by which the "wanting" and the "pointing" are accomplished, not the result of that process. That process is also indicative of the person's engagements in the world; indeed, the process symbolizes the engagement (Combs and Snygg, 1959, pp. 226-31).

The distinction between emotion as merely a sign and as a symbolization is addressed by Needleman (1968):

> The point here is that the essence of a sign, as distinguished from a symbol, does not involve the meaning structure of the signified, but only refers to the signified. The sign serves either as a substitute or a pointer in relation to the signified. In all cases the function of the sign is replaced or over-ridden by the presence of the signified. In this sense, the sign is a "stepping-stone" to the signified. Speaking phenomenologically, we posit the presence of the emotion, meaning, or object that is intrapsychically represented—this presence as *experienced* by the individual. There can be no experience of an intrapsychic sign because that which is to be signified is always already present....

> I am climbing the stairs of a strange house and before I enter one of the rooms I note that my palms are perspiring, my heart is beating faster, my throat is dry. Are these not signs of an intrapsychic phenomenon—fear? ...The condition of my palms, heartbeat, and throat are not intrapsychic phenomena—for the way the objection is phrased implies a state where the body is being observed other than the "mind." In the experiencing of fear, we do not experience signs of fear, signs that are of a qualitatively different order than what they signify. Let me, however, entering this same house, hear a rustling at the top of the stairs, and I fear a ghost, a bandit, and so forth. The fear of a ghost in this case represents a larger, more general fear of this strange house—but it expresses it, it partakes of the reality that it represents; it *symbolizes* it (pp. 82-83).

And it symbolizes more; it symbolizes the way in which I place myself in relation to strange places, to ghosts, and to those strange things that may befall me.

All emotion is tied to the object that is perceived. Emotion is a dialectic; it gains its impetus from an encounter with that object (Leeper, 1970). That encounter is subsumed under my way of being in the world, my projects, my engagements. It at once *expresses* my world and *is* my world. We do not merely flee; we flee from an object to which we have attributed value. We do not merely get angry; we are angry at someone. We are not merely sad; we *are* saddened. Indeed, we are saddening ourselves in our encounter with that person; we interact with that object in a sad way. We anger ourselves in terms of that object, and our anger becomes at once a function of how we structure our relationships with that object and an indication of our self-definitional structuring. We create our emotional relations with the world, and we *sustain* our feelings and emotions in accordance with our peculiar intentions to *be* a certain way in the world. In a difficult passage Sartre lays bare the outlines of all emotion when he speaks of sadness:

I am sad. One might think that surely I am the sadness in the mode of being what I am. What is the sadness, however, if not the intentional unity which comes to reassemble and animate the totality of my conduct? It is the meaning of this dull look with which I view the world, of my bowed shoulders, of my lowered head, of the listlessness in my whole body. But at the very moment when I adopt each of these attitudes, do I not know that I shall not be able to hold on to it? Let a stranger suddenly appear and I will lift up my head, I will assume a lively cheerfulness. What will remain of my sadness except that I obligingly promise it an appointment for later after the departure of the visitor? Moreover, is not this sadness itself a *conduct*? Is it not consciousness *which affects itself with sadness as a magical recourse against a situation too urgent*? [Emphasis supplied.] And in this case even, should we not say that being sad means first to make oneself sad? ... If I make myself sad, I must continue to make myself sad from beginning to end. I cannot treat my sadness as an impulse finally achieved and put it on file without recreating it, nor can I carry it in the manner of an inert body which continues its movement after the initial shock. There is no inertia in consciousness. If I make myself sad, it is because I *am* not sad—the being of the sadness escaped me by and in the very act by which I affect myself with it (1956, pp. 60-61).

Emotion is a certain way in which we choose to apprehend our relation to the world. We generate the machinery of our feelings, and we are the ones who must continue to maintain it. We are totally responsible for our emotions and our feelings. On the other hand, much of the way in which we choose to apprehend the world is not closely attended to; it remains in the prereflective mode. Recall, however, that prereflective behavior is *not* to be equated with unconscious behavior. It is, rather, what Sartre calls "nonthetic," not formulated but entirely, imminently possible of formulation if we but choose to attend to it. It is as if there is a not noted skip that focuses on the object that exists "out there" much like we "give" color to the jacket of the book upon which our eye falls. The color is in me, but I place it in the paper of the book. The world that surrounds me varies as a response to my choices and my vision, but in denying the encounter I choose to ignore this and place it all out there.

Often, the world (to which we give color or emotion) appears to be difficult—as if the difficulty were, again, out there rather than in our apprehension, our project in relation to it. I am not aware of *my* difficulty with the world; rather, the difficulty is somehow there in the world. It is a quality of the world that is given in the perception, exactly like the paths toward the potentialities in the world themselves and the exigencies of objects: books to be read, papers to be written, classes to be taught, and so forth.

It is when we respond to the world, as if the difficulties were out there, when we *must* act but we see that the world bars our acts, that we try to change the world *we* have inhabited with difficulty. This transformation of the world, this attempt to loosen the connection between cause and effect in the face of our having to act, is emotion. And further, the way in which emotions intend is by magic. Through our emotional responsiveness, we intend to change the "hard" world into a "softer" one over which we have some (albeit less than effective) retroflexive control.

When we perceive a situation as objectively insoluble, we intentionally, though prereflectively, alter it, see it in a new aspect in order to deal with it. And seeing this new aspect is emotional behavior. Significantly, emotional behavior is not effective. It really does not solve the problem we saw in the world. Nonemotional behavior intends to act upon the world in instrumental ways. If a tire is flat, we take out our Auto Club card and call for help. Emotional acts (kicking the tire, or crying) do not fill tires with air. Rather, without actually modifying them, emotions intend to confer upon objects and events another quality that *seems* more available of control and effect.

> For example, take passive fear. I see a wild animal coming toward me. My legs give way, my heart beats more feebly, I turn pale, I fall and faint. Nothing seems less adapted than this behavior which hands me over defenseless to the danger. And yet it is a behavior *of escape*. Here the fainting is a refuge. Let it not be thought that this is a refuge *for me*, that I am trying to save *myself* in order not to *see* the wild animal *any more*. I did not leave the unreflective level, but, lacking power to avoid the danger by the normal methods and the deterministic links, I denied it. I wanted to annihilate it. The urgency of the danger served as motive for an annihilating intention which demanded magical behavior. And, by virtue of this fact, I did annihilate it as far as was in my power. These are the limits of my magical action upon the world; I can eliminate it as an object of consciousness, but I can do so only by eliminating consciousness itself. Let it not be thought that the physiological behavior of passive fear is pure disorder. It represents the abrupt realization of the bodily conditions which ordinarily accompany the transition from being awake to sleeping.
>
> We do not flee in order to take shelter; we flee for lack of power to annihilate ourselves in the state of fainting. . . . Thus, the true meaning of fear is apparent; it is a consciousness which, through magical behavior, aims at denying an object of the external world, and which will go so far as to annihilate itself in order to annihilate the object with it (Sartre, 1948, pp. 62-64).

Emotional responsiveness is indicative of the magical qualities by which we intend to affect the world. Emotion is not an accident nor a remnant of the animal past. It is, rather, a way in which consciousness intends to understand and deal with a difficult world. The particular way in which emotion operates is prereflective, and it entails a leap into a magical way of dealing with what seems to be undealable, unbearable. The magic of emotion is the break with organic (nonhuman) reality where determinism and causality exist. It is we, then, in emotion, who constitute a magical act to replace a causal activity we cannot realize.

In depression, for example, where there is no way to undo what has been done or what has happened (a tragedy, or a terrible mistake), we depress ourselves with the *intention* of eliminating effective ways of dealing with what we see as an "undealable-with" situation. We have been frustrated in our projects, so we change the world by behaving "in such a way that the universe no longer requires anything of us. To bring that change about, we can only act upon ourselves, only 'dim the light' and withdraw the press of the world: depress ourselves" (Sartre, 1948, p. 65).

Another use of the magical world is expressed in the fact that our emotional responses often seem to be interpersonal statements, even though they may be carried out in absolute solitude. Faced with an absolutely insoluble situation, a reality we have construed as immovable, we behave in a manner that seems to be in terms of some existent other. Throwing a tantrum when one is alone, upon close inspection, will reveal the hidden magical notion that "someone really sees me and hears my plea." Persons wail at the Wailing Wall, the wail being in reality a plea to some other being who will supposedly hear and perhaps respond "if my plea or prayer is correct," and thus ensure a magical semblance of control over the seemingly uncontrollable. A man says, "I can't be thoroughly content any time" because someone (who takes account of my contentment) will punish me by visiting me with sorrow as a response to my contentment. Belief in a principle of reciprocity in life is such a magical belief. Here, a person who cannot tolerate the "all is hazard" nature of life, where persons respond out of their own freedom and events occur that are exempt from human control, changes that reality, annihilates it by placing it magically under his control: "I was not a good enough person"—if I were good enough (and I still can be good, can't I, Doctor, by being "cured") this would not have happened; if I had been good enough they would have loved me, she (he) would have acted differently."

In the final analysis, it seems, what keeps feelings of anger and resentment going in us is the magical belief that we can reshape the past, influence our dead parents, take revenge, and, therefore, undo the undoable—and maintain the belief that we still control events. "Since things cannot be what they were or are, I must be able to change them by changing myself, magically."

A client who had gone through three "complete" analyses by qualified analysts had remained profoundly depressed. The worrying, agonizing attitude of this woman was part of her view of the world, which expressed itself in statements like these:

Pt: I have to agonize, worry over things, I can't let things go. I believe that I avoid an even greater disaster. If I don't watch out, these bad things will really happen. I have to agonize over them, over almost everything in order to control them. I can't go out and have a good time 'til everything is in order. I can't enjoy myself until I have conquered all these things (carpets, doors, furniture, interior decor). I can't have a good time 'til I have my head cleared up. My dad always had to clear his calendar and clear his desk before he could leave his office to go home. And so do I, I can't leave things. I can't distract myself out of my depression. It is always there, like a pool of things that is always with me. I can't have a good time 'til it's all cleared up.

Th: But you are the one who invents that formula; sure, your dad may have "taught" it to you, but you are the one who keeps it alive, you must do that for a good reason. You must believe that it's somehow important to you.

Pt: I don't know why. It's so damned screwy, so bad, so painful to me. You see, I think I believe that I control things that way, as we've talked about before. I avoid even worse things by my agonizing.

Th: By worrying, you've got a kind of magic formula. If I worry about it, if I agonize, if I suffer, worse things won't happen to me. I've invested pain. I am the secret controller.

Pt: Yeah, yes, that's right. If I give up my magic, then I'm prey to surprises, to accidents, to haphazard things—things I can't control—that I seem to be prey to anyway. All kinds of bad things happen. My brother is dying of heart disease, but I can't give it up, I can't. If I do feel better, it's all gonna really crash in on me. I've felt great, and I really got it—right in the teeth. I really believe it, I believe in that kind of power [cries]— I've got to. Somebody someplace, something kinda knows and watches and counts the good days. If I have a good time, I'll be punished for it. My mother couldn't stand it if I had a good time. She'd love me only if I suffered.

Th: I guess you really do believe that if you suffer, you'll be loved, if you pay your penance, you won't be beset by bad things. Except that you still suffer so much. It's as if you bought that system and you're unwilling to fiddle with it, to dither with it.

Pt: I feel helpless to dither with it.

Th: Yeah, that feeling of helplessness is right in with your system. Something or somebody knows about you, takes you into account, is interested in you. "They," whoever "they" is, don't want you to have a good time. You seem to act in terms of some mythic "them."

Pt: That was the way it was with me, always; it still is. I can't face that there is nobody there! That there is no one to pay a debt to.

Th: That would be terrible, if you had only yourself to account to.

Pt: Yes.

Th: But you seem to be suffering anyway.

Pt: Yeah, but I don't know what will happen if I don't pay that kind of debt.

Th: That seems right. No one knows. And it's just that kind of "not knowing" that you seem to be trying to get around—and you're paying a hell of a price for it, it seems.

Let us demonstrate the magical use of emotion by another example of a married woman who speaks of her husband's past affair:

Pt: Yet there's still a feeling... about her... and in the past few days, I have seen that I'm just hanging on to the feeling that... I believe that my feelings about her now are histrionic rather than real ones. I think it's like a package that I've carried over from two years ago... and I've just kind of seen that... that I can at any time just lay that down.

Th: Hm, hm.

Pt: It's like to get into outraged feelings about her or anything real, I have to go into how I was two years ago, and how he was two years ago, and drum up the whole situation of two years ago.

Th: Yup.

Pt: And there's nothing real in that today.

Th: Not unless you want there to be, for some good reason or good purpose. You know, you seem to be talking about your ability, mine, everyone's, I suppose, of being able to resurrect an image...

Pt: Yeah, like that, like I'm making it happen.

Th: ...and inject it with feeling. But, Sue, there must be a good reason for your doing that; what do you want to accomplish by that?

Pt: Well, let's see; I guess I can blame him then, and he can be contrite, and sorrowful, about it. I come out on top. But you know, somehow, I know it's bullshit, this "on top" business. It just puts us farther apart in the long run—in the long run? In the short run. Now!

Th: It's that subject-object thing, isn't it?

Pt: Yeah, the only way I seem to be able to deal with him—and he with me—is from a position of power.

Th: And that interrupts the dyadic flow between you. It really is a way of *not* dealing with him. You structure the relationship as a sort of given. You break the encounter, deny it, deny that fact that your relationship is *now* and you have to create it constantly. It's a new relationship now, except that you recreate the past to keep it "locked in," stable, permanent, a thing.

Pt: Yeah, somehow I recognize that I do it. But something in me feels that's—it's done to me, like I was the object of his deception, his infidelity.

Th: I can understand that. It's like you say, "I'll put myself into an emotional stew," into a "state," otherwise it's just a charade. It's like ostensibly you are the object of your "state of emotion." You get all steamed up by resurrecting the past situation, and then your husband is all apologetic, worried, and consternated, and he says, "Oh, what am I going to do with you, with us; what will happen? I can't understand you, things have been going well, we've been talking...." You become the object of his concern. But there's a kind of secret subjectivity about you—you're the one who arranges the whole maneuver, the whole trick, and you have to pull if off regarding yourself too; *you have to feel it.* But secretly, you're doing it all, you're breaking the open encounter between you, the dialectic, the flow, by assuming that position. But listen, the important thing is that it also works between us, here—how can I break into your split, and create the flow between us?

We can "use" emotion in literally any situation, and the catalog of emotional responses is indeed long. But the major outlines remain: emotions establish a magical world where normal cause-effect relationships must not exist, and we use the "body as a means of incantation" (Sartre, 1948, p. 70). As opposed to the peripheralists, the HE holds that the behavior is *not* the emotion, just as when the cat whose thalamic nuclei are stimulated by implanted electrodes exhibits the bodily signs of rage and fear yet does not seem to be experiencing the same emotion as when it is presented with a dog (Masserman, 1943, Ch. 3).

Emotional behavior is accompanied by "true belief." It must, if it is to accomplish its intention of altering the world magically, be believed fully and undergone completely. The grapes must be green and sour. Our flight as a magical alteration and annihilation must be unbelievably felt. Thus, when all paths to an effective solution seem blocked, consciousness degrades itself into a magical world of emotions whose intention it is to survive, to act upon the refractory world in the only way it sees left open to it. But this must be a total bodily response:

> We understand in this situation the role of purely physiological phenomena: they represent the *seriousness* of the emotion; they are phenomena of belief. They should certainly not be separated from behavior. At first, they present a certain analogy with it. The hyper-tension of fear or sadness, the vaso-constrictions, the respiratory difficulties, symbolize quite well a behavior which aims at denying the world or discharging it of its affective potential by denying it. It is then impossible to draw exactly a borderline between the pure difficulties and the behavior. They finally enter with the behavior into a total synthetic form and cannot be studied by themselves.... And yet they are not reducible to behavior; one can stop himself from fleeing, but not from trembling. I can, by a violent effort raise myself from my chair, turn my thought from the disaster which is crushing me, and get down to work; my hands will remain icy. Therefore, the emotion must be considered not simply as being enacted; it is not a matter of pure demeanor. It is the demeanor of a body which is in a certain state; the state alone would not provoke the demeanor; the demeanor without the state is comedy; but the emotion appears in a highly disturbed body which retains a certain behavior. The disturbance can survive the behavior, but the behavior constitutes the form and significance of the disturbance. On the other hand, without this disturbance, the behavior would be pure signification, an affective scheme. We are really dealing with a synthetic form; *in order to believe* in magical behavior it is necessary to be highly disturbed (Sartre, 1948, p. 75).

Other writers have noted analogous (though not quite identical) views of the emotional process. In summarizing much thought and research on the issue of emotion, Magda Arnold (1960, 1970) concluded that emotion is aroused by the person's perceptual appreciation of some situations and that while physiologic changes are important, they play a secondary role to *reinforce* and continue the emotion:

> In the human adult and the older child, the estimate of weal or woe is both

intuitive and reflective. But the intuitive judgment is immediate; the reflective judgment follows. This is shown by the fact that the intuitive appraisal is often supplemented or corrected by later reflection. When this happens, the emotion changes with the new intuitive estimate which follows the corrective judgment.... Normally, the sequence perception-appraisal-emotion is so closely knit that our everday experience is never strictly objective knowledge of a thing: it is always a knowing-and-liking, or a knowing and disliking. There is hardly any object we simply note as such without appraising it (1960, pp. 175, 177).

It is interesting to note the position Arnold comes to when she states that humans are moved to action by an immediate appraisal that is a "sense judgment" on the prereflective first, and then by an intellectual or reflective judgment. Man's emotional and other strivings, for Arnold as well as for Sartre, are functions of overall original choices or projects. The similarity between Arnold's conclusions and the HE position is evident by the following:

What we call *appraisal* or *estimate* is close to such a sense judgment. In emotional experience such appraisal is always direct, immediate; it is a *sense judgment* and includes a reflective judgment only as a secondary evaluation. Perhaps an example will illustrate the difference. When the outfielder "judges" a fly ball, he simply senses where he is going and where the ball is going and gauges his movements so that he will meet the ball. If he stopped to reflect, he would never stay in the game. We ourselves are constantly making judgments of this sort without paying too much attention to them. Now the judgment that the ball is too far or too close or just right for catching is no different from the judgment we make in appraising an object as good or bad, pleasurable or dangerous for us. Such sense judgments are direct, immediate, nonreflective, nonintellectual (Arnold, 1960, p. 175).

Leeper (1970) extends this view by stating that emotions *are* perceptual processes. He means that they are perceptions not in an ancillary or marginal sense, but in the full sense of a process that has very definite cognitive content and that is endowed with rich informational terms. He believes, further, that the emotional process in man is a more authentic model of the processes of perception than is usually thought. Leeper proposes that emotional responses in man are perceptions of the situations in which the person finds himself, and that they tend to be long-sustained perceptions (much akin to cosmologies) of the basic and significant aspects of man's situations.

From this presentation of the HE view of emotion, one may conclude that the nonthetic, or prereflective, mode is somehow beyond cognitive inspection. On the contrary, in most cases of intense emotion, upon reflection, the "missing connection" between the situation that evokes the emotion and the experience itself is an image of the threat *in* that situation. And the words that accompany that intuitive image are there to be uttered *if one chooses to attend to them* and spell them out. Much depends on how we wish to view this situation. If the client and the therapist choose to believe in a depth, psychoanalytic, or mystical view of man, where things are deeply hidden and can be known only vaguely and symbolically (as in Freudian and Jungian cosmologies), then they will not be satisfied with the client's report but will search for even more abstract and "deep" concepts that fit that notion. Usually, the client's choice is not to look into the good reasons for his responses or to understand himself and to become aware of *his own* belief-system because he would be faced with his inescapable responsibility. Thus the client chooses instead to cloud the issue by repeatedly saying "I don't know." The result is the fulfillment of his choice to continue the machinery of his emotional responsiveness rather than enter into a realistic, responsible encounter with whatever needs to be faced. Unfortunately, because of their own needs, too many therapists are happy to stay in the morass of clouded images and symbolism.

I recall an emergency counseling hour with a theater arts student who had just broken up with his fiancee and was in a state of panic about not hearing from her.

Pt: I'm just shaking. I can't stop thinking about her, worrying about it. [shouting] I can't stop shaking—it's got a hold of me.

Th: You see something, something shaking you.

Pt: Yes.

Th: What is shaking you?

Pt: What?

Th: Take a look at what's shaking you, how you're shaking yourself.

Pt: I see me—me shaking me.

Th: How is that, tell me—describe it.

Pt: Hey, listen [thinks a while, sits down], it's like I'm trying to shake me free, to pull me free. I'm so caught up in this broad. I need her, man, I need her. I can't stand it without her. I'm no good without her. Ya see, she left me 'cause I got nothing—I'm a nothing. If I was more, more of a person, more of a man, she wouldn't have walked. It's really all my fault, ya know. I'm such a shit!

Th: She left you because you aren't enough. You're a shaky guy—on shaky ground.

Pt: Yeah. Yeah, that's right.

Th: What's the picture in your head, now, of you?

Pt: [quickly] Like a twig. I need a stake to support me. A thin, shaky, no-backbone twig. [long silence] Hey, ya know, that may be—that's why she liked me. She could be strong for me, to me.

Th: Being that way, shaky, is what drew her to you?

Pt: Yeah, but then it got too much. Ya know, there were times when I kinda put it on—the needing thing, I mean.

This was discussed further: how the client had an image that only by his dependence could he maintain a close relationship with his girlfriend, and how he was at some level actually cognizant of his "project"—to make himself weak to maintain the relationship. But he really had to believe himself weak (otherwise it would just be a charade) and, consequently, "feel" weak, and shake.

Th: In that sense, then, it was good to be weak—to play it to the hilt. You thought and probably still think that's the way to be. To hold a relationship together, by being shaky, in need of support. You seem to be doing it right now. Shaking, being weak, blaming yourself. What do you want from me?

Pt: The same damn thing—you'll take me on, where she left off. If I'm really hung up, you'll come through.

This young man had to believe that his fiancee did not commit an independent act (i.e., "she left me for her own good reasons") but, rather, left him because of the way *he* was, "a nothing," because that still left him in control ("If I were stronger, she would never have left me"). He saw later that in the face of insufferable rejection he would say, "If I shake enough, someone will shore me up." Despite his repeated failure at his way of being in relationships, he could not face a relatively independent mutuality with another and the creation of a relationship in an open encounter. He had to make himself shaky and weak, both to believe that he retained control over someone else and to keep from the nagging anxiety of his separateness from others, ultimately acting so as to preclude a genuine or open encounter with another.

The image that kept the machinery of his feelings going, then, was his belief that this was the only way for him to be, and despite repeated disconfirmations, he chose to maintain his image and his belief, rather than face the anxiety of the recognition that he alone was responsible for his existence and his feelings and that he was not omnipotently in control over other people's responses.

> Emotional man is dialectical man reasoning sophistically. Hemmed in by the import of his valued beliefs, a comforting situation which has nurtured meaning in the past, the man faced with an unacceptable alternative in the present now argues in favor of his belief with all the cunning at his disposal. He strives to cling to the meanings he wants to believe rather than accepting others [and so generates the machinery of his feeling-life] (Rychlak, 1968, p. 473).

It is entirely possible for persons to come to grips with their priorities, their commitments, and their projects in a relatively short time. What they are *willing* to do about them is another matter and awaits our discussion of authentic therapy.

3
Human Choice: On Behavior Therapy

I have very clearly taken sides in this issue between the objectivist and sub-jectist approaches to the study of man. I sincerely believe this is such a conflict as may well be termed a battle for man's soul. It is so not because behaviorism is following a blind alley but because it is clearly effective within its frighteningly limited perspective. Paul Tillich has said, "Man resists ob-jectification, and if his resistance to it is broken, man himself is broken" (Bugental, 1967, p. 9).

Behavior therapy, currently so popular in psychotherapeutic circles, stands in direct and basic opposition to the humanistic existentialist view-point. In this chapter we will explore briefly the assumptions inherent in behavior therapy and consider critically what this approach teaches the client about human reality. The HE counselor or therapist believes that there is no compromise possible between himself and the therapies that retrain a person's feelings or his habits using a conditioning or behavior-istic model. I emphatically do *not* agree with Rychlak's attempt to blend the two:

Psycho-therapy need *not* affect one's philosophical outlook in life in order for it to be effective. One might hold to Freudian theory yet gain considerably from a series of desensitization sessions regarding a phobia, let us say (1969, p. 214).

In the HE view, the phobic person has, in bad faith, given up his freedom in order to view himself as an automaton, controlled "from the outside" or possessed by his compulsion. At base, the phobia or com-pulsion is seen as a manifestation of self-enslavement. The phobic or compulsive person ostensibly gives up his autonomy and *expresses* that giving up in his worries, thoughts, and acts. His compulsive act is, at once, a result of and a strengthening of his "secret" basic choice: to be *as-if* unfree. This kind of person says in effect:

I have no freedom. See—I must do this thing. I have no control over it; I have no choice. I am passive, a mere responder to the stimuli arising in me or out there. In my passive, responding view of myself, I give myself over to you, behavior therapist, for *you* to do it *to* me. Since I am a hapless victim of external circumstances, I make you, therapist, yet another circumstance in my life. You see, I have nothing to do with it, with my compulsion; it does it to me. Thus I believe [and the behavior therapist confirms and strengthens this view] that there is nothing significant inside me; control over me is out there. I have nothing important inside me for which I need to be responsible, so condition me out of this state of mine. I don't have any control over it. You, therapist, do.

The behavior therapist, by consenting to this paradigm, affirms and reinforces the mechanistic, Lockean position. In effect, he falls right in with the system that consequently caused the patient to exhibit phobic behavior. The behavior therapist says, "Yes, your view is correct. You have no freedom. There is none. Give yourself over to me."

> So the patient, by definition terrified of being human, finds some false comfort in an image of non-humanness and the unrealistic, irrational hope of being made a more effective machine. In this hope ... he states that he looks toward a perpetuation of passivity, expects that he may remain basically passive, a machine activated by an outside source of energy, hopes that he may remain creature without becoming creator—and do so without discomfort (Singer, 1965, pp. 107-108).

To put it another way, the project of such a person is to make himself a complete object of his biology, his history, his impulses, others, and/or conditioning sequences impinging upon him—in effect to abandon his subjectivity. But note that although he ostensibly makes himself object to biology, others, etc., because *he has* decided on that position or view, he secretly remains the transcendental subject. The masochist *asks* to be made an object of another and so, in bad faith, blows the cover of his enterprise. The behavioral psychologist is all too willing to agree with this abandonment of subjectivity: "No one owns his own personality ... and society has the duty—and the means—to change it for the better" (McConnel, 1970, p. 3).

In the behavior therapies, both the therapist and the patient join hands to aid and abet each other's duplicity, passivity, and abandonment of responsibility.[1] And, both reaffirm the perception—the fundamental "ensickening" syndrome—that behavior is absolutely externally determined, thus confirming the view that the locus of personal causality lies in an

---

[1]Mowrer (1965, p. 242) has commented critically about the conceptualization of man as the hapless victim of emotional malconditioning that leads to irrational and abnormal behavior:

> Sober appraisal of our situation suggests that, in point of fact, it has contributed very little to the more effective management and prevention of psychopathology. A plausible case can, indeed, be made for the surmise that this theoretical position merely *reinforces a perception which the neurotic is himself almost certain to have* [emphasis supplied; this is the "joining in bad faith" of which we speak].... He will readily fall in with the idea, which flows naturally from the foregoing assumptions, that he himself is *not responsible* for what he now does. This type of theory—to the effect that so-called "neurotic" individuals act strangely (compulsively, irrationally) because their emotions have been perverted and warped—is thus part and parcel of the "disease" itself and is by no means its cure. Increasingly we are getting reports of iatrogenic... personality disorder. And it also appears that great social institutions (home, church, school, courts) which have assimilated this philosophy are afflicted by a mysterious, creeping paralysis and loss of confidence—to such a degree that our whole society is commonly said to be sick (pp. 242-43).

external rather than an internal point of reference. Further, the view is propagated that man *must* passively submit to the demand put upon him, rather than actively engage his environment.

As I have said, the foregoing is a moral position (Lowe, 1969; Singer, 1965). By acting in the manner I have described, the behavior therapist establishes his position as a value and teaches the patient *that* view of reality. Nowhere is the person confronted with his commitment *not* to choose. Nowhere is the person's symptom given the dignity of being a meaningful symbol *for* the choice the person has made but that he or she is fearful of declaring verbally and openly. Rather, the therapist and the patient lock arms and recreate the existential crisis that has led the patient to deny his freedom. Both say, "Yes, you are no good this way; let's both change you. You are indeed strange and bedevilled."

Laing (1967) has seen this dilemma and described it brilliantly:

> Why do all theories about depersonalization, reification, splitting, denial, tend themselves to exhibit the symptoms they attempt to describe? We are left with transactions, but where is the individual: The individual, but where is the other? Patterns of behavior, but where is the experience? Information and communication, but where are the pathos and sympathy, the passion and compassion?

> Behavior therapy is the most extreme example of such schizoid theory and practice that proposes to think and act purely in terms of the other without reference to the self of the therapist or the patient, in terms of behavior without experience, in terms of objects rather than persons. It is inevitable therefore a technique of nonmeeting, of manipulation and control.

> Psychotherapy must remain *an obstinate attempt of two people to recover the wholeness of being human through the relationship between them.*

> Any technique concerned with the other without the self, with behavior to the exclusion of experience, with the relationship to the neglect of the persons in relation, with the individuals to the exclusion of their relationship, and most of all with an object-to-be-changed rather than a person-to-be-accepted, simply perpetuates the disease it purports to cure (pp. 31-32).

It does *seem*[2] possible to *have* imposed *on* me temporarily, or to impose on myself, projects and behaviors that go against my predominant way of structuring myself in the world, (my cosmology) without modifying my cosmology. A psychologist once related that the wife of a prominent politician had come to him with a problem: she had lost the strength in her arms and was thus unable to serve coffee, cocktails, and dinners to her husband's business associates and important political supporters. She was unable to be his "hostess." The psychologist, the head of a

---

[2]In this regard, the phrase *it seems that way* has special significance in therapy and counseling. So many clients seem to ask whether certain aspects of their lives "belong" in their lives. "Does (should) conflict exist in a marriage; is pain a normal part of life, the pain I bear?" All these questions refer to an essentialistic definition of life, and the only possible answer to such questions *seems* to be, "It seems that way."

psychology department promulgating behavior modification as the "only" therapy, stated that he "cured" her of this "neurasthenia" by systematic desensitization in seven sessions—without ever asking why or what the symptom was saying *for* this woman! If sexual frigidity, for example, were a further expression of this person's choice, she could decide to be "cured" by progressive desensitization, progressive relaxation, or the various other methods currently available (Paul, 1969; Yates, 1970) and not understand her choice of inferiority and the "rating game" she plays—of which her frigidity is but a consequence.

> As an inferior person, [she might say] I cannot risk entering into equal exchange with others—into an open encounter; I view others, men in particular, as objects who are related to me in a hierarchical or positional manner. I must, therefore, maintain psychological aloofness lest, by relating, my cosmology comes under threat because I am bound to glimpse that all is, and we all are, in the end equal. I must remain detached and cold, frigid, hidden, and unrelated. The only way that I maintain a semblance of interpersonal potency is by an apathetic and detached pose. In detachment at least some people see me as composed and strong.

She can succeed in her voluntary submission to self-reform by behavior modification without having stopped to touch her basic choice: to feel herself and to will herself to be inferior among others. But if unity of consciousness is posited, and if symptoms are not accidental invasions or results of an unfortunate set of conditioning sequences, something else will arise to take the place of the infirmity she suffers in order to express in some way the cosmology she pursues. The behaviorist's cure alters only one expression of the way in which the person freely chooses to see herself.

A person's feelings of inadequacy and inferiority represent the way in which he chooses to make himself analogous to a thing, without accepting freedom and its twin, responsibility. At the same time, he maintains an excuse, a hope, and, above all, control: "If I were other than inferior, then...." But each tactic denies that his being-for-others acts as a *cause* and that this way of being is the person's free choice. This person does not wish to dither with this basic choice, with his commitment, or his project. *He wants to get rid of the results of his project while nevertheless maintaining his project.* This attempt at remaining in the fire—but "please, Doctor, take away the burning sensation!"—is the covert statement of many who come for therapy or counseling. On the one hand, the person works to get help that on the other hand he must ultimately refuse.

The person decides voluntarily to come to the therapist because he no longer can deny the negative aspects that accompany his project. But by that very fact, he puts himself in a dangerous situation. He runs the risk of being faced with his own commitment, his own responsibility, and his freedom. The risk of being cured is that the person may see that he has freely chosen his project, that he can tinker with it, and that any project he chooses has its negative as well as positive components. He will have to face that he is not omnipotent and that the world may answer his pleas according to its own independent will, that others are independent of him, and that he is independent of others. Others may not be in this world to fulfill his needs, and he may not have the control over others that he may think he does. This realization brings with it anguish, joy, freedom, and a stinging sense of absurdity. Often persons glimpse this reality and find it difficult to bear or even intolerable while some people come to therapy to be relieved of their ills, these individuals come in order to persuade themselves that they have done everything possible to be cured and that they are, indeed, "incurable."[3]

Therapy or counseling is in jeopardy whenever the client and the therapist come close to grasping the person's cosmology, his construction. The client may say "Yes, Doctor, I understand that must be why I do that, but it doesn't help." He abandons therapy or begins to lie:

> It would be useless to try to explain this resistance by a revolt or an unconscious anxiety. How then could the unconscious be informed of the progress in the psychoanalytical investigation unless precisely by being a consciousness? But if the patient plays the game to the end, it is necessary that he experience a partial cure; that is, there must be produced in him the disappearance of the morbid phenomena which have brought him to seek the help of the physician. Thus he will have chosen the lesser evil: having come in order to persuade himself that he is incurable, he is forced—in order to avoid apprehending his project in full light and consequently having to nihilate it and to become freely another project—he is forced to depart in full possession of the cure.... In this case the timidity will disappear; it is the lesser evil. An artificial and voluble assurance will come to replace [it], (Sartre, 1956, p. 475).

To the HE, human dignity requires the recognition that a symptom expresses the way the person chooses life. Frigidity, impotence, and inferiority, then, can be "cured," not by treating these symptoms, but rather by the person's assumption of responsibility *for* them. The person must see that the symptom is his unique way of expressing the truth *of* him *for* him. It is his way of asserting his project in life and how he conducts his relationships as *part* of that commitment. The HE is less interested in the solutions to specific problems than in the assumption of total humanness. Symptoms are seen as the total expression of the humanness of a specific person; they symbolize what he is and has chosen to be, but denies.

The only real way a person can be freed of his frigidity, his inferiority,

---

[3]Arthur Burton (1969) speaks of this kind of person in an interesting and illuminating article about long-term patients.

or his depression is by rechoosing his basic cosmology. When in counseling or therapy, the person comes to see, fully experiences, or affirms his basic project, and sees it in its totality, without having any basis but his own decision, at that *liberating instant* the person who calls himself a patient can, if he wishes, radically convert himself. He can put his choice in the past, live in the now and suffer the contingencies of an authentic real being. It takes courage, and that touches upon the real riddle of life: how to live in-the-now, to fully experience life in all its immediacy.

The behavior modification therapist, quite opposite from this view, sees man in a reductive, piecemeal manner. Such a therapist asserts, partly correctly, that there is no such entity as mental illness underlying the symptoms his subjects exhibit. For him, the symptoms *are* the disease.[4] The behavior modifier rarely considers or even attempts to justify the underlying value judgments that are part and parcel of his ostensibly "objective" descriptions of his patients' behavior. He ignores the contention (which is gaining ever greater recognition) that such concepts as pathology and especially psychopathology are wholly valuational notions.

But the behavior therapist replies, "My techniques work, damn it! And they work well." Since symptoms are merely conditioned forms of behavior, the therapist's task is prescribed: when a patient comes complaining of homosexuality, depression, or any number of symptoms, the behavior therapist merely conditions the symptoms away.[5] There is a certain appeal and simplicity in such a position: the woman wants her nose made smaller so that she can be more attractive, and the surgeon complies. The patient comes with an inability to lift trays full of canapes and decrusted sandwiches for her husband's cocktail parties, and the behavior therapist "reduces" her resistance, much as the plastic surgeon would reduce the nose. The patient wants to become a more efficient rapist ("Gosh, Doc, I lose my erection when the young girl screams too hard") and the behavior therapist reinforces his erectile response.[6] Needleman (1968) points out that,

---

[4]The view most often expressed by those who have approached the domain of psychopathology from the standpoint of learning theory has been to the effect that here the basic trouble lies in some anomaly in the *emotional* (or "attitudinal" life of the afflicted individual and that any irregularities in overt behavior are merely symptomatic of the underlying affective problem. More specifically, the assumption has been that psychoneurotic individuals have suffered from "traumatic" emotional malconditioning of some sort, as a result of physical accidents or overly harsh, perverse training at the hands of others. Irrational or irresponsible behavior on the part of the victims of such unfortunate treatment is thus merely an expression of the irrationality and abnormality of their emotions. This, then, is supposed to be the essence of "neurosis" and "mental illness" in the most pervasive sense of these terms" (Mowrer, 1965, p. 242).

This view, then, is essentially dissimilar to that of the classical Freudian.

[5]But for a balanced and critical review of learning and behavior therapies, see Murray and Jacobson (1971), and Breger and McGaugh (1965).

[6]cf., Rhinehart, *The Dice Man,* 1971.

when seen in this way, behavior therapy techniques might be more appropriately called "behavioral cosmetics."

Of course, the behavior therapist would deny that. He elevates his work to the treatment of psychopathology, neurosis, phobia, or maladaptive behavior. Thus he puts himself right back into what he denies: the injection of what as a natural scientist he wishes to eliminate (a project that seems doomed in an encountered universe)—value concepts.

> Obviously, to think of behavior as adaptive or maladaptive is to treat it as instrumental toward the realization of an end. But how is the goal or end to be known? For, surely, there are levels of instrumentality; that is, there are goals which are themselves instrumental for further ends. And, of course, the immediate goal of a particular pattern of "adaptive" behavior may itself be "maladaptive" with respect to a more fundamental goal, etc., etc. In addition, therefore, behavior therapy on its very own terms is obliged to consider the well-known problem of adaptation to a "sick society," that is, it raises the ethically and psychologically formidable issue of "the well-adjusted storm-trooper." And, of course, it must also consider on an individual basis the "adaptability" of the patient's relatively fundamental life-goals.

> Any refusal, under the banner of a positivistic rejection of the "unverifiable" [values], to scrutinize these more fundamental goals would be to lapse, again, though more subtly, into cosmetics. Thus, the very project of therapy should force the behavior therapist to question in the most serious way the often careless equating of what is desired with what is desirable. If he does not do this, he ought to change his title to cosmetician (Needleman, 1968, p. xi).

In summary, then, the HE believes that the view of man as a conditionable machine on which stimuli impinge or a machine that *is* conditioned, is at the core of what is called mental illness or human problems. For the humanistic existentialist, self-deceptive or bad-faith behavior depends on the degree to which the person makes himself into a machinelike thing, determined, nonresponsible, unfree. In contrast, to the behavior therapist symptoms are merely bad habits learned accidentally. Man is passive and determined by his prior states, his prior acts, or even his prior movements[7], not by his intentions. In this manner behavior therapy furthers the basic bad faith and irresponsibility from which the person suffers in the first place. In HE terms, the mere existence of an *act* implies its absolute autonomy and responsibility.

---

[7]Again, the theoretical and experimental literature, looked at critically, does not support this view. Personality factors and cognitive factors—that is, man's unique self-reflexive consciousness, come into play even in *classical conditioning* (See Grings, 1965, p. 85).

In *operant conditioning,* human awareness is becoming a relevant variable to be dealt with. In a number of studies, it has been found that with experimental subjects who are aware of the correct responses required (that is, of the response-reinforcement contingency), the acquisition and extinction of verbal behavior can be demonstrated; while in persons who are unaware (that is, have no cognition about the process), conditioning is relatively impossible to demonstrate (Dulany, 1962; Jacobson, 1969; Matarrazzo, Saslow, and Pareis, 1960; Spielberger and DeNike, 1960).

As to complex *human verbal learning,* Underwood (1964) has put the case well:

THE ETHICAL DILEMMA IN COUNSELING
AND THERAPY

More needs to be said about values and behavior therapy. Herbert Kelman (1968) points out that the psychologist, as he addresses himself to changing the behavior of the patient, finds himself in a situation quite analogous to that of the nuclear physicist working on the Bomb. It is known that under certain conditions persons *can* be manipulated, influenced, and brainwashed; that, in a word, man can be placed in situations where he can be used (Walker and Heyns, 1962; London, 1967; Kiesler and Kiesler, 1969; and Zimbardo and Ebbesen, 1969). The fact of that possibility—i.e., control and manipulation of human behavior—is fraught with most important of ethical ambiguities. The psychologist must accept the responsibility for the personal and broader social consequences of the conditions leading to control and manipulation. Kelman further points out that even the worker engaged in pure or theoretical research cannot demur by asserting that his knowledge is ethically neutral:

> It is impossible to carry out social research . . . that is unaffected by the values of the investigator and the groups to which he belongs. The choice of problem, the approach to it, and the interpretation of the findings inevitably reflect the value assumptions and preferences that the investigator brings to his research (1968, p. 110).

The social scientist, like the physicist, must consider how his findings and discoveries are likely to be applied. And the practitioner cannot find any comfort in the ethically ambiguous position that he is helping others or doing good, nor can he relinquish his responsibility by doing only what the patient says he wants him to do. In addition, there is always surplus value or a metacommunication inherent in the therapist's acts; that is, the therapist asserts the value of his actions merely by performing them. In terms of behavior modification therapy:

> the danger is, to quote Seeley once more, that as man "becomes to himself . . . a scientific object, an object of mere curiosity or curiosity in the service of manipulation, he ceases, *pari passu* to be a self . . . ceases to be his own habitable home, and becomes what he has made himself, a true object for engineering, the true fruit of science. . . . It is not at all clear . . . that a science of man in the traditional sense of the word "science" is possible without self-destruction—by each of himself, or of most by some" (Kelman, 1968, p. 112).

To the HE therapist, the central therapeutic effort is (or ought to be) directed at precisely this and perhaps nothing more: attaining a constantly spelled-out awareness of *the particular* person's freedom-and-responsi-

---

The image of a subject in a verbal learning experiment as being a *tabula rasa* upon which the investigator chisels associations, and quite against the S's wishes, is archaic. The S is far from passive and the tablet has already impressed upon it an immense network of verbal habits. A more accurate description of the verbal-learning experiment is one in which the S actively "calls upon" all the repertoire of habits and skills to outwit the investigator (p. 52).

bility. And that is a fundamental value growing out of the HE conception of what it is to be a person. From this position, any manipulation of another's behavior violates him. It matters not at all whether such manipulation is requested by the patient, whether it is for his own good, or whether it is based on aversive reinforcement or positive reinforcement. The central ethical issue with behavior modification not merely over what *ends* are achieved but also concerns the use of manipulation and control (either subtle or overt).

While any manipulation is a violation, on the other hand, any effort at change or interchange, no matter how minimal, seems to include some degree of influence, control, or manipulation. Any therapy, then, faces this dilemma, and those directed at *changing the person*—even toward freedom—represent a potentially manipulative situation. I disagree with Kelman's (1968) statement that the manipulative situation can be mitigated by an awareness of the "important differences in degree and kind of manipulation" (p. 16). He underplays what I consider central: the explicitly aware struggle, the *dealing* with influence and manipulation. More importantly, it is that subject-object split (*re* the self and others, and the self and the self) that is the exquisite heart of the matter of personhood and interpersonality. Manipulation, influence, and control are not epiphenomena in human relations; they are central facts that make up the very fabric of human relations, and as such they need to be constantly dealt with in careful and explicit awareness. We shall address this issue further in discussing the concept of authentic relationships (Chapter 4).

The dilemma is crystallized in the debate between Rogers and Skinner (1956). Skinner ignores the first horn of the dilemma (that violation is intrinsically bound with manipulation), and Rogers minimizes the second (that it is impossible to avoid manipulation in influencing another). Of Skinner, Kelman (1968) writes:

> Skinner is well aware of the inevitability of control in human affairs, and argues for a type of control that is based on intelligent planning and positive reinforcement and is not "exercised for the selfish purposes of the controller." ... But Skinner fails to see the basis of many of the criticisms directed at him, because he is concerned about the control of human behavior only when that control is aversive, and when it is misused, that is, when it is used for the benefit of the controller and to the detriment of the controlee. He seems unable to see any problem in the mere *use* of control regardless of technique or purpose. This inability is inconsistent with his value position, which does not recognize the exercise of choice as a good per se (p. 17).

With equal balance, Kelman writes of Carl Roger's position:

> Rogers tends to minimize the second horn of the dilemma presented here: the inevitability of some degree of manipulation in any influence attempt. He makes what appears to me the unrealistic assumption that by choosing the proper goals and the proper techniques in an influence situation one can com-

pletely sidestep the problem of manipulation and control. He seems to argue that, when an influencing agent is dedicated to the value of man as a self-actualizing process and selects techniques that are designed to promote this value, he can abrogate his power over the influence and maintain a relationship untainted by behavior control. This ignores, in my opinion, the dynamics of the influence situation itself (p. 18).

Jourard (1971) points out that patients come to him because they have become so estranged from themselves that they are unable to show important people in their lives their "real selves." Jourard appears to differ from Rogers when he questions how a therapist can reacquaint his patients with what is real in themselves while he engages in subtle manipulations and withholds his "realness" from patients. But he falls right into the dilemma when he writes:

> It reminds me of the sick leading the sick. In point of fact, if my experience means anything, it has shown me that *I can come closest to eliciting and reinforcing authentic behavior in my patient by manifesting it myself.* This presumes that I am able to do this. Probably, by virtue of my own training, and whatever was real in my own therapy, I am better able to do this than an untrained person (1971, p. 141).

Thus Jourard, too, uses manipulation (in this case "modeling") and influence, but of a special kind: authentic modeling. He believes that by being in a genuine dialogue he can obviate or somehow neutralize the issue of influence, control, and manipulation in counseling and therapy. I do not wish to disparage Jourard; however there is an issue here that is being ignored, and by his position, this brilliant and effective therapist also denies the encounter.

On the other side, London (1964) argues blatantly that the therapist is *mainly* a manipulator of other persons, and as such he must accept that he functions as a moral agent whether he likes it or not. This being the case, he concludes that therapists ought to accept their roles as "secular priests" who draw their authority from their superior knowledge of human nature. By virtue of that knowledge they are best qualified to decide upon the nature and kind of moral indoctrination their patients should receive. London writes:

> [The therapist] would be a secular priest, whose justifications are not in a theology revealed from heaven, but one discovered or intimated in the laboratory. The genesis of his consideration would then be the nature of man, and his gospel the fulfillment of that nature, its decalogue the medium of behavior—and all preached from the altar of science (1964, p. 163).[8]

---

[8]And yet, at the same time, London (1964, p. 25) writes:

So little is actually known about the principles of behavior that all personality theories of much relevance to psychotherapy are thoroughly speculative. Insofar as they are neither tested nor currently testable, the implications for morality that derive from them have no more scientific validity than do the moral adjurations of revealed religion. They are predictions based on faith, not fact.

Thus London has grasped the first horn of the dilemma and made making a transcendent virtue out of a problematic necessity. He cannot conceive of a situation where he and the patient are both priests, grappling with the problem inherent in such a relationship.

SKINNER'S CHOICE: CAVEAT ACTOR, CAVEAT EMPTOR

Let us examine Skinner's latest book, a propaganda piece espousing the application of Skinnerian technology to the basic question of how we *should* lead our lives. As I have said previously, one of the rallying cries of the behavior shaper is that his procedure is based on laboratory findings and that "it works." We have alluded to methodological difficulties in a "black box" conception of S-R bonding, but a deeper reply to the argument "because it works" must be offered now.

As many who are concerned with technology have taught (cf., Muller, 1970; Chein, 1972; Kelman, 1968; and Wheelis, 1971), the choice of a methodology *merely* on the basis of its being rigorous or its being efficient is narrow and unacceptable. The central question, raised by Skinner's book and by the film *A Clockwork Orange* (Burgess, 1963), is whether a laboratory-based technology is valuable. Do we, in the long view, really want it around? What, besides manipulating man efficiently, does it *do* to man? What else does it make of him? What kind of world will the *Clockwork Orange* world be?

In Skinner's conception, the idea of autonomous man must be discarded and control over him accomplished by "the environment." According to Skinner, this need not make man a slave to his environment because that environment would be of man's own design. But this is precious; it is within everyone's experience that if we are not careful, we can and do become the victims of our own doings and of our own self-deceptions.

Further, there are serious problems with basing our future upon the findings of the behavior laboratory. As we have pointed out before, the *findings* of that laboratory are not neutral of value and may be the result of a circular, restricted, and self-fulfilling prophecy. As Sartre has aptly pointed out, "We find only what we are looking for." Importantly, the findings of the laboratory reflect passive man; a world designed to model the attributes of the lab can provide modes or paradigms only for the maintenance of a world presided over by the passive status quo.

I merely call into attention here Zimbardo's demonstration that persons who are "objects" in an experiment respond (unless they are treated differently) according to the narrow limits and constricted condition demanded by the design. If the experiment is to be rigorous, the experimenter:

(1) defines the goal of the experiment;
(2) manages the environment strictly and tightly;

(3) expects (hopes) the subject will do as he is asked—the subject should be dependent upon the experimenter; and

(4) provides the subject with as little information as possible—indeed he may even distort information (Argyris, 1971, p. 553).

It is no wonder, then, that to structure man as pigeon finds him, indeed, to be so. This is just one of the reasons that experimental or laboratory science may not necessarily produce valid information on which to base a model of man.

Krasner (1971) points out that one of the major goals of the Skinnerian behavior shaper is to inject this kind of laboratory-science approach into the very fabric of all of life. It is important to note that if your life is to be designed—as an experiment is designed—by this kind of person, then life will produce a particular kind of person. If it were rigidly structured, a laboratory-based family would produce a certain kind of person. Kibbutz rearing has an effect on people! The concentration camp produces a certain kind of person; so does Madison Avenue. The question is what kind of person do we want? Do we even dare to raise that question? When we raise it, we cannot cop out to a value-free "experimental" approach or science. Argyris (1971) points out that the kind of world created by the Skinnerian would be exactly like the one we now have: "If anything, it will become bureaucracy squared" (p. 554).

I resurrect now the central argument that technology is not neutral in terms of value. But Skinner insists that his technology is neutral:

[Skinner] cites as an example of neutrality the generalization to the effect that positive reinforcement will encourage the behavior reinforced. No position is taken about what kind of behavior should be reinforced.

Is this the kind of primitive generalization that has given Skinner his fame? If he and his students had remained at such a primitive level then he would not be the honored and respected scientist that he is. The reason that Skinner has become famous is that he has much to say about the sequence of reinforcement, the conditions under which it should occur, who should do it, and how much the "subject" need know. It is therefore not precise to say that Skinner has discovered the importance of behavior being shaped by reinforcement, because this position leaves open the logical possibility that the subject can design and do his own reinforcing. As Skinner has repeatedly pointed out, the reinforcement comes from the environment.

Once we dig into how the environment should be designed, the normative position becomes clearer. One would predict that the world Skinner designs requires human beings who enjoy, rather than resist, dependent relationships and whose influence on the environment is minimal.

One indication in support of this prediction is the history of successful application of Skinner's ideas in helping human beings. The great majority of the successes reported so far have come primarily with such groups as younger students in schools, delinquents in institutions, with patients with varying behavior disorders, and the mentally retarded. It may be argued that these delinquents and patients have chosen to participate because they see their present

state as aversive. Or, as in the case of the mentally retarded, they may be induced to participate by being offered better living conditions and a better
environment (e.g., toys). Or, as in the case of students, they may be confronted
with a new way to learn which they strive to use as best they can.

In these cases the subjects find it worthwhile to be placed in situations in which

    1) they are dependent upon the experimenter or therapist
    2) they are submissive to the experimenter or therapist
    3) they have a short time perspective; and
    4) they perform only those tasks assigned to them.

These are the identical conditions to which animals or humans are exposed in
experimental situations.

In addition, the people whom the Skinnerians have helped have been primarily
people who wish to adapt to the present environment [emphasis supplied]. . . .
As we suggest, if a technology developed directly from, and following, the
properties of the experimental method, is applied to people, it tends to reinforce certain types of behavior (dependency, submissiveness) and refrains from
rewarding proactive attempts to resist and alter the reinforcement schedule
(Argyris, 1971, pp. 556-57).

Skinner wants to give complete control over the person to the environment and to others in that environment. The HE therapist, however, wants
the person to be the locus of control.

The HE therapist values an individual's ability to be centered in his own
values, where he can respond effectively when he is being seduced or bribed
by positive reinforcement, when he is being confronted, when he is being
aversively reinforced, or when, as in most situations in life, there seems to
be no clear positive or negative reinforcement. Life is ambiguous. Upon
what, then, shall a person rely?

We need situations where a schedule of reinforcements does not come
from anyone "out there" because the important "out there" must be "in
here" a schedule that comes from the person himself. When a person dares
to become aware, when he dares to spell out the engagements in his life, he
is less susceptible to Madison Avenue and to brain-washing and to group
pressure. Such a person can stand alone when he needs to; he is a free man
even when he is in prison for his beliefs. Christ, Galileo, Abraham, Einstein,[9] and Freud were such men.

For Skinner, freedom is escape from aversive situations. He writes:

It is possible that man's genetic endowments support this kind of struggle for
freedom: when treated aversively people tend to act aggressively or to be reinforced by signs of having worked aggressive damage [p.29] . . . . Man's struggle for freedom is not due to a will to be free, but to certain behavioral processes
characteristic of the human organism, the chief effect of which is the avoidance
of or escape from so-called "aversive" features of the environment (Skinner,
1971, p. 42).

Skinner seems to ignore the experimental evidence (for example, Zim-

---

[9]cf. C.P. Snow's (1967) excellent description of Albert Einstein.

bardo's work, 1957, 1969a and b) and the thinking of humanists and existentialists who have dealt with an idea of freedom in terms of personal responsibility, personal causation, and the acceptance of freedom by persons *as a central,* causal issue. In this view, as Binswanger (Needleman, 1968) pointed out, if the external environment and other people are being controlled by others, it is precisely because some persons are denying their human responsibilities and are thus electing to live under the control of the environment.

> This literature, in contradistinction to Skinner, conceives of the running away from aversive phenomena as superficial and shallow. The most important issues about freedom are how man moves toward aversive phenomena; how he actively or proactively manages them and his environment; how he maintains an active vigil to make sure that he does not become a happy slave (Argyris, 1971, p. 562).

I cannot accept the behavior modifier's retort that he will "condition" the person toward that kind of autonomy, just as I cannot accept the Leninist or Bolshevist claim that all that is needed is two generations of a dictatorship of the proletariat to eventually achieve democracy. I reject the claim that one can attain democracy through undemocratic means or that we can attain autonomy through behavior control.

As I shall point out in a moment, the therapist's influence in a behavior-shaping paradigm is just as potent as in any other. A recent study has shown (Ryan and Gizynski, 1971), that what seems important in even this kind of therapy is the quality of the relationship between patient and therapist, and it is that relationship that influences and teaches the person about "how it really is," should be, or can be.

> A key variable in the social science universe is the nature of man. Skinner's concept fits the nature of man that an engineering-technologically oriented society generates. Others seek to develop a concept of autonomous man which is quite different from Skinner's. Their autonomous man is not defined only by what he runs away from but what he goes toward; what initiative he takes; what and how he confronts, alters, and manages his environment. . . . This flexibility of man means that ultimately [as was pointed out in our discussion of perception] man *selects and designs* his environment, and not the other way around. Man is responsible to develop the design of his nature (Argyris, 1971, p. 565).

THE DILEMMA, THE PARADOX, AND THE ENGAGED ENCOUNTER

The HE maintains that the behavior modifier and his subject have succumbed to the bad faith proposition that since manipulation cannot be avoided it is best to do it well. "I am nothing but a manipulated man," says the patient, "consequently, let me be manipulated in the right direction, at least." And the therapist supports that contention tacitly or openly, saying, "That's right, you are nothing but for others. Then be for me, let *me* do you right." The moral scheme underlying such a proposition is expressed thus:

> The trouble with letting people identify their own goals, desirable as it may be in other respects, is like the trouble with letting children learn some things by experience; they are patently incompetent to judge either the stability of their aspirations or the consequences of their experiments. (London, 1964, p. 161).

Both therapist and patient have denied the basic encounter around which life seems to revolve, namely, the paradox of how two humans can *be* together, each exquisitely aware of the paradox, and grapple with it (that, by the way, *is* the relationship) in a dialectic fashion—where no party succumbs, where one is not slave, and the other not master, but where each is reciprocally engaged with the other. The basic issue, then, is how to live (love?) together, as two or more equals, one no lesser or greater than the other. There may be no ultimate or final solution to their paradox; life, love, may just be a dyadic engagement with the paradox.

I should like to draw an analogy here that might clarify the problem of the paradox in human life. Max Planck (1949) has written of his conception of a duality in human existence. As he speaks of freedom and its opposite, determinism, he assigns to these polarities the significance of *right* and *left*—a perspective dependent upon one's spatial position. These orientations depend on the *person* who is looking, on his perspective. Freedom and determinism are not "out there"; "really" it is our perception, arising out of our encounter with reality. To follow Planck's thinking, we can conclude that the problem of freedom-determinism can be denied or can be resolved once and for all. But the issue does arise, constantly. It cannot be disposed of as being merely a chimera, an artifact. The analogy to manipulation can be stated in this manner. Man is the one who sees left and right, sees freedom and determinism, from *his* position, and what that position speaks of or symbolizes is precisely the *paradoxical nature of the encounter itself.* To put it another way, the concern with manipulation and nonmanipulation, or freedom and determinism reflects, perhaps, the ambiguous nature of human existence. Just as light may be thought of both as corpuscular and in waves, so human existence can be determined and manipulated, or free and self-determined, depending upon the perspective one takes or attends to;[10] it is a paradox. While a permanent resolution may not be possible, a local or temporary resolution may be available. The importance of the whole issue is that *it is an issue man raises,* and as such it may speak to the fundamental ambiguity of human life. Such an issue must not be ignored or denied; it must be dealt with; it must be encountered.

Both the behavior modifier and the humanistic psychologist (not the

---

[10]See an allied view in Laszlo (1972) especially pages 234-56.

HE psychologist) deny the encounter by equal though polarly different positions, each by grasping one horn of the dilemma. The behavior controller says, "There is no way out. Let us, then, frankly manipulate and do it well." The humanist says, "We must overcome, somehow, the basic issue in human relations by ignoring it and focusing instead on love, creativity, emotionalized expression, and an enhancement of 'self-actualization'—a kind of lifting oneself up by one's own bootstraps." The experiental therapist, however, does indeed engage at times, and when he engages the "usness" (which the Gestaltist ignores) and our "dilemma," he approaches the HE position of an aware appreciation, a confrontation, and grappling with the subject-object issue.[11] The behavior modifier, on the other hand, is clearly in bad faith.

The way out of the dilemma is that there is no way out. It is a constant, engaged dealing or encounter with the central human paradox: the issue of manipulation, control, freedom, and determinism. The encounter is not a denial of the dilemma or a capitulation to it, but a struggle with that central fact and a laboring *toward* a true subject-subject meeting.

---

[11]cf., Gendlin, 1973.

4
We: The Therapeutic Relationship

Psychotherapy is not so much a science or technique as it is a way of being with another person (Jourard, 1968, p. 57).

THE CONCEPT OF RELATIONSHIP—SOME MODELS

Therapy occurs within the context of a relationship. This special kind of relationship has been envisioned in numerous, varied ways. To introduce this discussion of human relationships as they occur in the therapist's office, I want to present several different models of relationships that are written about in the literature.

It should be apparent that it is extraordinarily difficult to write about relationships. Written words cannot express the feelings or nuances that spoken words carry with them—the body attitudes, the facial expressions, the tones of voice, the tears in the eyes, or the choked-up voice. The same problem seems to occur, though perhaps to a lesser degree, in the tape-recorded interviews and videotapes. They are pale reflections of what really transpires between two people as they struggle to be as real as they can be with each other.

The Analytic Relationship—Model 1

Working at peak efficiency, the therapist must, within the first few minutes of the interview, appraise not only the nature of the patient's illness, but much of his underlying personality structure and his characteristic defenses, as well. Observation of the patient's general appearance, dress, speech, manner, and affect is crucial. Knowledge of semantics, kinesics, and linguistics, the essentials of character analysis, is indispensable. An initial impression of a "baby face" or childlike voice may be the only clue necessary to recognize the infantile personality. The patient who uses a euphemism for death, such as "passing away" or "being no more" reveals strong fears of loss and separation. A clenched fist on the lap discloses poorly repressed anger. Fluttering eyelashes and histrionic manner unmask an hysterical character. Evasiveness gives away the paranoid, reasonableness the obsessive, psychomotor retardation the depressive. . . . Furthermore, if there were situations in the patient's past which could have been conflictual, it is likely that they were. If a patient has siblings, for example, there will have been sibling rivalry whether or not the patient has stated so, or even is aware of it. No matter what the family constellation, the therapist can assume that there was conflict over wanting sole possession of the patient's mother's love. When the therapist acquires skill through practice, his evaluation has begun long before the patient's entire revelation of the content of his life history, which follows the chief complaint. In fact, the content of the history should be mostly confirmatory, revealing the why and the how of the illness. . . . The first real therapeutic effort should be made to confront the patient with his masochism, his self-defeating, self-destructive actions. *No interpretations or confrontations should be made in the initial interview, except those which are tied directly to guilt and self-punishment.* The symptoms themselves should be translated as mechanisms meant to harass or to torture the patient. Compulsions, phobias, insomnia, fear, conversion reaction, anxiety, depression, angry outbursts, anorexia and worry should all be explained as components of self-punishment, products of a guilty conscience. The patient should be shown how each symptom hurts him in some way, by mental anguish, by destroying his feeling of well-being, or by provoking others to hurt him or to leave him. . . . Confrontations of masochism should be made incisively, directly, and with the confidence of certainty. No matter what other factors are involved in the patient's symptoms, conflicts, and defenses, the therapist can be absolutely sure of the elements of self-punishment. The patient's very illness that necessitated his being in the doctor's office is in itself incontrovertible proof of the presence of some self-punitive drive, even in acute situational reactions, and in identity or family crises. It is the need for self-punishment that prevents most patients from bumbling into a spontaneous resolution of their problems without anyone's help. There is no need for hesitancy, doubt, timidity, or obscurity. The doctor's confrontation must be firm, direct, and insistent: "Look what you are doing to yourself! See how you hurt and torment yourself!" This is the one time in therapy for forcefulness. There can be no wavering. Either the patient is willing to examine his role in hurting himself or there can be no therapy (Lewin, 1970, pp. 50-52).

Lewin is a clinical assistant professor of psychiatry at the University of Pittsburgh School of Medicine. His position is that of the classical medical-model, doctor-expert, who is watchful for every sign of "sickness" or pathology—psychopathology in this instance. He expresses one side of the object-subject relationship: the all-knowing, superior observer. This position permits him to evaluate, diagnose, judge, and disclose to the patient the patient's illness. Everything in the patient's behavior becomes a clue to the underlying pathology about which the doctor possesses a secret. Everything is a sign of a regressive pathological process.

Further, there are rules to follow ("no interpretations should be made") so that the theory and its technology take precedence over the person sitting opposite and direct the interaction. Despite what the patient thinks, he should be shown that "each symptom hurts him in some way." This must be so because according to the theory, masochism is man's basic tendency. "No matter what other factors are involved . . . the therapist can be absolutely sure of the element of self-punishment."

What is the metacommunication in this type of treatment; what does the therapist teach the patient? Regarding the relationship, the patient learns that there are people in this world (doctors of any stripe) who can know more about him than he himself can. He learns also that he is wrong, ill, or inhabited by forces of which he is unaware and that only the doctor can understand. He is a helpless victim of masochistic forces that serve no beneficent purpose other than to hurt and torment him. There is no dignity, no positive aspect to the patient; these Thanatos-induced structures must be gotten rid of through a punishing interpretation by the doctor: "See, see how you are punishing yourself!"

In this model the patient is irresponsible and must place himself in the hands of an omnipotent expert to effect a "cure." It is the image of man and of this man in particular as a victim of his own self that is transmitted and taught. The patient must "knuckle under" to the authority and will of the therapist. Either the patient is willing to examine his role in hurting himself or there can be no therapy. That is not an offer a troubled man can refuse.

The therapist here reenacts the essentially violating conditions that, probably more than any others, are instrumental in bringing persons to a state of self-obliviousness. The patient, both as a child and as an adult, is told overtly and covertly that he is not good or acceptable the way he is and that it is necessary for him to change, grow or mature in order to be cured, adjusted, or normal according to the doctor's or parent's model.

This is the traditional model of psychotherapy and counseling—albeit a bit more blatantly put than most—a model that establishes a sharp gulf between the doctor and the patient, between the healthy and the "ill." The person's basic problem—that he has compromised and failed to declare his reality for the sake of another's—is only furthered by the stance and position of the therapist.

Moreover, the hope is held out to the patient that conflicts, guilt, and anxieties, *can* be eradicated by accepting the therapist's interpretations. The bleak, authoritarian picture goes on. The reality of conflict, social injustice, and others is obviated and traded in for a solipsistic, totally intrapersonal, omnipotent position. From this analytic position, all is within the person; his toilet training, for example, directs his illness today. This quasi-relationship emphasizes provocative events in childhood and focuses on reteaching through well-timed silences, responses, interpretations (punishments), or withholdings. In this way, the relationship furthers unreality in the person.

The basic thrust of this kind of therapy is to *tell* the patient in one way or another about the inevitable traumatic circumstances that directly cause the problem or the symptom. The intended communication is, "You must see that because this happened to you in the past, you act as though it were either happening now, or were inevitably going to happen." The implication is that the patient is wrong in his thinking and if he sees that this is wrong, he will stop acting that way. The repetition compulsion will be broken by the machinations of a paternalistic, all-knowing therapist.

The implicit message to the patient is that all things are not as they seem:

> Now what does the analyst do? (1) He helps the patient eliminate his resistance as far as possible. . . . (2) Knowing that the utterances of the patient are really allusions to other things, the psychoanalyst tries to deduce what lies behind the allusions and to impart this information to the patient. When there is a minimum of distance between allusion and what is alluded to, the analyst gives the patient words to express feelings just rising to the surface and thereby facilitates their becoming conscious. . . . This procedure of deducing what the patient actually means and telling it to him is called interpretation (Fenichel, 1945, p. 25).

In this therapeutic relationship, the patient is considered helpless on his own. He is oblivious to himself and must rely on the doctor's expertise, because the doctor knows him far better than he can know himself. The patient is the victim of his past and of an aversive superego, and his best adjustment is to displace or to sublimate.

The therapist is the Knower. There is no possible mutuality in the relationship since all personal statements are seen as transferences or distortions. The patient's statements are not taken at face value. Since all persons are viewed as basically neurotic, the patient is violated in this way merely because he has chosen to become a patient (Storr, 1968).

The analytically oriented therapist's relationship with his patient and his communication to him follow from his image of man and his conceptions of psychosexual maturity as the *sine qua non* of psychological healing. The therapist's basic intention is to "mature" his patient and to interfere with regressive and defensive processes, to help the patient accept his traumatic experiences, to become aware of the inevitably conflicted nature of his instincts, and to displace and sublimate them. But the therapist's participation is reduced to a minimum (Glad, 1959). In the most orthodox instance, the consulting room is arranged so that the therapist will be as innocuous and bland a figure as possible. Personal contacts are few and the therapist is usually not visible during the hour. In most instances, the patient lies on a couch and the therapist sits behind him, unseen. This arrangement is supposed to permit the patient maximum freedom to enter into a dreamlike state where his thought processes are entirely internal, and to express his inner life rather than relating to external reality. The patient can see the reincarnation of important figures in his childhood in this nebulous therapist, and thus can transfer onto him feelings and rejections that belonged to those earlier models.

Though some aspects of psychoanalytic psychotherapy have changed in recent years, the essential features of the patient-therapist relation remain the same. Everything is arranged so that the patient has nothing else to do but to imagine, and then those imaginings are used as proof of the reality of the transference (Shepard & Lee, 1970). A modern psychoanalyst exemplifies this further:

> There are two basic requirements which the analyst must fulfill in order to promote the growth of the transference neurosis in the patient. The analyst must consistently frustrate the patient's quest for neurotic gratification and reassurance and he must also remain relatively anonymous. . . . The analyst must also serve as a guide in leading the patient into the strange world of psychoanalytic treatment. At the proper time he must explain the many strange and artificial instrumentalities and rules necessary for conducting psychoanalysis. In a sense *he has to teach the patient to become a psychoanalytic patient* [emphasis supplied]. . . . The analytic relationship is a complicated and fragile human predicament for both parties. The expert in the situation must not permit his responses to intrude upon the patient and thus obscure the patient's individual and unique reaction. The analyst's responses must be restrained, muted, and in the service of the therapeutic commitment, which recognizes insight and understanding as its most potent single instrumentality. . . . I believe this outline indicates how the analyst may solve the conflict between the deprivational, incognito attitudes required for the transference development, and the humane treater of the sick necessary for the working alliance (Greenson, 1967, pp. 377-79).

Let us compare the analyst's and the HE therapist's responses to a patient who does not feel alive and who often looks in mirrors:

Pt: I don't feel alive at all. I feel anxious, tense, and I cannot fall asleep for fear of not awakening. I dream of falling into a bottomless abyss.

We would imagine the inner and outer responses of the dynamically oriented therapist to be something like the following:

Analyst: Through my interpretation, I, as his doctor, have to get him to relate to me since "This shows starkly and simply [that] the deepest root of mental illness in a schizoid patient may [be] . . . a lack of sheer mothering, which somehow the therapist has to understand and find out how to remedy" (Guntrip, 1971, p. 187).

In response to the analytic patient's statement, a humanistic existentialist therapist might think and say:

HE Therapist: You may be right. You might not wake up, and your attempts at convincing yourself that you exist seem to be correct also. I guess what you are saying is that your sense of identity does not have an independent existence of its own in you—that is, independent of what you do and what you are in the world. If you have to believe that you are a "somebody" in societal, collective terms, then you are going to have to seek that validation everywhere and at all times. Mirrors may be one way.

Here the therapist addresses himself to the way the person has freely structured his identity and the ways that project (to be *somebody*) affects him in his life. In HE therapy, we wish merely to elucidate the simple, underlying need as the person has established or "forged" that need (in this instance to feel valid and important) to *affirm* it, to help the person see whether the way he is going about fulfilling that need is effective for him, and to help him be aware of (a) his free choice of that project, (b) the hope for his project, and (c) the negative and positive aspects or consequences of his basic choice.

The therapist might bring the relationship itself right into the hour by having the client explain why he is telling the therapist what he is telling him, what he hopes the therapist will do, and how that desire to "be somebody" works "between us." We will address ourselves to a therapy in this context later on.

On Gestalt Therapy—Model 2

Gestalt therapy, the approach developed by Frederick Perls (1966, 1951, 1969, 1973) is often called an existential therapy that has a procedure or technique appropriate to an existential framework (Naranjo, 1968).

The basic goal of Gestalt psychotherapy is to help the person come back into awareness.

> So, we come now to the most important, interesting phenomenon in all pathology: self-regulation versus external regulation. The anarchy which is usually feared by the controllers is not an anarchy which is without meaning. On the contrary, it means the organism is left alone to take care of itself, without being meddled with from outside. . . . And I believe that this is the great thing to understand: *that awareness per se—by and of itself—can be curative.* Because with full awareness you become aware of this organismic self-regulation, you can let the organism take over without interfering, without interrupting; we can rely on the wisdom of the organism. And the contrast to this is the whole pathology of self-manipulation, environmental control, and so on, that interferes with this subtle organismic self-control (Perls, 1969, pp. 16-17).

The Gestalt therapist emphasizes the concept of awareness instead of consciousness and has as a major goal helping the person contact his immediate, here-and-now, ongoing process, i.e., his organismic self. Much of that contact is brought about through attention to the sensory and feeling bases of this process as they are expressed in the therapy hour.

Towards this end, the communication of the Gestalt therapist to the person does not consist of questions, interpretations, explanations, normal conversation, or usually the therapist's *response* to the person. Rather, intervention is directed toward a reawakening of the person's acute awareness of his own ongoing activity and feeling. The major thrust seems to be to let the person "be" and to help him perceive how his being in fact *is*. Thus the person most often is asked merely to express or act out what in fact he is experiencing.

The *intent* of the Gestalt therapist's intervention is to lead the person first to identify, then to become, and finally to reclaim his previously repressed feeling, sensation, or action. To accomplish this, Gestalt therapists use many techniques or resources. The primary technique seems to be to make the person aware of what he is actually doing at that instant and to avoid thinking about the past or the future. The therapist constantly directs the person's attention to the immediate experience of his current self. Often, this awareness of what is going on leads to an impasse, a conflict between two polarities, and the person is then helped to fully recognize that impasse or dilemma, and perhaps even to dramatize (take on the role, or "be") both sides of that dilemma toward the end of owning the whole of the dilemma.

The role of the therapist and the relationship is well expressed in the following excerpt:

Adelaide Bry:	Dr. Perls, what is Gestalt therapy?
Dr. Perls:	Discussing, talking, explaining is unreal to me. I hate intellectualizing, don't you?
A.B.:	Sometimes, but I want to interview you. I want to know about Gestalt therapy. So...
Dr. Perls:	Let's try something else. You be the patient. *Be real...* no more intellectualizing.
A.B.:	Well, if it's what you want, I'll try it. I'll *try* being the patient.... Here's what I'd say to you then: "I'm Adelaide and I come to you, Fritz Perls, as a patient. I'm depressed and I also have this physiologically expressed fear of flying. My hands get clammy. My heart beats rapidly." Now what?
Dr. Perls:	I'd cure you of your physiologically expressed fear of flying in five minutes.
A.B.:	Oh, you would? All right. How would you do that?
Dr. Perls:	Close your eyes. Go into the airplane. Realize you're not in a real airplane, just in your fantasy. So fantasy is going to help you see what you experience when you are flying.
A.B.:	Already my heart begins to beat faster...
Dr. Perls:	Don't open your eyes...
A.B.:	All right...
Dr. Perls:	Your heart begins to beat faster...go on.
A.B.:	I see the back of the pilot up there, and you know I'm not sure whether he can do it.
Dr. Perls:	Good. Get up and tell him that.
A.B.:	I tap him on the shoulder, he looks around, I say, "Are you keeping your eyes on the road?" He shoves me away and I go back to my seat.
Dr. Perls:	Now you don't go back to your seat. Change seats. You're the pilot. (Dr. Perls asked me to get up, sit in another chair facing the one I was previously sitting in. Each time I changed roles, I changed seats.)

A.B.:	I'm the pilot. What is this woman doing interfering with me? Get out of the cockpit and get back to your seat. *I know what I'm doing.*
Dr. Perls:	I don't believe your voice. Listen to your voice. (Bry, 1972, pp. 59-60).

The Gestalt therapist, then, takes the role of a "Zen master who guides his apprentice on the paradoxic road to self-mastery, discipline, and freedom [and] teaches the patient to do what he wants with every moment of his life..." (Cohn, 1970, p. 136). In doing so, he grasps one horn of the influence dilemma in human relationships. By his therapeutic manipulations, he plays a game with the client for therapeutic benefit. Just as in psychoanalytic therapy, there is no mutuality, no real encounter of the basic struggle for a relationship. The mutually human and humanizing reciprocal process that forms the essence of HE therapy is ignored.

Another example of how the therapist plays a game on the person (and does not admit it) is shown by the therapist's demands on the father in a family therapy situation:

> The husband... has now whimpered at his wife, and when confronted by the therapist, whimpers at him also helplessly asking, "What can I do? She stops me at every turn."

[1]*Th:*	(sarcastically, to provoke him) You poor thing, overpowered by that terrible lady over there.
F:	(ducking) She means well.
Th:	You're whimpering at me, and I can't stand to see a grown man whimpering.
F:	(firmer) I tell you I don't know what to do.
Th:	Like hell you don't (offering and at the same time pushing). You know as well as I that if you want her off your back, you just have to tell her to get the hell off your back and mean it. That's one thing you could do instead of that mealy-mouthed apology: "She means well" (Kempler, 1970, p. 157).

Therapy of this sort violates the person in teaching him how he can behave since there is an implied criticism that he is wrong, sick, weak, or "screwed up." The therapist's interest is in change, rather than in helping the person face the good reason for his choice and his possible denial of his choice. This process fails to attend to the consequences of the way the patient has chosen to be.

Rewritten to fit the HE position more adequately, the dialogue might sound like this:

F:	What else can I do? She stops me at every turn.
Th:	Your sentence is quite clear. It says to me that whatever your hopes and good reasons are for whatever you are doing (whining, etc.), it seems to end up, as you say, in stopping you at every turn.

---

[1]*Th* is the therapist; *F* is the father.

F: She means well.

Th: I guess that expresses the attitude you assume. If she means well—which
         she probably does, everyone behaves for the best of all possible reasons—
         then your position is that you will *not* confront her. You seem to disarm your-
         self on the basis of her good intentions. Do you see anything wrong with that,
         I mean, in terms of your marriage?

Here the therapist merely points out the father's belief, *affirms* his good
reasons for it, but asks him to look at how it is working. In fact, the father
might reaffirm his position, "I believe in disarming myself more than I
believe in not facing the troubles in my marriage," and the HE therapist
would go along with affirming that. HE therapists are not interested in
change or in the salvation of marriages in and of themselves, but rather in
helping persons *see* the reality of what they have chosen to be and what it
brings them. It is in this sense that humanistic existentialism and Gestalt
agree—that awareness and its attendant responsibility are central. The
major differences between them are in the superior, distant position of the
Gestalt therapist—the "Zen Master" approach—which denies the existential I-Thou encounter central in HE therapy.

The importance of a mutual process in therapy has been stressed by
various recent writers. Some of the following views of the therapeutic
relationship are a salient preface to considering the concept of the struggle
for relationship and HE therapy.

Model 3

If you were to tell me the main belief of *Jung's* on which you base your theory
and your therapy, what would it be?

Dr. Hart: I guess it's respect for the whole person or for the psyche, and the
              wholeness which is trying to be realized. I can't think of any better
              approach to psychotherapy than that. It means to take a person
              at face value.

A.B.:   Face value?

Dr. Hart: When a person comes to me, I try to take him as he is. This is not
              always the case with therapists. Some therapists say to themselves,
              "What does *that* really mean? What is he *really* saying? What is
              he hiding?" I take it as it comes—not always successfully. When
              I can do that, I offer more basis for development. If a person is
              taken seriously, as *he is now,* then he has additional self-respect,
              which he needs. Out of this he can begin to examine himself. I think
              you have to play it very carefully and respectfully with the way a
              person presents himself. If you say he's resisting and so on, that
              may be true, but it doesn't mean that what he is presenting is
              wrong. In presenting his feeling he is doing the very best he can
              just as he is, and this is the best that he can offer, whatever he is.
              The very fact that he is seeing me means that he is offering the
              best. He wouldn't be bothering to see a therapist if he weren't
              after something. I have to be very careful not to judge, if I can
              help it, on preconceived ideas like, she ought to be doing more,

she ought to be making money, or she ought to be working or away from her parents. I can think of a lot of things like that. Every time you judge a human being this way you undercut him where he is. So, you have to be very careful. It may look like a hopeless situation to you, but you must not judge because your standards are not being used.

A.B.:   So what you strive for is complete acceptance of this human being...

Dr. Hart: I think you strive for it; you never reach it. You never reach it (Bry, 1972, pp. 38-39).

Model 3A

Dr. Singer: I'm not sure . . . I suspect that it has something to do with the therapist's willingness to constantly reexamine himself, what he believes, and by what standards he lives. I have a notion that this willingness on the part of the therapist to face himself and to change creates a climate in which the patient starts to feel free to grasp his own emotional life (Singer in Bry, 1972, pp. 54-55).

Model 3B

When, as a psychotherapist, I set myself up as a medical authority over my patient and on that account claim to know something about his individuality, or to be able to make valid statements about it, I am only demonstrating my lack of criticism, for I am in no position to judge the whole of the personality before me. I cannot say anything valid about him except in so far as he approximates to the "universal man." But since all life is to be found only in individual form, and I myself can assert of another individuality only what I find in my own, I am in constant danger either of doing *violence* [emphasis supplied] to the other person or of succumbing to his influence. If I wish to treat another individual psychologically at all, I must for better or worse, give up all pretensions to superior knowledge, all authority and desire to influence. I must perforce adopt a dialectical procedure consisting in a comparison of our mutual findings. But this becomes possible only if I give the other person a chance to play his hand to the full, unhampered by my assumptions. In this way his system is geared to mine and acts upon it; my reaction is the only thing with which I as an individual can legitimately confront my patient (Jung, 1966, p. 5).

A therapy independent of the doctor's personality is just conceivable in the sphere of rational techniques, but it is quite inconceivable in a dialectical procedure where the doctor must emerge from his anonymity and give an account of himself, just as he expects his patient to do. I do not know which is the more difficult: to accumulate a wide knowledge or to renounce one's professional authority and anonymity....Just as all doctors are exposed to infections and other occupational hazards, so the psychotherapist runs the risk of psychic infections which are no less menacing. On the one hand he is often in danger of getting entangled in the neuroses of his patients; on the other hand if he tries too hard to guard against their influence, he robs himself of his therapeutic efficacy. Between this Scylla and Charybdis lies the peril, but also the healing power (Jung, 1966, pp. 18-19).

Model 4

Before the therapist is a patient of his own age; the opportunity and challenge lies in the recognition of their equality in confronting problems and asking the questions each asks in his other relations; the irony lies in the attitude of the doctor, that he can leave his life stage at home while the patient cannot. Before the therapist sits a youngster grappling with his career or his choice of mate. The opportunity for the therapist lies in remembering the struggle which beset him or, if the choice were clearly and happily made, the recollected humility of being a lucky person. In either case, the therapist is called to be compassionate more than knowledgeable, wise more than informed and hopeful more than assured. The irony is in the doctor's assuming that age gives him the right to know better. . . . No longer does the doctor have any special knowledge or even wisdom unless he believes in or is called upon to provide a palliative, a sedative, or lies about the true condition. . . . What has become more impressive to me than all this is the ways in which the patient endows me with significance and the negative and postive ways he asserts this power. I used to call his negative power, "resistance," but I don't any longer because I resist him as much as he does me. If I am to reach him, he must also feel I have been affected by him. If he is to change in our relation, I must change too. If I am to teach him something about his mind, he will teach me something about mine. I think that the dedicated interest I show in his thought is more important than the particular comments I make about his mind, but I also know that his interest in what I think is as important as my concern for him. If he agrees to what I say and my reasons for saying it, it is because I have allies on my side. Unseen are all those who have ever shown him affectionate respect. They speak again through my tongue. If he objects to something I say, I may react defensively and accuse him of resisting the emergence of some painful Freudian, Jungian, Adlerian or whatever complex. Or when I get down from my high horse, I will state that we misunderstood each other (Steinzor, 1967, pp. 96-97).

Model 5

I try to help him (the client) re-invent himself and his situation, and then help him try to fulfill the invention, just as an artist paints what at first was a private image. To implement this project, *I respond in any way and every way that is available to me in the context of dialogue.* My commitment in the dialogue is not to a theory, technique, or setting, but to the *project* of abetting another person's wholeness and growth. Of necessity, there are technical ways of embodying this project, but these always reach an impasse, and at the impasse, the seriousness of my commitment receives its test: Am I committed to my theory and techniques? Or to the project? In the context of dialogue I don't hesitate to share any of my experiences with existential binds roughly comparable with those in which the seeker finds himself (this is now called "modeling"); nor do I hesitate to disclose my experience of him, myself, and our relationship as it unfolds from moment to moment. Nor do I hesitate, when it becomes relevant, to tell a joke, give a lecture for a few minutes on my view of how he is being mystified by others in his life, and how he is mystifying others, thereby increasing his estrangement from his authentic experience. And I might give Freudian or other types of interpretations. And I might teach him such Yoga know-how, or such tricks for expanding body-awareness as I have mastered, or engage in arm-wrestling, or hold hands, or hug him, *if that is the response that emerges in the dialogue.* I encourage him to try experiments with his own existence like trying the risky business of authenticity, or changing living arrangements. Our relationship begins almost always in the seeker's expectation that it will unfold in a technically predictable and prescribed way. ... In fact, I feel pressure from him to keep me in an impersonal and technical role. I respect this and respond with the invitation to dialogue. If he accepts the invitation—and gradually he does—the relationship becomes a shared quest for authentic ways he might live that generate wholeness and growth. I do not hesitate to play a game of handball with a seeker, or visit him in his home—if he unfolds in the dialogue. In short, I've come to see that much of the rigidity of our professional practice is similar to an experimentally produced character disorder and character armor. The training which produces it serves to wean a person from the disorders and armor produced by his life with his family and his early schooling; but then it persists after graduate training as a *badge* as well as armor. The technical ways of behaving [that] we have called "psychotherapeutic practice" have relevance as authenticated paths to enlightenment and liberation if that is, indeed, what they have been for someone. But to congeal them as orthodoxies is to meet a seeker's "hangups" engendered in an academy. They (technical approaches) limit the capacity for relevant response in dialogue, and confuse commitments. *A therapist is defined by his project, not his means (Jourard, 1969, pp. 50-51).*

Model 6

Current developments in psychotherapy have obscured the lines between different orientations. For example, contrast psychoanalysis and client-centered therapy. What a sharp difference that once seemed to be! Today, looking back, we see the similarity: Both were highly formal denials of a real relationship. One role-played a relationship of transference; the other role-played a perfectly neutral acceptance. We see two of a kind—artificial, formalistic avoidances of genuine interaction between two people. The patient's real feelings were considered invalid (transference). The analyst's feelings were also considered invalid (counter-transference). Similarly, in client-centered therapy, it was a mistake for the therapist to interject his own feelings into the therapeutic situation. Today, client-centered therapists make "genuineness" the first condition for therapy and therapist-expressivity and spontaneity main therapeutic factors. Psychoanalysts are also moving toward real involvement and commitment as persons, with less reliance on technique (Gendlin, 1970, pp. 72-73).

The present explorations in psychotherapy reflect a period of transition. The new essential dimensions, shared very broadly by some therapists in all orientations, are *the relationship process between two humans and the therapeutic feeling process....* [This process points] at the concrete living personal relationship, something that is much more than two people and their individual patterns, more than what each thinks of the other or how each sees the other, more than units of meaning communicated from one to the other. Martin Buber as quoted in "The Existential Moment" says of the therapist that "if he has really gathered the child (or the 'other') into his life then that subterranean dialogic... is established and endures." This is no mere professional relationship to a patient; it is a life relationship of two humans. They both live really there, in the "reality *between* them." And this reality is a "subterranean" connection and interaction. It isn't something perceived and communicated, or specific reactions of one to the other. It involves one's whole ongoing aliveness. Poetic language—but we have no well-established technical terms for it (Gendlin, 1970, pp. 73-74).

I believe that successful psychotherapy of any type has always centrally involved this concrete type of encounter. Yet, there has also been a great deal of artificiality, of therapists limiting their involvement as persons (as if it were an error betraying the therapist's weaknesses, needs, or softness), much painfully distant dealing with patients as though with forceps. Therapists have often felt they had to sit behind screens of various kinds—fully seeing the patient, but themselves neither visible nor visibly involved in an encounter (Gendlin, 1970, p. 74).

Individuals are not boxes full of entities into which a therapist tries to put new entities (information, example, insight, values). We have no way to get such entities into somebody. Personality change is just this shift of a person from being unable to learn, to take in, or to perceive accurately to being able to do so. Hence, even if information, example, insight, and values are "communicated" from therapist to patient, the question of change is: what happens in psychotherapy so that the patient "becomes aware," "learns," "accepts," "takes in from his living what, at first, he was unable to be aware of, or learn," what happens to alter his self-defeating patterns? If the essential nature of human being is conceived of as a being-with and a being-in, then it is most easily explainable that people change when their surroundings change, that people are different when they are with someone different. If there is a puzzle, it is how we avoid being alive in new ways, how we repeat patterns that are not a being affected by the situation or person, here, now (Gendlin, 1970, p. 83).

Model 7

Walter Kempler, a psychiatrist, has written well of an existential model for interpersonal relationships in counseling and psychotherapy. Kempler sees psychotherapists as offering for sale a subtle, though valuable and definable product—that which he calls "The Therapist's Merchandise." He begins his discussion by assuming, much as we do, that people are created into patients via certain interactions with others: interactions that are based on duplicity, the placing of the person in a double-bind, by distortion and violation. The essential therapeutic ingredient that the therapist has to offer is just the opposite—self-disclosure presented with straightforward clarity.

Broadly then, the therapist's merchandise can be envisaged as his ability to know and to reveal himself forthrightly as he is in relation to his patient. . . . It includes the ability to reveal his inability to present himself when he can't. The degree to which the therapist has developed these skills is the degree to which he will be able to influence others therapeutically. In other words, his own freedom from deviousness, duplicity, and self-deception—conscious or otherwise—is his power. His ability to disclose himself is the activation of that power. This activated personal power is his product: Manifest Presence. The manifestation of presence is not the "just-be-who-you-are" oversimplification of existential principles. It is more than "being" the composite therapist —the person one "is" at any given moment. It has more precise characteristics. Presence comes from self-awareness and it is a most difficult skill to achieve (restore). It is not the relatively easy job of picking up on the verbal and non-verbal behavior of others [which many Gestalt-oriented therapists seem to see as their main task]. Presence is discerning the internal repercussions from such external awareness. Manifesting that presence, revealing that internal awareness with clarity and in full voice, is no less challenging.

Presence means more than awareness of internal responses to current experience. It also means the ability to translate those inner sensations into language... If, despite alert sensory antennae, the therapist becomes aware that nothing is experienced within, then this becomes a significant bit of knowledge.

Presence is not the therapist's ability to observe and describe what he sees happening around him. Observers and reporters are not therapists. His unique therapeutic skillfulness lies in his ability to circulate within himself those phenomena that he experiences, and to bring forth not an observation or a report, but rather an expression that reflects who he is as a consequence of what he experiences [That is, unless the therapist becomes totally psychologically alone—his experience is coupled to that of the other, of the person with whom he is relating at that moment. The therapist is in the world with the person, and his response, if the therapist is attending, is to the relationship *between* the two].

Manifesting presence means self-disclosure, often frightening or embarrassing. It means responding with words, thoughts, feelings, and behavior as is, rather than as they should be. It means a willingness to expose the anguish felt when unpleasant consequences occur. It means revealing an unwillingness to risk unpleasant consequences, if that be the case. It means returning to an encounter the feelings aroused by the encounter, with all attendant concerns about doing so.[2]

Manifesting presence means action. It may mean a vigorous confrontation; it may mean a watchful silence. But whether it be warring or a waiting, it is deliberate; it is active. It is not mere words. It is laughing, not saying in a monotone, "That's amusing." It is perhaps crying along with; it is never just

---

[2]This is a crucial point in helping define authentic relating. Many, especially "humanistically oriented" therapists with a rather naive view of relationship, think that authentic responding implies "giving the person hell" whenever they feel like it. Authentic functioning means, to the HE therapist, sharing with the person the totality of his response to that person. Rarely, except in extreme and relatively rare instances, is a person so enraged or so enraptured that he is quite literally "carried away" by the situation and the feelings that have been built into that situation. More often, if one observes clearly and if one really attends to oneself and to the situation, feelings are mixed—a mixture of wanting and not wanting, of desiring and being afraid, of hating, and of yesses and noes. Authentic responding means sharing with the person not only the predominant feeling, but the ongoing ambivalence, conflict, and perhaps even the opposite feelings as they occur and change in the interaction and as a function of the interaction. Undoubtedly this is a difficult process, especially since we are riddled with essentialistic notions of what fully-functioning means.

The attending to only one of our responses and the essentialistic attempts at perpetuating them over time, denies the reality of the flux of relationship, of the full melange and the meaning of an intense relationship. It is most often exhibited in a kind of touch-and-run or hit-and-run responsiveness that denies the totality of a sustained encounter where two persons engage in a mutual exchange or reciprocally shared interaction in all its fullness. The kind of hostile or loving hit-and-run so redolent in encounter groups, the instant intimacy, denies the reciprocal nature of human interactions. It merely exposes one person's process to the other so that the other then becomes a silent witness to it, but not an ongoing participant.

words of comfort. It is writhing through an embarrassing exploration; it is not a clever confession. It is revealing a distaste for a patient by word or gesture; it is not an innocent query such as, "How do you think people respond when you act like that?" It means saying, "I won't talk to you now," and shutting up until you want to speak. It is not offering a clever accusing interpretation such as, "You must like to get people to talk and then not listen."

Manifesting presence means that the therapist must reveal who he isn't as well as who he is. Therapists often suffer from a tendency to be who they are when they feel positively, e.g., pleased when pleased. But when their experience is negative or unacceptable to themselves they merely verbalize who they are not, usually in a quiet voice, e.g., "I feel uncomfortable when you. . . ." Manifesting presence demands full expression on all occasions. It means, for instance, that the therapist is obliged to reveal and pursue his inability to present himself until such time as he becomes present. If this cannot be achieved the therapist's limitation could reasonably become the basis for going *with his patient* to a colleague for consultation. If he is reluctant to do this he should admit it and then transfer his patient to someone else.

The reluctance of therapists toward self-disclosure is most often expressed in the camouflaged garb of professional responsibility: "Patients can't take an honest confrontation," or "It's not fair to burden patients with our problems." Patients—people—therapists—can take and prefer an honest presentment [*sic*] to deception. Furthermore, patients share the therapist's "problems" whether they are manifested openly and directly or not. The therapist who presents himself forthrightly offers his patient the greatest opportunity to evaluate the relationship for himself and not as the therapist would wish his patient to see their relationship. By doing so, the therapist places his patient on equal terms; and although the patient may not like his therapist's action he cannot feel inferior or diminished by it. Full and forthright personal expression on all occasions is considered and considerate. It is neither impulsive nor irresponsible since it contains the therapist's personal concerns. . . .

Manifest presence is not the same as undivided or continuous attention. Continuous attention is impossible and the pretence of it is a seduction.[3] Patients plan and pay for a period of time with a therapist. Manifest presence can be purchased; attention cannot.

Manifest presence can say, "My attention is elsewhere at this moment" and the therapist may explore his needed migration. Manifest presence reveals where the therapist is or where he would like to be but can't. Manifest presence is not a physical, spiritual, or emotional presence but rather the expression of the therapist's current identity *pertinent to the present moment* (and the manifest interaction) [emphasis supplied]. It is not sufficient for him merely to know his current identity. It is his obligation to present it. Away from the therapeutic experience, presence need not be manifested; the therapist has the option of revealing his identity or not. In therapy it is all he has to offer and it must not be withheld. His task is to manifest it during each interview. HOW he does it is shaped by his personality and the discipline he reflects. THAT he does it is his responsibility to his patient and to himself.

It is not the duty of the therapist to reveal himself in a continuous monologue.

---

[3]Even worse, it teaches an essentialistic notion to the patient or person that such undivided attention is possible, and that somehow, when he (the person) gets "better" as the therapist is, then he will be able to be capable of sustained constant attention also.

That, of course, would be absurd. As long as he is a full participant in the present with those about him he is fulfilling his obligation. His presence is committed. It is only when there is some loss, some discrepancy, some absence on his part that he is obliged to disclose this aspect of himself. Initially these revelations may be his most painful moments. But by these self-disclosures he establishes a context in which everyone, himself included, has the opportunity to grow...(Kempler, 1969-1970, pp. 57-60).

Model 8

Martin Buber speaks of relationship:

Human life and humanity come into being in genuine meetings. There man learns not merely that he is limited by man, cast upon his own finitude, partialness, need of completion, but his own relation to truth is heightened by the other's different relation to the same truth—different in accordance with his individuation, and destined to take seed and grow differently. Men need, and it is granted to them, to confirm one another in the individual being by means of genuine meetings. But beyond this they need, and it is granted to them, to see the truth, which the soul gains by its struggle, light up to the others, the brothers, in a different way, and even so be confirmed (1965, p. 69).

Man wishes to be confirmed in his being by man, and wishes to have a presence in the being of another. The human person needs confirmation because man as man needs it.... It is different with man: sent forth from the natural domain of species into the hazard of the solitary category, surrounded by the air of chaos which came into being with him, secretly and bashfully he watches for a Yes which allows him to be and which can come to him only from one human person to another. It is from one man to another that the heavenly bread of self-being is passed (1965, p. 71).

Now we turn to the HE conception of human and therapeutic relationship, the concept of the struggle for relationship, and the philosophic underpinnings of the HE view.

WE: THE PHILOSOPHIC BACKGROUND

In his writing about relationships, Martin Buber emphasizes dialogue and the concept of the essential we. Briefly stated, Buber distinguishes between two modes of human interaction, two modes of being: the I-It relationship and the I-Thou relationship.

What characterizes the I-It and the I-Thou modes is not the receiver of the relationship (i.e., not the object addressed), but the *way* "I" come to the relationship, the way I constitute my being in the relationship as I present myself to the other. In the I-Thou mode, my relationship is *immediate,* direct, and wholly present. It is reciprocal and mutual. In such a mode, the person to whom I come is immediately grasped as unique (not "considered," thought about, or deliberated about). He is perhaps the only one existing at the moment for me, and I am seriously affected by that person. I am, at that moment, available to the "we" and devoid of preconceived notions, images, or categories in which I place him; I experience *him,* not a chimera of him.[4] I live that moment with him immediately, spontaneously, totally responsively, and what occurs is unplanned and unpredictable. None of us can know in advance to what the "betweenness" of us will give birth. No one of us can know in advance what it is that you-and-I have to say. What is said is not to be "discovered" at all; it is a unique invention between us and of us, and that invention belongs to the specific you and me and to our specific encounter. If it bleeds over to another, different person or to a different situation, it is degraded into a repetition, a performance, a "line":

> Each should regard his partner as the very one he is. I become aware of him, aware that he is different, essentially different from myself, in the definite, unique way which is peculiar to him, and I accept who I thus see, so that in full earnestness I can direct what I say to him as the person he is.... I affirm the person I struggle with: I struggle with him as his partner, I confirm him as creature and as creation, I confirm him who is opposed to me as him who is over against me. It is true that it now depends on the other whether genuine dialogue, mutuality... arises between us. But if I thus give to the other who confronts me his legitimate standing as a man with whom I am ready to enter into dialogue, then I may trust him and suppose him to be also ready to deal with me as his partner (Buber, 1965, pp. 79-80).
>
> In the atmosphere of genuine dialogue, he who is ruled by the thought of his own effect as the speaker of what he has to speak [the characteristic "therapeutic" position], has a destructive effect. If instead of what has to be said, I try to bring attention to my *I,* I have irrevocably miscarried what I had to say.... Because genuine dialogue is an ontological sphere which is constituted by the authenticity of being, every invasion of semblance must damage it (p. 86).

In such a responding as Buber speaks of, there is a certain "irritability" (irritability in the sense of protoplasmic irritability), an availability to be affected by the person before me, and to *respond* with my whole being, not to mute, "consider," dissemble, or manipulate. For Buber, and for the HE, a manipulative or helping position places a superiority and distance between us that is arrogance. That distance collapses any real living, since "all real living is meeting." Relationships are not to be used. Such uses for the HE are obscene, even if the end sought is sublime. Using the dialogue, the relationship, the transference as a *means* to any end beyond itself breaks, defeats and degrades the genuine encounter.

We can fail to respond fully by withdrawing to a distant, manipulating, hidden, even lying, superior position; by not permitting the situation between us to evolve as a function of the mutual process, and by not trusting each of us enough to allow the we-situation to control. Such failure

---

[4]But what of all that I have learned? My past, my training, my schooling? If I have really learned it, it is now me. I incarnate it immediately in my responsiveness. And I am to respond with it by forgetting about it. I do not withdraw to deliberate and come up with a prepackaged response.

to respond produces guilt, and the distrust (born of past violations) breeds a further withdrawal, a deepened mistrust, and a suspiciousness of myself and others. Thus, guilt is the failure to act authentically, and to declare my existence; it is being less than fully human. This inauthentic, duplicitious stand not only violates another human; it also injures the interhuman, the we, the genuine. Its healing is affirmation.

> The relation to the Thou is direct. No system of concepts, no foreknowledge, and no fancy intervene between I and Thou. The memory itself is transformed, as it plunges out of its isolation into the unity of the whole. No set purpose, no greed, and no anticipation intervene between I and Thou. Desire itself is transformed as it plunges out of its dream into the appearance. Every means is an obstacle. Only when every means has collapsed does the meeting come about (Buber, 1958, pp. 11-13).

THE STRUGGLE FOR RELATIONSHIP AND THE ENGAGED ENCOUNTER

To begin to understand the concept of the struggle for relationship, we must understand how the HE views the nature of a dyad. The basic question involved is how is it that two (or more) persons can stand in a relation of concrete mutuality, in which two free humans are face-to-face on an equal plane together, aware of their separateness, yet without violating each other—without one robbing the other of his subjectivity?

It is my experience and, I suspect, the experience of most of us—that real relationships rarely run smoothly. As Kaiser (1965) has pointed out, the fusion-delusion where all is bliss, *is* a delusion. We are separate, and the dealing with that separateness—with two subjectivities (freedoms) coming together toward an essential we—is what a relationship is all about. We might restate the problem in quasi-religious terms: how can we be two gods together, neither one losing, neither one winning, each nourishing the other? There is no answer to that question, other than a temporary one specific to each dyad.

Just as individuals deny their own freedom and responsibility by bad faith, so in relationships they attempt to deny their selfhood and that of others by various ideal or essentialistic maneuvers. These are attempts at occluding what the HE accepts as the human task: the dealing in an *engaged encounter.*

Human relations, then, present a paradox since there is an inherent conflict in the desires of two free subjectivities. But conflict is not a sign of a sick or disturbed relationship, and therefore something to be overcome. Rather it seems conflict is the *very meaning* and fabric of relationships in general, of every relationship where two persons are in committed psychological contact. We might even define two beings in relation as: (a) perceiving or attending to each other (Esterson, 1972), and (b) dealing, or engaging each other, fully recognizing the implicit violation involved, and continuing to "hang in there," with neither member denying that the struggle with the paradox may have no resolution, but rather each member affirming that "our difficulty," "our struggle," *is* the relationship, and as such it has its ecstasy and its pain.

Perhaps the essential significance of a relationship lies in the fact that two people ask and continue to ask themselves how they can be two gods. In the HE view, there is, ultimately, no solution to the paradox of two equals, other than the engaged encounter that revolves around and deals with the paradox. Assuming an onanistic, omnipotent position is not a resolution of the paradox. The only solution seems to be the acceptance of the fact that the problem of us is *ours;* it exists *between us.* More broadly, it is the problem for us all; there is no exit from it, merely an exquisite sensitivity to it at all points of our coming together.

The hope of a *resolution* is seductive and can lead to interminable therapy, where the only relationship that exists is in the family therapist's office, or to fleeting multiple relationships where like Don Juan, one tries to replicate what cannot be sustained. Or, in another instance, one might sense the struggle and adopt a superior and aloof stance, or succumb to a subservient position (Sartre, 1963). Yet another course is to entirely deny the reality involved and to try to *cure* oneself instead: "I have to cure this hang-up of mine, and you *wait* until I do, and then things between us will run smoothly."

Many of the inexorable violations involved in human relations have been described by Sartre, de Beauvoir, Camus and Barnes (1959 and 1967). But the basic violation, which to the HE is also the usual sickening act, is the *denial of the problem or the paradox of the violation.*

In HE terms, violation stems from the notion that the other (another free subjectivity) possesses me by looking at me. By looking at me (perceiving me) he creates or outlines me as a person while, reciprocally, by my looking at him, I at once create him and seek to possess him. At the moment that I attempt to free myself from the other's hold, the other is trying to free himself from my grasp; while I seek to enslave the other, the other seeks to enslave me. But note, that while I am trying to free myself, so is the other. At no point are we dealing with unilateral relations as we would when we deal with objects such as rocks or tables. We are dealing with reciprocal and fluid relations—with an *exchange.*

Neither *love,* nor union by love lead us out of the paradox, as some theistic existentialists promise (Sadler, 1969). Sartre's statement here illustrates both the issue and the paradox:

> It is in this sense that love is a conflict. We have observed that the Other's freedom is the foundation of my being. But precisely because I exist by means of the Other's freedom, I have no security; I am in danger in this freedom. . . .

Why does the lover want to be *loved*? If love were in fact a pure desire for physical possession, it could in many cases be easily satisfied.... The notion of "ownership," by which love is so often explained, is not actually primary. Why should I want to appropriate the Other if it were not precisely that the Other makes me be?... it is the Other's freedom as such that we want to get hold of. Not because of a desire for power ... the man who wants to be loved does not desire the enslavement of the beloved.... He does not want to possess an automaton, and if we want to humiliate him, we need only to try to persuade him that the beloved's passion is the result of a psychological determinism ("I cannot help it, it's chemistry!"). The lover will then feel that both his love and his being are cheapened. If Tristan and Isolde fall madly in love because of a love potion, they are less interesting. The total enslavement of the beloved kills the love of the lover. The end is surpassed; if the beloved is transformed into an automaton, the lover finds himself alone. Thus the lover does not desire to possess the beloved as one possesses a thing; he demands a special type of appropriation. He wants to possess a freedom as freedom.
On the other hand, the lover can not be satisfied with that superior form of freedom which is a free and voluntary engagement. Who would be content with a love given as pure loyalty to a sworn oath? Who would be satisfied with the words, "I love you because I have freely engaged myself to love you and because I do not wish to go back on my word"? Thus the lover demands a pledge, yet is irritated by a pledge. He wants to be loved by a freedom but demands that this freedom as freedom should no longer be free (1956, pp. 366-67).

The struggle that lovers experience (actually, the struggle of each of us to grasp the freedom of the other and by that grasp to make it our freedom yet at the same instant to be loved freely) is the *hopeless* and yet engaging aspect of relationship.[5]

There are many patterns of bad faith that occur in human relationships. Basically, they deny the relationship in denying the struggle or the paradox. Sartre (1956) described three basic patterns of bad faith that break an encounter: *masochism*—I choose (but deny choosing) that position wherein I consent to be nothing but an object for the other; *indifference*—I become indifferent, an alienated observer upon the human scene, merely unengagedly observing the behavior of the other, remaining untouchable, invulnerable, lonely and in control (this is the characteristic "Doctor" role, where the major concern is the fulfillment of the role, where one cares "about" the object, but does not care "for" the object); and *sadism*—I choose to make the other succumb to my will through my exertion of power or influence over him.

I prefer to diagram the relationship and how the encounter can be engaged, denied or broken as in Figure 1. In each instance except the

---

[5]I believe that love is an absolutely unique invention between two people who are lovers. Loving someone is a genuine experience of that specific, unique person who is being loved. Any other conception leads to the following of a "love" paradigm that is socially proscribed. Such an essentialistic, Platonic conception of love is redolent in our culture.

Figure 1
Possible positions or tactics in a relationship.

DUOLOGUE
- We are side-by-side, mere witnesses to each other's inner processes
- Decoupling
- Subtle violence

FUSION DELUSION
- You are not you—you are me
- Self-deception
- Covert violence

ABSOLUTE VIOLENCE
- Absolute subject-object relation
- Manipulation, influence
- Superiority, masochism, sadism
- Overt objectivity, but covert transcendent subjectivity

ENGAGED ENCOUNTER
- Two gods openly struggling with their subjectivity, constantly asking "How can we permit each other to enter into the other's system for a while, for as long as is possible"
- I-Thou
- Affirmation
- Authenticity
- Struggle toward the establishment of mutual process and the essential we
- Avowal of implicit symmetry

engaged encounter, the basic tactic is that one person in the dyad assumes a falsely-safe omnipotence, takes control and is unwilling to see that *he exists in the world,* and that others are free entities in their own right. Many individuals deny the independent existence of others via their project of change. In effect they say,

> It is not that he wants to do such and such. I can steal his will from him by somehow changing or curing myself: I will be in control when I change. Then our sexuality will not express the reality between us (the quality of our relationship) but will rather be better, and more ideal, and if it does not happen, then I have not changed enough, or I must find yet another doctor.

In most broken encounters, the parties adopt a safe, omnipotent, encapsulated position where the risky business of unpredictable, surprising mutuality is diminished. Instead, a kind of mechanomorphic, instrumental, manipulative, or automanipulative position is taken towards the other, oneself, and the world. Fritz Perls speaks of this controlling aspect in somewhat analogous terms.

> Once we recognize the structure of our behavior, which in the case of self-improvement is the split between the topdog and the underdog, and if we understand how, by listening, we can bring about a reconciliation of these two fighting clowns, then we realize that *we cannot deliberately bring about changes in ourselves or in others. . . .* Every external control, even internalized external control—"you should"—interferes with the healthy working of the organism. There is only one thing that should control: *the situation.* If you understand the situation which you are in, and let the situation which you are in control your actions, then you learn how to cope with life. (1969, p. 19).

Many of us would rather exchange the reality of the other and of the world for a project which withdraws us from the situation. We thus maintain our omnipotence by the retroflexive project of self-change or self-improvement.

One person in therapy refused to see how another in her life was affecting her. She stated, "I have to make myself sad in order not to permit him to make me sad." She made herself into an omnipotent, predictable, controlled system that was seemingly impregnable. One day she said that there was something wrong with her: she was sad and lonely. She later revealed that she had unexpectedly dropped into her husband's office and he was chagrined by her unannounced intrusion. Her refusal to see the possibility of *his* affecting her was expressed in her "feeling sick—there's something wrong with me" that she had to handle and work through alone.

This woman would not see that her problem lay between her husband and her, to be worked out in a mutual relationship. There, in encounter, she would have to declare her wants, he his, and they would be engaged, in relation, working on their different needs, wants and selves. Each would have to become available to the other, and in that find a self-enounter. Each would have to declare himself in unambiguous terms, much as a child does:

"I want this," and by implication, "This is who I now am," and her husband would have to see that and respond with himself and to her. Part and parcel of this process is that each would have to accept that his feelings are correct; they are appropriate to the situation between them. Instead, she broke the encounter by withdrawing herself and her feelings from the world into herself alone.

Feelings and emotions inform us at once of our project or myth and of the independence of the world and other entities. This person preferred to say, "I am lonely because there is something missing in me" rather than "I am lonely because I do not get the attention I want." The former leads to a further encapsulated self-analysis and a project of self-change, while the latter puts the person squarely in the world and thus lays open the possibilities of a genuine encounter and consequent self-encounter. "Being in touch" here means being aware that my feelings are a correct response to the world, and that they inform me of who I am and what the situation is for me.

Many persons, especially those with psychological training, refuse this kind of man-in-the-street or childlike dialogue and the declaring, authentic responsiveness. They would prefer duologue, that is, reveal their own process to the other in his presence but without reciprocity. It is as if, in the duologue, each person is an actor on a stage "doing his own thing" to an audience composed of the other. Another instance of this kind of broken encounter, called "decoupling," is expressed in a dialogue that has the following features:

Person One: I come at you with the declaring truth of how I feel about you and the criticisms I have of you, or whatever it is that I feel about you, is fully expressed.

Person Two: Comes back with his own forceful response; he may "slam back."

The *Decoupling* position which breaks the engaged encounter is then expressed by the first person.

Person One: Oh, well, if you are going to come back at me with that, that way, then I'm not going to declare myself. Don't you want me to be honest with you?

The first person's *intent* is to break off the encounter by "spinning off" upon the second. He wants Person Two to be only a container for his (Person One's) affect. An authentic response from Person Two would be,

Person Two: Yes, I want you to be honest, but I want to be in full fidelity to my feeling as well. I don't want you to hold anything back at all; to do so would obviate me and you. But you want me to obviate me, and I want us to continue to engage even though it is difficult.

Only a psychotherapist would respond to a client stepping on his toe with, "I am aware that you are stepping on my toe," instead of the direct response, "Get off!" Statements starting with "I am aware" permit one person to spin out his decoupled position *upon* the other. In making such observations, the therapist teaches the person that that is the way to respond. Here is an example of such a transaction:

M: I was aware, when I sat down in the chair and put my hands on the arms right here, of the warmth that was still here from Leo and experiencing the warmth in my cold hands. And...I'm perspiring, and... my heart's beating fast, and I'm feeling...I'm swallowing, I'm holding my breath. A feeling, a stiffness in my shoulders and...

Th: Sounds like you're doing a lot of squeezing.

M: Yes, I'm squeezing, squeezing in.

Th: Can you either go with your squeezing in, or the reverse?

M: Squeezing in and pulling. Being very cl-close, closed...just kinda all in a knot. And when I'm not like this, I feel like I let people—the room —come in, and can be aware of what is going on in the room or aware of Jim, Leo, Bill, and all the rest, and then when I'm like this (arms folded, legs crossed), then the rest of it—you—begin to disappear; I'm aware of only me.

Th: Yeah. What did you just do?

M: I swallowed. And I experienced a cutting off of my breath, the jerkiness of it in here and here (points to chest).

Th: (talking ostensibly to the group) I'm always impressed with the phenomenon that I see over and over again—somebody will learn something about himself: if he does this, something happens; if he does that something happens—and then he discards what he's learned immediately. I don't understand.

M: It's a beautiful avoidance.

Th: Yes. "I'll work on this tomorrow." "I'll tuck it into my computer and explore it next week."

M: Um-hum (pause). And it always leaves me with unfinished business.

Th: *It.*

M: *I* leave myself with unfinished business.

Th: How?

M: By not staying with my feeling.

Th: I'd like to reinforce your *this* and *this* (referring to Mary's hand gestures of squeezing in). And I object to your avoiding the experiment. (Pause) Now I'm stuck. If I don't do anything, Mary will sit there. (Sighs) A perfect trap. I wish I had Fritz's cigarette (to wait out Mary's helplessness).

J: I don't know where to go from here.

Th: (Beginning dialogue with himself) Jim, shall Mary squeeze herself? Yes, but if you ask Mary to squeeze herself, then *she* isn't doing anything. She's just doing what *you* want. So how can Mary get out of her bind, Jim? The hell with Mary, how can I get out of my bind? (General gentle laughter) You've got yourself stuck. (Long pause) What do you experience now? (Simkin, 1970, pp. 162-163)

In this tableau, the disavowal of the therapist's part in the process of getting "stuck" and the therapist's decoupling is, I think, aptly expressed in his comment, "The hell with Mary." Violence is exhibited in the therapist's superior, observing attitude and in the overt compliance but covert control ("I'm *giving* you the power") of the patient; however, that violation is not attended to. The master-teacher contract is carried forward to the delight of the other witnesses in the room. The underlying decoupled relationship is also expressed by the arrogance of the therapist in beginning a dialogue with himself and in addressing the group during his "experiment" with Mary.

How different is the following piece from a brilliant Jungian therapist!

Mutual process is characterized by being a *psychological relationship* in which the partners recognize and work with the unconscious[6] as it manifests itself within and among them. It requires an increasing degree of mutual *openness*, of *intersubjectivity*, and a recognition of their *equality* before the gods, the archetypes. It normally enchances both relationship and consciousness, by promoting both differentiation and union. It results in a *creative work*, often one of joint concrete products, such as in art or science, or in aspects of relationship itself, such as mutual healing, mutual deepening. It is recognized as a *spiritual task*, a relationship requiring work. Each process, like individuation itself, is unique and requires that both partners recognize that there is a potential for uniqueness at the outset which remains to be realized, made manifest. There is therefore, always an *uncertainty* in the relationship, both between and within the partners, just as there is in individuation, and this provides part of the motive power for change. Mutual process recognizes all the trials and joys of individuation, including the characteristic struggle for union of the opposites of spirit and flesh, mind and matter, and continues this struggle as a shared experience, with mutual individuation, alone and together, as the outcome. . . . I have found that my concept of openness, and of surrender and control were not entirely clear to others. By openness I mean not the self-disclosure of facts about one's life or problems, necessarily—though these are not excluded—but the bringing forth of those fantasies and dreams, particularly, but also impulses and ideas which have to do with the other person, analyst or patient. *It is an openness of the subjective aspects of one's self which entwines the other person in any way.* It is work with these images and impulses, jointly, and openly, which is at stake. As to surrender and control there has been even more suspicion. Surrendering to the flow of imagery and impulse in not "acting out," since I assume that in this imagery there is also fear as well as closeness, retreat and withdrawal as well as advance, conscience as well as desire. Attention to surrender and control in one's self, as well as in the other, and going with that flow will tend to preclude violation or hurt. . . . That is the psychological relationship which can emerge in analysis itself. Psychological relationship is not limited to analysis, but is any relation-

---

[6]We need not be disturbed by Spiegelman's use of the term "unconscious" here. In HE terms, of course, the term is misleading since it is the person who makes himself unconscious or oblivious to himself by his own intention, though only by a charade. For the purpose of our illustration, "not attended to" or "unwilling to explicitly recognize" could just as easily be substituted.

ship in which both parties recognize the unconscious background going on within them and between them, and that they both share this realization and work on it. That is mutual process. . . .

I recently began analytic work with (a young person) who had undergone a number of months of therapy with a Freudian analyst. . . . so I would like to quote her very expressive words about it. . . .

> My pain is the pain of not being in connection with myself and not connecting with others. So, I went to a therapist, and he constantly told me to look into myself to find the reason for a question, and maybe when I knew that reason he would answer the question. That constant turning [me] back [to myself] *denies that there are two people involved* [emphasis supplied], that the therapist's emotional, physical being is also present. That must be acknowledged, for I can take in a look, a mood, the subtlest of things as being a response to what I am saying, to what I am. That (lack of response) is wrong. That is destructive of my being. I have the right to ask for clarity in what is happening. If I am disconnected, and all he gave me was that I was disconnected. He would not connect with me, risk for me, be with me. That was too hard, so he played with knowledge. All I could give him was my sickness, which kept me sick out of my need of him (Spiegelman, 1972, p. 22).

THE STRUGGLE FOR RELATIONSHIP; AN EXAMPLE IN THERAPY

Let us look at an example of the struggle for a relationship in therapy. This is one hour of "supervisory" therapy with a courageous and astute practicing psychologist, who was kind enough to supply a transcript of his session with his therapist. He brought to the session the tape of his hour with one of his own patients (whose permission he got to both tape and transcribe his interview).

Pt:	(pointing to the tape recorder that he brought in with him) I want you to listen to the flow of me and this patient for a while, O.K?
Th:	O.K.
Pt's patient:	Well, I think I understand, because you told me part of it, somehow, and I figured out part of it myself—that this feeling that you are always talking about, and my inability to confront it, to face it . . . or to be able to pull it off, to do w . . . it and have that deep feeling, that deep emotional feeling with people and to be able to communicate with them . . . I think that one of the reasons that I haven't been able to do that—to relate—is because I've been afraid. I think that you told me that whenever you have that deep personal communication, there's risks, there's responsibility . . . you might get hurt. I think that I've gone through life a lot of times not having very close friends at all. I've only had one close friend called _____ and that is not too much of a friendship. He just understands me, he tries to help me.
Pt:	(to his patient) Are you afraid now?
Pt's patient:	I don't think so.

Th: (to *Pt*) You know, *Pt*, I think that comment came a little late. Hey, what do you want me to do, give you Gestalt supervision or really what I think?

Pt: Do what you want to do.

Th: All right. I'd like you to be your patient for a minute, I'd like you to role-play your patient.

Pt: O.K. "Yeah, I remember what you told me . . . that I wasn't really coming across and relating, really. And I have been really thinking about that. That's what you the doctor told me. Uh, and the reasons that I don't relate well, I've been thinking about that . . . my reasons are that I'm afraid and it's pretty risky for me to take responsibility. I remember your saying those words."

Th: What's your name?

Pt: Frank.

Th: Now, Frank, we have something of a relationship right here between us. How does that fear exist between us, with us? Otherwise, *Pt*, it is all up here, in the head. Now, *Pt you*, you and me, how does that analog that Frank was talking about on the tape exist with us?

Pt: Between you and me?

Th: Yes.

Pt: I do that a lot with you.

Th: What do you do a lot with me?

Pt: I talk *about* situations a lot rather than to you. I talk triangular to you.

Th: Yeah, I'm aware of that.

Pt: It's a less intense way of relating.

Th: You must have a good reason for that, *Pt*.

Pt: I'm not afraid of you, I just want different things. I'm not wanting to get into relating deeply with you right now. I'm wanting more with the tape.

Th: I understand that . . . what does that do to us . . . to me . . . that you want to talk about the tape, your interview with Frank? I mean that is a legitmate request, it sounds as if . . .

Pt: It doesn't do anything with us.

Th: That's right. I guess in terms of what we have been talking about, you and I, you would think that you can become a better therapist, whatever that is, by my teaching you how to respond to that guy Frank on the tape.

Pt: I was a little shook by Dr. _____ [his internship supervisor] to what I thought was a very good hour with another patient of mine.

Th: Well, we can talk about that now, we can talk about that (points to the tape). But when we do that, I feel that we're missing the boat about which Dr. _____ was referring. We'd be doing the very same thing. See, see us now. You're moving your head back and forth and looking out the window. I feel alone—here, now.

Pt: I'm thinking.

Th: That's right. What would happen, *Pt*, if you didn't think about *how* to respond to me? But rather talked to me? It feels to me that when you are thinking like that you are moving into your own personal world and excluding me.

Pt: I don't know what to do or to say to you.

Th: Yeah, I can see that . . . when it comes to dealing with us, with me and you, you don't know what to say. You're at a loss. So you want me to reinforce that by teaching you how to nonmeet in therapy with someone else. There's no way, *Pt,* no technique. You're going to have to risk it with me. But you move away from me all the time.

Pt: I can only go so far with you.

Th: How do you know that . . . it must be right somehow.

Pt: I know because I've tried.

Th: You mean you don't, aren't willing to go any farther?

Pt: I'm unwilling to keep trying, when I don't get anywhere.

Th: With me?

Pt: With you.

Th: You don't get much from me, is that what you are saying?

Pt: I get a lot from you in an hour. I get as much from you in an hour as anyone could expect. I believe you give me all that can be given in this hour.

Th: I don't believe that. But you seem to settle for very little . . . even in his hour—where are you now?

Pt: I'm thinking I don't want a lot of things from you.

Th: Tell me what you do want?

Pt: (long silence)

Th: What's happening?

Pt: I'm thinking.

Th: Yeah, you're thinking, and that is your response to me. But you are not responding in a way that I can tell what's going on. It's like you're withholding yourself from me. You're responding internally, and then you give me the results of that internal process. But not your process, not your immediate direct response to me.

Pt: I'm feeling upset.

Th: (loudly) Look, don't tell me that you're feeling upset. Don't report to me about your internal state. I'd like to see and feel your upset directly. When my two daughters feel upset with me they don't say, "I'm upset"; they say something to me directly.

Pt: You seem to want some kind of action from me.

Th: You are talking at me about you. But you are not giving me you directly. See, what's happening now—you're thinking, I bet, "What shall I do now?"

Pt: I'm puzzled.

Th: Yes! Well, I guess you have good reasons for retreating as I see you are doing now. Retreating into your mental world . . . and . . . work it all out and then give me the finished product, the end result.

Pt: I'm just aware of feeling constricted inside of me.

Th: Now you are talking to me *about* what you are feeling. You prefer to describe you to me. I don't need that, it seems. See, *Pt,* you want to turn me off, like right now, I feel into you, understand—and I'm going to tell you exactly what is going on with me as you sit here with me, and I feel that you are withdrawing, and withdrawing *from me,* from *me;* it is not just happening to you. I am involved. I exist here with you now. So when you pull back into that fucking chair, it seems as if I push you back. Maybe I do. I *am* here. And when you do that I feel two things, like I want to go forward, but more that I want to sit back and to relax.

Pt: I *feel* like pulling back.

Th: I see that. I mean, that is precisely what I am talking about. And I would want you to engage me. I want us to be engaged. But that is my want now, it doesn't seem to be your want. I see that what you want to do is to talk about it or to describe it, to describe what you have felt without giving it to me more directly. See, I am aware right now that I don't want to talk to you anymore. I got turned on to you, I gave you it, and it's like . . . I entered your cunt, and it is dry, you dig?

Pt: I hear you.

Th: A lot of good that does me. Where are you with it?

Pt: I don't like what you are saying.

Th: Well, what is your objection? Talk to me, tell me to shut up, to fuck off, hit me or something.

Pt: Well, I'm not sure you're not correct.

Th: So . . .

Pt: If you are correct I don't like it in me.

Th: O.K. So what are you going to do with it? What are you going to do with me? What are *we* going to do? I feel all shut out of you. Is there some way that you can let me into your system, into your world, so that we can look at the world together? Let me in! Look, *Pt,* how can I get into your world, now, right now. *Pt,* there it is right now, this is where it is at. It's all here. The quintessence of you, of us is here right now. All of it. That is what Dr. _____ picked up. You are looking sideways at me, your head is turned towards the window, you are sitting quietly. I don't know what is going on. You are excluding me. I feel like I am in a different room.

Pt: I wanna get out!

Th: Where to?

Pt: Anywhere!

Th: Away from me?

Pt: Right.

Th: Yes, I see that, and this is what I keep responding to. You know, somehow I'd like to touch you, make physical contact with you. If I were a woman I'd want to touch you sexually—almost as a last resort. To turn you on, somehow, to make you respond to me. Can you understand that—my frantic feeling?

Pt: Hm, hm. (nods assent) Barbara often says that to me.

Th: O.K., now you are looking at me with a puzzled look and with closed fists. What are you saying to me?

Pt: I'm really anxious—whadya know! You're pressing me.

Th: You are describing what is going on between us. Look, I don't need that. You are not writing your book now. It's as if you're writing an annotation to an interview: "He's really anxious now because the therapist is pressing him." You've seen interviews transcribed and annotated with commentaries.

Pt: I do and I don't want you to continue. I am right in the middle. I do and I don't—that's where I am at with you.

Th: I feel effectively neutralized and pushed away. Look, I'm aware that even my voice has changed. It's more quiet and distant. Do you see me now? Do you hear me and see me?

Pt: You look pushed away. You are pushed away. You are sitting way back in your chair.

Th: Yes. Look, *Pt*, I'm not at all blaming you now for it. I merely want to bring the reality of what is happening down *between* us. It's the thing between us. We are *both* in it. We are responding to—one to the other. I want us to look at it, to taste it, to probe it, to prod it.

Pt: I'm puzzled. I see how you feel with what I do.

Th: Yeah.

Pt: And that's where I'm at.

Th: You want me to teach you what to do? Give you a tool, a technique, a method, something? I ain't gonna do that. You are going to have to do something. Do something, man, I'm stepping on your toe!

Pt: Inside of me I hear a voice saying, "Get the fuck off my toe!" but I'm not saying anything.

Th: That is correct! That's the shape of things. What happened just now is the shape of things between us and between you and others. That's what your suffering is all about. That's what you told me you came here for—your distance. Inside it all goes on, and I am effectively excluded. Safe, but lonely.

Pt: It takes me a while to tune in to people, to you.

Th: Let me tell you how I see what you've just said. It takes you a while. What happens is that you say, "Get off me, I'm going to my room and work it out alone and then when I'm good and ready, when the moment is past, I'll come out and respond."

Pt: Yeah (excitedly), that's what I do. It's like I'm a day late. When it's gone, when it's past, I'll come out and respond.

Th: *Pt*, that is what you seem to want to do, and you must have your very good reasons for that, for wanting to remain aloof, closed, enclosed and safe.

Pt: I feel upset.

Th: Oh?

Pt: Go fuck yourself?

Th: Oh!

Pt: I don't even like to say that because it seems like that's just what you want from me.

Th: *Pt,* I don't know what I want from you. I have no plan. I just seem to want to be "on" you, and I don't wanna let go. Not today.

Pt: Boy, you really are on me, and onto me.

Th: Why do you say that to me?

Pt: I've never felt so... this strongly before... this strongly engaged by anyone.

Th: Well, I don't feel like you're engaging me. I feel like it's all going on inside of you and I'm doing all the work.

Pt: I still feel like backing off. Going to my room. If I were doing anything else with you now, I would be faking it.

Th: I understand that, man; do I understand that! That was and is me all over. But play with it. Stick! Don't leave. Stick with us.

Pt: I wanna move forward, and I hold myself back.

Th: Yeah, I see that. I sense it. Everything is going on inside of you, and on the outside nothing much is coming out. Have you left now? You know, *Pt,* sometimes you're embracing a woman and she's with you, you feel her with you, and then all-of-a-sudden something happens and you know she's somewhere else. Do you know that feeling?

Pt: I know that feeling from me because it's what I do.

Th: Well, I just felt it.

Pt: Yeah, I was somewhere else. I do that with Barbara too.

Th: It makes good sense that you would. You must have good reasons to withdraw.

Pt: You know, I can't argue with what you're saying.

Th: (cuts him off) I'm not interested now in your making speeches about you.

Pt: That's clear to me.

Th: It's like you're uninvolvedly involved with what's happening. It all seems to boil down to this. You don't want anybody in. You don't want a dyadic flow, the engagement, the encounter. You want the pale shadow of it, so that you can stay cool, and remain, aloof, and have it all in your own little hands. Omnipotent. In control. Insulated. What's wrong with that? It seems to have a lot going for it, doesn't it?

Pt: It does all right. But it doesn't entirely get it for me.

Th: Oh?

Pt: You know, it's a bit vague to me. You want somehow to be together with me. I'm not even sure I know what you're talking about up here in my head, but I don't seem to really know it or want to know it in my guts.

Th: I can understand that. Oh, *Pt,* do I understand that! *Pt,* I've been there for most of my life. That's how you choose to encounter me and others now, intellectually, cognitively, in your head. Do you see that, can you sense it?

Pt: Yeah. It feels like all I'm doing is talking from this part up (puts his hand on his throat), you know. I don't like being that way. I don't feel enough. I see that is what I do, and even though I'm a psychologist, I'm befuddled as to how to get out of that. It doesn't seem groovy to me.

Th: I hear your saying to me, "Help me!" but I don't hear the call for help. I hear you saying something...

Pt: I don't want to ask you for help.

Th: I see. You come here every week and pay me good money, but you don't want to ask me for help.

Pt: That's what went through me. I don't want to ask you for help.

Th: You must have a good reason for that.

Pt: I don't want to be dependent on you. That way.

Th: You're afraid of me. You're afraid to be with me.

Pt: I'm afraid to need you or anyone that much. That's like being like a child.

Th: You limit the quality of our relationship by what you project into the future—you'll become needy, dependent, a child.

Pt: Yeah.

Th: I hear you. That is a good reason. You *would* want to limit our relationship if that is what you projected—that you would become a helpless child in my arms. I wouldn't want to go near anybody if I thought that. It makes very good sense if you define it that way. Good sense.[7]

Pt: But it's expensive. The cost is like you were feeling like you wanted to split. You engaged me and if you didn't continue to push back you would have split. Like the others.

Th: No. I would have sat back in my chair and relaxed and let the wheels roll on until I couldn't stand it anymore.

Pt: That's what I meant by split.

Th: I see. But look what you demand of me, look how much work I have to do. I guess it's like your girlfriend who says, "I have to beat at you all the time to get you to attend to me." I feel tired now.

Pt: I don't know how to respond to you or to anyone. Like there's all kinds of puzzlement going on inside of me now. Like yeah, you're tired, I believe you. And yet I'm really not sure of what you or they want from me.

Th: What the hell do you care what I want? What do you want?

Pt: I wanna understand...

Th: You can understand all you want, and you can sit in that chair for six years full of understanding, and say, "Oh, yes, Doctor, that must be why I do that," and nothing happens. I would like you to stand under it, feel it over you, be wet with it.

Pt: When you said that I had a feeling of not feeling anything, of closing up, that must indicate what my position is. That what I prefer to do

---

[7]An essential, affirming response.

	when someone really touches me like I feel you have, I close up, and go away. I guess that's how it is between us.
Th:	You make yourself an object to you. You hold yourself all in your hands, like behind your back, and you prefer not to give yourself to a relationship, to the process between us. You want me to be the surgeon who operates on you while you observe and say, "Oh, yes, now I see what has been hurting me."
Pt:	I am very silent.
Th:	I see that.
Pt:	I am reporting.
Th:	Yeah, and looking away; looking around, for what, *Pt?*
Pt:	I was just feeling sad.
Th:	That's something. Now, I feel your sadness, I see your eyes brimming over with tears.
Pt:	I'm really sad because that is how I am. It hurts so much. (cries) I'm so lonely, I don't wanna be like that forever.
Th:	But, *Pt,* it seems like there are good reasons for your remaining that way, and you are feeling the loneliness and the sadness which are the negative sides of the way you have chosen to be. I feel with you about that. I feel very close to you right now. I can feel you (reaches out and touches his hand).
Pt:	I feel close to you, and at the same time I feel all fucked up inside of myself. It's so hard for me to be this way. Maybe psychology is not for me? (cries)
Th:	It seems as if you are right with the conflict. How you want to be insulated, how that does some good things for you, and how it also hurts. You are feeling it now. That's something.
Pt:	What's gonna happen?
Th:	I don't know...I don't know. A lot depends on how you want to live your life.
Pt:	Yeah...yeah. It's my choice, isn't it?
Th:	See you next week.

By way of summary, let me quote Buber's description of the engaged encounter and its denial.

> The relationship to the Thou is direct. No system of concepts, no foreknowledge, and no fancy intervene between I and Thou.... Every means is an obstacle. Only when every means has collapsed does the meeting come about (1958, pp. 11-13).

I would paraphrase Buber as follows:

> The relationship between us is direct—coupled. No theory, no system of concepts, no hypotheses regarding psychic mechanisms, intervene between I and Thou. Every technique is an obstacle. Only when we engage, hand-to-hand, heart-to-heart, now, does the meeting come about.

THE THERAPEUTIC RELATIONSHIP

Counseling and psychotherapy in the HE framework take place within the context of two people who see each other as unique entities. HE or Affirmation Counseling and Therapy constitute a relationship based on the concepts of humanistic existentialism presented in this work and elsewhere (Ofman, 1967, 1970; Rios and Ofman, 1972). Basic to the therapeutic enterprise is the concept of violation that the HE sees as the essentially ensickening act (cf., Esterson, 1972). One person violates another's phenomenological or experiential world by objectifying him and trying to change him or raise him according to the subject's (the changer's) view of reality and then denying that he is attempting to do just that. The violation, then, is a double denial; it is a denial by another of one person's view of reality, and it is a *denial of that denial.* The violation says, "It is not that there is you and there is me and I shall try to influence you to see things my way; it is, rather, that you are wrong, and I am right." The denial of the violation by the violator is maddening.

Unfortunately, often what is called therapeutic treatment is in reality getting the person to once again abandon his subjective experience for the therapist's or society's "objective" reality. But the person's experiential perspective is *his correct invention to be able to exist in his situation.* Such therapeutic treatment is a reliving, albeit much more subtly, of the basic violating paradigm. Here, as before, it is given for the person's "own good." This danger of violation in counseling and psychotherapy is perhaps inescapable. Comments on this issue by Blount, a practicing therapist, are included in Appendix II.

Although Szasz (1961), Weisskopf-Joelson (1968), Wheelis (1970), and Rosenhan (1973), have also pointed out the possibility of violation in the therapeutic relationship, I want to emphasize that the *kind* of relationship (i.e., how the two persons communicate, their basic intent) and the position the therapist takes with the client denotes the relationship that they form. The quality of that relationship—reciprocally mutual or hierarchical—teaches the person about relationships, and what it is to be a person in general. I fully agree with Hora (1960) and Colm (1973) that psychotherapy is much less a science or a technique than it is a way that one person *is* (a way of being) with another. Here again, with every act that he performs, the therapist asserts that way of acting *as a value* in the world.

A hierarchical, superior kind of relationship with a doctorly expert is also deleterious to what I consider to be the main job of counseling and therapy. To the HE, the therapeutic task is not the discovery of connections between family cathexes and current relationships, nor is it the discovery of connections between the past and the present. It is, rather, the fostering of explicit awareness. The goals of HE therapy are for the person to utter and clarify his priorities and basic projects, to assume ownership, validity, and responsibility for his projects and to accept the positive and negative aspects of his projects, so that the divided, unattended-to parts of his personality can be integrated. Progress towards these goals is sought by means of affirmation and authentic relating.

Being authentic in relation to a person does not mean entering into his phenomenological field, as the Rogerians used to teach, for no man can rupture another's subjectivity, enter into his mind, or see through his eyes. Rather, it means a *mutual* quest for the denied integrity in life—for both the therapist and for the person who faces him. Such a quest for unity, meaningfulness, and affirmation of the person's *unique* existence (Friedman, 1972) seems to occur in genuine meetings based on the recognition that both the therapist and the person are in the same boat—life; or on the recognition that we are all more human than not (Farber, 1966). Hanna Colm points out the importance of the therapist's adopting such a mutual reciprocity with the client:

> It is essential that the patient can share the therapist's own feelings, his associations evoked by a patient's problem, his dreams at times, or his counter-transferences. Then he will, in the framework of therapy as encounter, experience how seriously the therapist takes his partnership and the feelings and reactions he brings into the partnership. Encounter reveals itself as a slowly developing process on both sides, which centers around the patient's needs especially in the beginning, but then slowly develops into a genuine relationship, with growth on both sides.... Growth towards reality is achieved faster through the experience of genuineness than an experience of prescribed frustration which the Freudian unresponsive and unqualified acceptance may actually create.... The closeness, which will remain between patient and therapist, will eventually be that of two friends, who now do not any longer need to see each other at regular intervals. They see each other when both feel like it and when conditions permit it (1973, p. 172).

Affirmation can never emerge from a hierarchical, even benevolently hierarchical, manipulative position (Pandé, 1968). Such a position not only denies the frankly paradoxical influence relationship between two entities and denies the denial, but masks pronouncements and interpretations as truth or even as "hypotheses" to be tested by the patient. When such pronouncements are challenged or not accepted as valid, the patient is considered resistant, and so the violations continue. Any time that it is assumed by either party in the therapeutic encounter that the therapist has access to a "secret" about the person to which that person is not and cannot be privy, the genuine, mutual encounter is broken, decoupling takes place, and violation occurs.

Ambiguity and anonymity on the part of the therapist merely aid the process of *mystification,* which violates and keeps the person in a one-sided, decoupled encounter (Bordin, 1968). By this tactic, the therapist, cloaked in his safe, knowing ambiguity, promulgates a furthering of the rift in an already unintegrated view of self.[8] The process of mystification needs to be commented on further at this point, since it is closely connected with the notion of the basic violation.

A NOTE ON MYSTIFICATION

Laing (1965) says that Karl Marx used the concept of mystification to mean a *plausible* misrepresentation of a situation offered to the exploited by the exploiters. The misrepresentation took the form of calling exploitation "benevolence," by deluding the exploited into believing that they were at one with their exploiters, or making the exploited feel grateful for their "being done to" on the basis that it was for their ultimate benefit. The double denial works here, too. The exploiters may not want to face that they are frankly exploiting; consequently, they deny the fact of exploitation and deny that they deny. They leave the scene of the crime that they have committed, as it were, and leave the second party there—feeling mad! This process, mystification, is one of the major ways in which people violate others in their encounters with them.

To mystify, then is to befuddle, to mask the true state of affairs to the other, and to deceive oneself about the process. It is an inherently confusing situation since there is failure to explicitly attend to and be aware of what each party of the encounter *really* experiences. When one party in the encounter points to the mystification process, the other denies it, lays it *all* on the perceiver (see pps. 171ff. on transference) or calls it such names as projection or transference. The *state* of being mystified is expressed in the

---

[8]Perhaps a little more needs to be said about the psychoanalytic therapeutic ritual. It has been pointed out (Stein, 1973; Glad, 1959; Greenson, 1967; Giovacchini, 1975; Strupp, 1968) that the major thrust of psychoanalytic therapy is the attempt to establish a non-aversive, or counter-repressive climate in the therapeutic hours. The goal is the permission, via free-association, ambiguity, and non-involvement on the analyst's part, for the patient to express words and other utterances as freely as is possible. Thus, by such expression, the repressive mantle is lifted and the person is better able to make conscious all the forgotten, unattended-to, hostile and guilt-ridden thoughts and their accompanying emotions.

The analyst, as does the HE therapist, considers the essential human relationship to be the basic ground for psychological development and personality growth. It was this realization that led to the then and current view that the creation of the transference neurosis and the analysis of the transference phenomenon is the central issue in analytic work. The goal is, of course, the mitigation and sublimation of the person's instinct-life, especially as it pertains to interpersonal relationships (Singer, 1965); and this goal is to be achieved via the working through of the relationships between the patient and the analyst (Greenson, 1967).

But, the ritual demands that the analyst consciously maintain an objective, superior, and aloof distance from any personal or human involvement while, on the other hand, the patient is encouraged to completely succumb to emotional entanglement and deep involvement (and punished for hesitating to do so via the interpretation of resistance to it). Such an asymmetrical ritual is a strange distortion of a possible human connection. Primarily because the analytic model is acted out in a largely non-mutual and asymmetrical human relationship, it fails in the very goal it sets out for itself: ego regulation in creative human relationships. Because the model is so nonmutual, it may even be obstructive to mutuality and growthful encounters.

person by a feeling of being muddled, seemingly all within himself. There seems to be no perpetrator of the act of befuddlement; the violated person is left confused, holding the whole bag, as it were, with the person who gave him the bag, invisible.

The major purpose of mystification is the avoidance of an authentic engaging encounter where each party *declares* what he really is all about, what he intends, what his motives are, and what he really wants. In such an encounter, each person asserts what he is ready to engage about in a clear, reciprocal exchange of wants—a mutual declaration. Often that kind of declaration leads to genuine conflict of interests, but the conflict may be judged bad or unhealthy. By means of mystification, the conflict is avoided, at least in appearance.

The essential violation involved in mystification is the rupture of another person's subjectivity. Thus if there is a contradiction between your perception and mine, I choose *not* to encounter you, I tell you that it is in your imagination, that you are distorting, projecting, or acting out—in sum, that you are unreal. And all too often, after such treatment, the person begins to feel unreal and eventually acts unreal.

Another way in which a person mystifies another is by disconfirming the *content* of that person's experience and replacing it with his own view of the other. In the following examples, the therapist "lays his trip" on the patient:

Pt: I really got angry with you for being late for my appointment today.
Th: You are an angry person. Let's look into your anger. How have you been frustrated by your father?

Or,

Pt:. I really got angry with you for being late for my appointment today.
Th: Can you *be* your anger? Let your anger speak.

Or,

Pt: I really got angry with you for being late for my appointment today.
Th: (silence)

In each instance, the encounter between the two is decoupled in order to avoid a possible conflict between two subjectivities. Instead, the problem is pushed back on the patient. The feeling that person invariably gets is, "There is something wrong with *me* for feeling angry. He seems OK. I am wrong."

A nonviolating, nonmystifying exchange might be:

Pt: I really got angry with you for being late for my appointment today.
Th: Of course! I was doing what *I* wanted to do...and so, I did not want to be on time and wasn't.

Another example of mystification is when a mother, in speaking to her child, substitutes her demand, "Go to bed! It is your bedtime and you are tired," for a more authentic: "*I* am tired, so go to bed. I want to be alone now." Or still another example occurs when a wife tells her husband she is unhappy, and he responds with, "You can't be—you're nuts. You have everything—a housekeeper, a house, a pool, a Porsche. How can you be so ungrateful, especially when I work so hard!"

The violating aspect of mystification occurs when one party cannot tolerate to reveal himself *as he is,* so he tries to make the other feel bad, guilty, or mad—anything other than what he is in fact experiencing—in order to befuddle real feelings, i.e., the reality of both the parties and the situation between them. That is one reason for some very "sick" persons not being tolerated easily by many people. In their struggle to demystify themselves, they see through or at least are very sensitive to the parent, friend, or therapist, and it is hard to take. The truth often is.

Psychotherapy in the HE modes is conducted in a mutual, often painful, authentic fashion. If we explain away the person's view of us as a transference or a projection, we further mystify. We need to understand that the person *probably is* seeing something correct in us.

THERAPY AND COUNSELING AS AN HE ENCOUNTER

Since the therapist has no secrets, what does he have? What is he paid for; what is his merchandise? In the main, he is paid for what he, himself, has gone through in his quest for authenticity, and for his willingness to manifest presence—*to be there;* for his willingness to unmask himself and perhaps thus help the person sitting before him. The therapist knows that just as he himself is able, the person too, is capable of declaring and affirming himself *as he is;* and he knows that the person can also know who he is *if he wishes to look*—if he is willing to experience reality directly by paying attention to his life as it is in fact experienced, and if he will be explicitly aware of his projects and of what they may bring him.

An absolutely affirming, real relationship where the engaged encounter obtains *is* the therapeutic event. Psychotherapy and counseling, then, consists mainly in the mutual paring away of all that stands between us and leads, finally, to the basic dealing with two (or more) realities as we confront each other in life. The only basis for an authentic relationship is the conviction that the other person is a separate, free spontaneity who has some integrity, some unity, and some cohesive project of which he can become aware, and that is expressed in the fabric of his life.

In contrast to the Rogerian approach, the frame of reference and the matrix of the authentic relationship may not include prizing the other person as a prior condition. For the HE, loving, caring, or prizing may grow out of an authentic meeting, but one cannot will oneself to love, to prize or to trust, for these are unwillables. They either grow out of the ground of two people committing themselves to becoming in relation or they do not.

There is no rule, image or mythology at all that one should live up to as an HE therapist save the following: to be free, to be all that one is, to pay attention, to take the transaction and life seriously, to "get wet" by the other, and to respond. The only thing, perhaps, that the client has a right to demand of the therapist (and his lover, his spouse, or true friend) is his *full response.* And in a deeper sense, that is impossible also; either the therapist chooses to respond or he does not, and the client will then know him by the quantity and quality of his responsiveness. Nevertheless, the content of the response is unwillable by the therapist in any authentic sense.

Often, the difficulties experienced in life that bring people to therapy are the consequences that attend wants, but many deny this. Clients deny that the negative aspects of their lives belong to their projects just as much as the positive aspects that they hope to attain. They thus create a disunity or an opacity in themselves and end up playing a kind of charade. People want power, esteem, glory, wealth, or whatever, but at the same time they say, "Doctor, why is my stomach so constantly upset at my executive job where the pressure is so great?" Or "There is something wrong with *me* that I have a hard time making difficult decisions. I can't face that my reality, and thus my priorities, have included in them difficult decisions. Difficult decisions should be easy; there must be something wrong with me that you can cure, so that difficult decisions will be easy. Life really *is* beautiful and easy, so when I find that it is difficult, it is an imperfection in me. Ideal life does not include this imperfection."

Many people come to therapy saying, in one way or another, I value my projects, my goals, and my priorities, but there are elements attending my project that are negative, and these I choose not to admit (friction does not exist in a relationship, or death will not come, or I have all the time in the world to wait for my secret lover to divorce and come to me). Instead, I choose to blame myself, call myself sick, and ask you to cure my illness, thus salvaging my mythology about the essential nature of life. To put it another way, "I want to continue to sit on this hot seat, but please take away the burning sensation."[9]

Some of the key elements in the denial of the negative aspects of one's wants can be seen in the following transcription. This is the eighth interview with a man who came to therapy because of a stomach disorder that was becoming progressively more dangerous.

Pt: Yeah, and I, I wondered this morning why, you know, why do I always drink too much wine. I drink it, and I wondered if, uh, subconsciously I could sort of like being in a hospital. Bleeding, getting all that attention.

---

[9]cf., Eliot quotation on p. 28.

Getting all of that, yeah, that's it, yeah, attention. Possible?

Th: You need attention?

Pt: I don't know. You tell me if I need attention. I, I . . .

Th: It's, it feels to me like you need caring.

Pt: So it's possible. 'Cause it, it's, you know. It doesn't make sense.

Th: What doesn't make sense?

Pt: Well, my drinking *any* wine. It doesn't make a great deal of sense in my, you know, the way my gut spills acid. But drinking a lot of it makes no sense at all. I mean, not from a health standpoint, not from a business standpoint. Oh, and eating the foods that I eat. You know, like last week I came I was sick—I had Mexican food; shit! I had Mexican food at lunch yesterday again.

Th: You had what? I didn't hear.

Pt: I had Mexican food for lunch yesterday.

Th: Again?

Pt: Yeah. I gotta be trying to put myself back in . . .

Th: In the hospital.

Pt: Gotta be.

Th: Well, let's take a look at that. What does the hospital give you?

Pt: Care.

Th: The hospital makes you well.

Pt: Right.

Th: Go with your hope for the hospital.

Pt: Well, when I'm in the hospital I, I don't have to do the things that I have to do when I'm not in the hospital. You know. Dealing with work responsibilities. Yeah, it's a great cop-out. Can't do it, pal. Can't do it, team. In the hospital.

Th: What's the cop-out?

Pt: Well, the cop-out is you get sick you go to the hospital.

Th: What's the cop-out? What's the cop-out?

Pt: Getting out from under responsibilities.

Th: Oh, evidently you can't get out from under it some other way.

Pt: I guess not. I guess that's, yeah. So, I, I felt that that was very likely. That's, what makes me do stupid things. I mean, uh, stupid. To not take care of myself.

Th: Well, let's understand uh, what the underlying need is. The good, valuable, for good reasons need. You need to be rid of the oppressive responsibilities which you seem to be suffering from. You need to rest, to be healed, to be taken care of.

> [*Here the therapist merely organizes what the person has said so far and makes a succinct statement of the underlying, simple need that the patient has expressed and denies in the next statement, "... my subconscious thinks that. In actual fact it's not so."*]

Pt: Right. Oh, well, I think I need, you know, I, I guess my subconscious thinks that. In actual fact that's not so.

Th: What do you mean by that?

Pt: I don't think that I carry, uh, overpowering responsibilities at all. And I don't think that I fail to get uh, a fair and you know, pretty decent share of attention. Now, uh, that's my conscious. So, obviously my subconscious is, is not satisfied. It's not satisfied with the attention that we get, and it's not, in my, uh, something with it may, drives me to really want to get out from under work responsibilities. I don't like it. I'm really getting fed up with me.

[*That is the basic transformation and denial of which Eliot (1959) and I speak. "I'm really getting fed up with me." Here the denial is in refusing to see that* he is in the world, *that his ulcer is his response to his situation. Instead, he blames himself, and makes it a project of self-changing "adjustment." He denies the facts: "This work is hard for me."*]

Th: It, it's very interesting that you say that, *Pt,* that you're getting fed up with you, rather than getting... It's like uh, you're wearing tight shoes, right? These fancy Gucci's...

[*Therapist recalls that* Pt *was wearing expensive but tight shoes at the previous session and tries to point out a simple analogy.*]

Pt: Hurt. The black ones hurt.

Th: Right. It's like you're saying, well, I bought these great Gucci shoes for $50.00 or $60.00, right? How much were they?

Pt: $50.00.

Th: Fifty bucks. And uh, because I want status, and I want attention and I want to, to, to have people respond to me and in a status and warm, and uh, admiring way, and uh, but the shoes hurt like crazy. You know, and they hurt. They just plain ordinary hurt. And what you do say is, "Well, you know, there's nothing, there's nothing wrong with the shoes; I'm sick of myself hurting because my shoes are too tight. There's something wrong with me." And that's exactly what you said just now. And I wonder if you heard what you said?

Pt: I heard what I said. I realize you've got a beautiful, wonderful box here...

[*Reference is made to the tape-recording process.*]

Th: Yeah. The tape recorder. You know, it's, it's like you're saying, um, I'm carrying a 3,000 pound weight on my shoulders and my shoulders are hurting and my arms are shaking and my stomach is rumbling; I'm sick of myself for responding appropriately to a 3,000 pound weight. Which is what you're saying.

[*Therapist continues with the analogy.*]

Pt: Okay.

Th: Okay, what? What . . .

Pt: Okay, I go for that.

Th: What are you doing? I feel like you're placating me by saying that.

Pt: I'm not. I'm not placating you. What the hell do I want to placate you for?

Th: I haven't the foggiest idea.

Pt: It's a waste of time.

Th: That's right. That's right.

Pt: You don't need placating.

Th: Oh? Oh, what was that?

[*Th thought he detected a hostile note.*]

Pt: *You* don't need placating.

Th: Well, what was that? You need it but I don't need it?

Pt: I don't think you need placating. You don't need placating in the context that, of, of, of my visit to you. Uh, I don't need to come here and placate you.

Th: Why not?

[Th *objects to being made into a superior doctor, and the implicit denial of responsibility on the Pt's part.*]

Pt: I don't think, I don't think you require it.

Th: Well, how do you know; how, how do you figure that?

Pt: I think that your responsibility, I hope your responsibility is to get me better.

Th: Oh?

Pt: Not to be placated.

Th: Really? Okay. We'll tackle that some other time. I think you're putting me in some kind of doctor position. It's really a, something else.

Pt: What, what kind of a doctor position?

Th: Oh, man, you know, it's *his* responsibility to cure me. I'm not gonna . . .

Pt: Oh, well, no it's not. Oh, fuck me, you don't mean that.

Th: I don't know what I mean. All that I know is that when I'm with you I respond to you. And the best damn thing I can give you is the totality of my response.

Pt: I agreed with what you said. I agreed that . . .

Th: That's what I wanted to know.

Pt: I agreed that, uh, and the, but I wasn't placating you, what you said made sense. Now, shit, you may, uh . . .

Th: How did it make sense? I want to know. I forgot what I said.

Pt: You, ah, you are a piece of work. You use the example of a man with a 3,000-pound weight who hated himself for reacting as you must react if you're carrying a 3,000-pound weight. Okay, I'm hip. I'm reacting because of the action that is, there is; there is an action and this is the reaction. I'm aware. I agree with you. It was well said. I, I hadn't thought of it before you said it. You said it. I grasped it instantly. I'm bright.

Th: Yes, you are. I experience you as being bright.

Pt: Uh, you know, seriously, I, I am getting very upset lately.

Th: Well, here, here we go again. We're right back where we came from. Uh, you're like the uh, uh, the big company executive that used to come here, who said, you know, I'm burdened with terribly difficult decisions. And, I don't know why I should find them difficult.

Pt: I see that parallel.

Th: Evidently you refuse to see how difficult for you what you're doing is.

Pt: When do we get to that part?

Th: What part?

Pt: When do I begin to see this?

Th: I don't know. If you could see it maybe your stomach wouldn't have to respond. Maybe you have to lose your whole stomach.

Pt: My stomach is not responding. Now. I'm trying to force my stomach to respond.

Th: Oh, that'd be good. If you became aware of how in fact it does respond, like when you're at, at dinnertime and eating Mexican food and uh, if you become exquisitely aware of what you want or when you drink, when you drink too much wine, of how much care you need, it won't have to respond. If you can accept the reality of what *Pt* is, of who *Pt* is, your body won't have to tell you constantly who it is. I mean, all, all, all I do say is: look at your tummy, you're bursting out of your pants, to understand how much succor you in fact do need.

Pt: Okay. If we accept that, when do we get to the part that I, I receive succor?

Th: You will receive succor when you understand clearly, in exquisite aware-ness, what it is specifically that you need, when you need it, and how in fact, what's happening in your life now is not satisfying it, as a matter of fact, may be taking it away from you. Now, you're going to have to stop and think about that.

Pt: What you just said doesn't make any sense.

Th: No?

Pt: It's so far away. Whatever it was you just said is not attainable quickly.

Th: That, I think that's true. You could, if you really open your eyes, (snaps fingers) like that. But what you do, you, you, what you do is you don't want to see, uh, what, what your life is like. I mean, you are suffering from your life. From the way you lead your life.

   [*Here is expressed the basic HE belief that people suffer from the nega-tive aspects attending their choices.*]

Pt: Do I change the way I lead my life, or do I learn to live the life I lead?

   [*Again, the emphasis on change, which denies the basic awareness of what* is *happening.*]

Th: I'm, I'm not even going to begin to answer that because it is totally out of my hands and I don't care how you do it. What you do with your life is entirely your affair. Whether you *see* your life clearly and respond to it responsibly is my affair.

   [*Th states his position, and this* is *essentially the HE position.*]

Pt: You didn't say anything just then.

Th: I didn't say anything now. You mean you didn't hear me, or, or it was unimportant what I said, or what?

Pt: The object of this whole thing is to straighten my head out.

Th: The object of this whole thing is to make you see reality clearly, is to help you come into reality clearly. What you do when you in fact see it is none of my affair. I'll be a, a kind of Frankenstein, Dr. Frankenstein if it were.

Pt: Why don't I respond as I should, to the reality I see. I see . . .

Th: You do.

Pt: I see that I'm bursting out of my pants. Why don't I stop eating?

Th: Because (laughs) why don't, why doesn't my foot stop hurting? Gotta take the fucking shoes off. I mean, if you're wearing shoes that are too small for you, as indeed you were, two times earlier when you were here, you keep saying, I see that my foot hurts, why doesn't, why don't I, why

Th: doesn't my foot stop hurting? Gotta take the fucking shoes off. I mean any two-year-old kid could see that. Hey, do you see your belt is too tight?

Pt: Yeah, yeah.

Th: Okay. Well, what's to do about that?

Pt: I'm not gonna get a bigger belt. I'm gonna suffer.

Th: Well, then, there's your answer.

Pt: I'm not gonna get bigger pants. Okay.

Th: (laughs) Those pants will get small too. Look, do you see what we're talking about? Do you see my point? You said to me . . .

Pt: I, I . . .

Th: When do I stop eating? When you're satisfied, right, in your life, so that you don't have to eat to get what you want.

Pt: Haven't you got a pill that can get me off for the next couple of weeks?

Th: Yep, I do. It's a hard pill.

Pt: I'm going to miss, uh . . .

    [Pt *refers to his frequent business trips.*]

Th: I don't want to hear about that now. I want to hear what you're going to say, um, what you said in fact, about what's this next couple of weeks.

Pt: There's nothing especially significant about them.

Th: There must be.

Pt: No, there, isn't. There, there's nothing significant about the next couple of weeks, but if I could not eat for the next couple of weeks, Bill, my pants would fit.

Th: You could. You could.

Pt: I know I could, Bill.

Th: If you wished to.

Pt: Well, I'm, I am consciously, desperate, to get myself in order.

Th: Well, again, you're using the analogy of attacking the uh, result of . . .

Pt: Well, I also want to add that I don't want to die fat.

Th: Say that again. Say, say it again. I didn't hear it.

Pt: Why did I want to add, and didn't, I don't want to die fat.

Th: I don't know.

Pt: Which was really there before I said I want to get myself in order. That's a kind of, that's a farce (laughs).

Th: Yeah. Yeah. I think you want rest. Surcease.

Pt: Yeah, I think, I do, Bill, because there is no opportunity for it. I mean, I, I have things I must do. They gotta be done. Nobody else to do them. I gotta do them, and they gotta be done. Very normal, very natural to want rest. So, because I can't go someplace to lie down and rest I'm going to pour the fucking wine in and they're going to take me down to Cedars and . . .

    [*The affirmation of connection, "There are things my choice forces me to do, and these have consequences."*]

Th: Force you to rest.

Pt: I'm going to have rest and cheat on them. Oh, I'm sorry fellows. You gotta do the show.

Th: But I'm not responsible. I got an ulcer.

Pt: Right.

Th: Well, that's as good a tactic as any, isn't it?

Pt: It's a shit thing. I can't, I can't like myself or respect myself. For that, and I'm desperate to overcome that.

Th: Overcome what?

Pt: To overcome that, uh, tactic. If in fact, that's what it is.

Th: You will overcome it when you take what's happening to you seriously. And when you take the rest that you need. That you *need*. I mean, you've been denying how much pressure, how much tension you in fact are under and how much satisfaction you have to pour into yourself via wine, Mexican food, and whatever else you shove down your gullet, to, uh, to kind of uh, uh, then hope to die. Because that'll be restful somehow. You deny the fact of the difficulty of what it is that you're doing. For you. The difficulties for you, in what you're doing.

Pt: I don't think so. I think I'm quite aware of the difficulties. I think I'm painfully aware of the difficulties.

[*Note the totally different position from Pt's position on pps. 145-146.*]

Th: Are you?

Pt: I'm trying, you know, to get out from under.

Th: See, what you do, what I heard you wanting to do to yourself, is to say, uh, well, I want to sit in a frying pan, but, Doctor, don't let me hurt. Don't let me burn. Uh, by saying to me well, uh, my life is difficult, how do you make me not feel it? Well, that's death. If somebody throws a spear at you and you don't feel it, you're dead.

Pt: Oh, I, uh, I haven't been, um, I really haven't been despondent or upset since we began. I am today. I just don't like me today. At all.

(silence)

Th: Well, I believe that there's a good reason for you not liking you. I believe that you see things fairly clearly, about yourself, now; I feel that there's a good reason, some, somehow, somewhere you're selling out yourself. A good reason for selling out.

Pt: Well, we'll just have to keep, uh . . .

Th: Well, let's keep at it right now. Where, where is it?

Pt: I don't know where it is. You know, I, I get back to things we've talked about. We could talk about again. You know, I wonder if I'm up to doing what it is I have to do. Which is primarily this show.

Th: That's a very wonderful thought.

Pt: What's a wonderful thought?

Th: That you wonder whether you're up to doing it.

Pt: What's wonderful about it?

Th: That sounds like it's right on the right track.

Pt: Okay. So I, I'm aware of, uh, I'm aware that, uh, I don't know.

Th: Say it. Finish the sentence.

Pt: I lost it. I just, you know.

Th: Try to get it back. I want you to get it back.

(silence)

Pt: Well, you know, you, uh, uh, I, uh, I, uh, apart from the fact that I wonder whether, um, you know, whether I'm up to doing this uh, thing, today, right now, I also wonder whether I'm up to really being anything. I mean, just stop beating, stop spreading. Stop drinking far too much wine. I, I, uh, you know, I'm really very, very disgusted.

Th: Uh, what, what, what I see is that your eating and drinking is a correct and adequate response to uh, things that are happening in your life. And what you're doing is your, it's like, um, again, I, I, um, when somebody hits you in the face with a baseball bat and you fall down, what you're disgusted about is the fact that you fall down.

[*Clarification of the basic denial.*]

Pt: You have made your point.

Th: I want you to pay attention to the fact that you get yourself in the situation where you're being hit in the face with a baseball bat. That's what to be disgusted about. That's what to look at, at any rate.

Pt: I don't see that at all. You know if we, if we can achieve that uh, in fairly short order. I think that would be splendid. If in fact that is what . . .

Th: Well . . .

Pt: I don't, I don't honestly conjure up any image of being hit with a baseball bat or carrying a 3,000-pound weight around (grabs his stomach and rolls a roll of fat around in his hands).

Th: Oh, you do feel that?

Pt: Yeah.

Th: Well, when you carry a 3,000-pound weight, uh, and you say well, I've got to eat in order to bear it; what you're disgusted about is the eating rather than the fact that you have to carry the weight around.

Pt: We're going around in a circle.

Th: Oh, we're going, can you see it?

Pt: If I, if I, if I'm carrying a 3,000-pound weight, then I'm reacting . . .

Th: Appropriately to it.

Pt: Appropriately. Okay, but I am finding myself trying to put the fucking weight down.

Th: That seems right.

Pt: But I'm putting the weight down while they haul me off in an ambulance bleeding to, to the hospital.

Th: Yeah, well, what you're saying is that it's too late. Well, what you're saying is . . .

Pt: No, I hope it's not too late.

Th: Well, what you're saying is that the way you put it down is . . .

Pt: Yeah, I mean.

Th: I understand that.

Pt: I mean, why don't I just put it down? Put it down.

Th: Well, you tell me. You must have a good reason for carrying the weight.

Pt: I don't know.

Th: Well, I have a good suspicion about that from what you've said to me the last couple of times we've been talking together. That somehow you feel, or you believe that that is the way for you to get what you want.

>   [*Again* Th *addresses himself to the underlying project, his want, and the hope he has for it.*]

Pt: Okay. I, uh, I'll accept that. I, uh, I said it so I'll accept it. What's, how do we get out of that?

Th: How do you get out of it?

Pt: I don't know.

Th: I know how I get out of it. I constantly look at the price that I have to pay for what I want and whether what I do in the hope of getting what I want really gets me what I want. Now that's a very painful process to keep paying attention to that concept, but, but at least it keeps me straight.

Pt: Why can't I do it?

Th: You don't want to do it. Aw, you're trying to do it with me here.

Pt: So I do want to do it?

Th: It seems that way.

Pt: Why can't I do it?

Th: It seems that what you really want is to be rid of your ulcer without doing anything about yourself.

>   [*Again, the basic structure.*]

Pt: Right.

Th: I mean, your coming here is just a, one step away from your being in the hospital. It's the same kind of thing. You can use this therapy here as the biggest cop-out in the world. Say, hey Doc, fix up my ulcers, but don't make me do anything about myself and the way I live my life—which has caused the ulcers in the first place.

Pt: I'm, I'm really not very responsive today. I'm, I'm, really down, uh, and I didn't realize how down I was 'til I came in to see you. I'm just, you know, bubbled out. Spewed out. Bubbled out. Uh, shit. (sigh) I ain't happy I tell you that. I'm not happy.

Th: Well, your unhappiness is a correct and absolutely adequate response to uh, what you're doing, what's happening around you. That is, you have very good reason not to be happy.

(silence)

Pt: I wish I didn't have to go out of town.

Th: Yeah. Well, that's merely the consequences of, um, you, your working, how you're working, and where you're working. I wish you didn't have to go out of town either. I hate that. I hate your going out of town.

Pt: I, I, you know, I meant it only in, I meant it because of the therapy.

Th: Yeah, well, I hate it when you go out of town. I hate it when you miss hours with me. I feel that we, that I, I feel that I, I'm uh, abandoned by you.

Pt: Yeah. I've got one more and then I'm, and then I'll be here for a good while.

Th: Yeah.

Pt: Well, I'm here until I, uh, uh, uh, further notice.

Th: Yeah, but I, I tell you how I respond. I feel like you're abandoning me. I know there are good reasons.

Pt: I know. You, you, you have told me that. Uh, but you, you don't appreciate, you don't appreciate the enormous, uh, uh, discipline that I follow in seeing you when I do and, and in trying to move trips around you know, so that I . . .

Th: I'd like you to tell me. I, I'd, I'd—how could I appreciate it without you telling me?

Pt: Well, you know, I do it because I have to do it. But, you know, I, I do, very often, you know, think in terms of the therapy, when I'll say I'll see you so and so, such and such a day, such and such a time.

Th: I like that. I, it indicates to me that you're committed to this process.

Pt: Oh, totally. Abs—, totally. Boy, you know, I have, I have a thing I have to do next week, and I'll miss, this is the last, and I'll miss Tuesday and Wednesday, and I dwell on that. I think about that a lot, and I say to myself, well, well, I suppose I say a little bit of so what, not, not to therapy but to group. And then I find that I think of it every day, which, gee, I'm going to miss the group for two weeks. And I think about not seeing you privately, that's, as I say, at least I, I can see where—I'm going to try and get back Wednesday evening, at 6:30. . . .

I believe that a healing relationship is one based on mutuality, on a conviction that the person is the way he is and that there is a unifying, underlying meaning to his existence, a meaning that he chooses to hold onto in the face of the aversive consequences attending his project. People are willing to suffer terribly for the results of their priorities and their images rather than face the fact that these are the outcome of the way they have chosen (and keep rechoosing) to live their lives. These consequences are often expressed in the way a person feels, and the feelings are seen as somehow bracketed and self-generating.

An example of such a project, and the commitment which the person has to it, despite the difficulties in maintaining it is given by the heroine in Erica Jong's book (1973), *Fear of Flying,* in this touching monologue-dialogue with herself.

If I was trapped, I was trapped by my own fears. Motivating everything was the terror of being alone. It sometimes seemed I would make any compromise, endure any ignominy, stay with any man just so as not to face being alone. But why? What was so terrible about being alone? *Try to think of the reasons,* I told myself. *Try.*

ME: Why is being alone so terrible?

ME: Because if no man loves me I have no identity.

ME: But obviously that isn't true. You write, people read your work and it matters to them. You teach and your students need you and care about you. You have friends who love you . . .

ME: None of that makes a dent in my loneliness. I have no man, I have no child.

ME: But you know that children are no antidote to loneliness.

ME: I know.

ME: And you know that children only belong to their parents temporarily.

ME: I know.

ME: And you know that men and women can never wholly possess each other.

ME: I know.

ME: And you know that you'd hate to have a man who possessed you totally and used up your breathing space . . .

ME: I know—but I yearn for it desperately.

ME: But if you had it, you'd feel trapped.

ME: I know.

ME: You want contradictory things.

ME: I know.

ME: You want freedom and you also want closeness.

ME: I know.

ME: Very few people ever find that.

ME: I know.

ME: Why do you expect to be happy when most people aren't?

ME: I don't know. I only know that if I stop hoping for love, stop expecting it, stop searching for it, my life will be as flat as a cancerous breast after radical surgery. *I feed on this expectation. I nurse it. It keeps me alive.* [emphasis supplied] (pp. 277-278).

No feeling—love, fear, anxiety, depression, or agitation—exists merely as a habit or autonomously. Feelings are a consequence of a person's way of writing his biography or living his basic myth. Most people choose not to face this fact. They would rather believe their feelings are under complete external control, and so they seek behavior therapists and others who indeed affirm this view.

Instead of seeing the meaningful connection between his priorities and his feelings, a person will choose to blame himself and call himself sick. His goal here is to deny the negative aspects of his life, of his own decisions and what Sartre (1956) calls the coefficient of adversity (i.e., the unavoidable difficulties in life). Yet the very feelings that the person complains about are the absolutely appropriate responses to his desire to maintain his world view.[10]

A woman says she wants to be perfect and decries the resulting frustration of her failures. She is unwilling not only to face her choice to be perfect, but even to tinker with the fact that if she only had the courage, she could change her basic choice, convert herself. She cannot acknowledge her personal myth: "It is too risky to approach someone on an equal basis; it is too risky to see life in its contingency. Perfection, the ideal image of me, is an ordering security operation in my life that I cherish." But she feels her frustration and depression indicate that something is wrong with her.

---

[10]cf., Rychlak (1958, p. 473).

A young man continues to abuse women, to take revenge on his unloving mother, and feels lonely, somehow detached from life and feeling. He wants to be loved but chooses not to face the fact that the past is the past, that it cannot be rewritten, and that revenge is in fact an attempt to remake what is true: that his mother did not love him as he wished her to. That fact, he hopes, can somehow be redone. If he discontinued feelings of anger and revenge against his parents, he would become a psychological "orphan," needing to be responsible to and for himself. He could then look only to himself for the source of his project and its resultant difficulties. But the avenging person does not wish to do that, and for good reasons. It is, admittedly, a risky venture to take back the puppet strings that he has given over to others (parents, habits, biology, God), and so he continues to give up control over himself. To give up one's life for others has the consequence of self-awareness. Thus neurotic anguish is substituted for authentic anguish that seems to be attendant upon the realization that there is no basis for commitment other than the courage to leap in the face of ambiguity (cf., Singer, 1965).

Consider a married couple who cannot tolerate any more than a sparse degree of intimacy and who have covertly "contracted" to be exactly as they are. They choose to ignore the validity of their choices and their needs and focus instead on blaming each other for the negative aspects of their limited relationship. They say covertly, "Yes, I want to be just this close and no more," but this declaration is intolerable in light of the social and personal images and myths each harbors and cherishes about how they should be and what the ideal marriage should be. When they faced in therapy their choices to maintain a limited degree of intimacy, both seemed to be freed from the images they held. This explicit awareness led to a greater freedom based on living and declaring what in fact *is*. At one point the husband said, "I know, baby, that you are not the greatest lover in the world. I've been around, I've had some real swingers, I guess I want you the way you are. I don't know how I could be with those other chicks." Their relationship cannot compare to the bliss described in the *Ladies Home Journal*, but it is now more authentic, and so less blaming, and includes the *possibility* of a deepened relatedness, if they so choose.

The basis for the real relationship for which the HE therapist strives is equality. The relationship entails respect, taking the person seriously, facing free choices, and seeing that both are undetermined and completely without excuse. I agree with Singer (1965) that the necessary condition for the therapeutic happening is an authentic relationship, where as Kaiser (1965) says, "The person stands behind his words." Not all therapists are for all persons, but each person absolutely deserves the therapist he *stays* with because psychological therapy is not a medical art. It is, or can be, the deepest of human encounters. Perhaps that is all that can be asked of any relationship.

ACCEPTANCE AND CHANGE

One of the basic propositions of most psychotherapeutic approaches is that acceptance is an absolutely necessary condition for personality growth. The common admonition is to accept the person as he is and where he is. Yet acceptance, like love, cannot be willed, though it can be put on, acted, or pretended. True acceptance is born of a cosmology that includes in it a belief that persons are free, that they are all potentially aware, that there is no black box of an unconscious that introduces an inescapable disunity into the personality, and that persons are capable of explicitly knowing and sharing the reasons for their actions if they only wish to look.

When a person says in therapy, "I don't know," we often respond by saying, "That sentence means 'I don't care to look or pursue it.'" This is a critical juncture that separates HE therapy from other types or ways of viewing persons. If one believes that there is on principle an obscure and inaccessible part of the person (Hall, 1954; Freud, 1949), then one will be likely to respond to "I don't know," with tolerant, benign understanding: "Of course you don't know, it's unconscious." Overtly or covertly, the message of the reality of an unknowable, obscure part of the person is transmitted. On the other hand, if one holds, for example, that there cannot be censorship without a censor who knows what needs to be censored, that the person is quite potentially lucid to himself, then one might say, "Look, when you say, 'I don't know why I don't get an erection with her,' you are saying that you don't want to look, to attend to what you are doing and feeling or not feeling, and the possible good reasons for it. It's not so deeply hidden that you can't find out. Of course, finding out might mean that your penis is right about your relationship with her. There's some risk in looking." In any way that we respond we inform the person what we believe to be true about people. Wheelis (1969) has stated it very nicely when he discusses the rewriting of a patient's history in terms of subjective, arbitrary necessity vs. objective or mandatory necessity (see chapter two).

In this context, let me restate briefly the HE attitude towards the determining unconscious and towards the determining past. The unconscious exists only insofar as the person deems its existence, through the choice not to be explicitly aware. The past has no reality other than that which the person himself chooses to give it. In fact, for many persons, the construct of an unconscious or of a determining past *is* the project that leads them to do what they want, to constantly escape the responsibility for their lives (see also Singer, 1965, p. 79*ff*.).

On what basis then, can we really accept a person as he is without being saccharinely romantic or inauthentic? I believe that an accepting attitude can follow the recognition that a person has freely chosen to do and to be what he is and that he has chosen this way *for the best of all reasons* (cf., Corey, 1966). Why else would people tolerate so much suffering in their lives? A hypothesis of suffering based on the idea of repetition compulsion or of masochism born as a child of Thanatos is untenable, logically indefensible, and succumbs to the myth of naming. I prefer Nietzsche's view that "Man always acts rightly" (Clive, 1965, p. 368). In the most apparently destructive and painful of relationships and events, if one looks clearly, one finds the best of hopes, the most optimistic of goals and pursuits.[11] People choose to maintain that hope in the face of the most massive deleterious consequences and disconfirmations of their hopes and their images; they refuse to believe what they see. Instead, they maintain the image of their fond hope and discount the reality of what is. Rather than attend to the reality that choices carry their own duties, that life contains its own independence and may answer the demands persons make upon it with yeses or noes, persons attempt to evade that independent postion and tend to blame themselves and call themselves inadequate. Such maneuvers are designed to deny others and the reality of a causation independent of them.

The inauthenticity of most feelings of inadequacy or self-hate and guilt is exemplified by the statement, "If I were other than I was, then he would have married me. If I were better, sexier, more beautiful, then he would have acted differently." These comments deny the other's independence, and deny the reality of the self. They maintain the myth of omnipotence: "I can determine and control his responses still, by more skillful manipulations." The other *must not* be independent; he must not make his decisions as a function of his own reasons, independent of the person who is speaking. "I cannot bear this freedom; I have to be able to do or be something to manipulate him and so place him under my control. I cannot bear to see that he is he and I am I—that no matter what I do, he might still act in a way that displeases me." Since this person cannot bear an independent position, she chooses to maintain her self-deception of inadequacy. She cannot bear to be able to say, "Listen, this is who I am. Here I stand before you as I am, in my full reality. If you like it, come and we shall deal with us. If you don't, tell me clearly."

Consider the example of a young woman who believes that her life is run by a committee of elders who have direct control over her and over the events that occur in her life. When her therapist returned from vacation, he was greeted with the statement that this hiatus was planned against her by the committee who did not want her to be involved with anyone. For this woman, the recognition that people go away on vacation of their own

---

[11]This is put well in the following excerpt:

Secondly, while I listen—and this is very helpful to me—I try to look at his disturbed behavior not as "pathology," but in terms of what this behavior and what his symptoms possibly express in terms of their meaning to his whole living. What is it he tries to tell me? Often, "neurotic behavior and symptoms" express as much as possible the degree to which a patient can live with integrity in an adverse family or cultural situation. I look not for his pathology but for his integrity (Colm, 1973, p. 153).

independent choosing, that they do things for them, and not against her, and that there is no ruling body to which she can appeal is frightening because it leaves her essentially powerless to control the behavior of others that hurt her. In believing that there is a structure in which everything is mapped out, that controls everything, she escapes the ambiguity of independent others, of surprises in her life, of the ambiguous future, and believes that she has some recourse.

> The future is *in principle* unknown and unknowable, which means that all habits, defenses, and coping mechanisms are doubtful and ambiguous because they are based on past experience . . . I am convinced that much of what we now call psychology is the study of the tricks we use to avoid the anxiety of absolute novelty by making believe the future will be like the past (Maslow, 1960, p. 59).

A client says, "I really don't believe in masturbation. I am a nun, after all, but I did it, do it, and feel guilty about it." Such a statement clearly denies the person's reality. An honest man does not steal, and a person who really believes that masturbation is wrong for *her* does not masturbate. Obviously this person believes that masturbation is not wrong for her, simply *because* she does it. In some general, abstract sense, she believes it is wrong for others, but she denies what she really believes about herself. She will not face her own reality and must generate feelings of guilt to justify her acts and be able to say, "After all, I am getting help for it!" Such persons cling to the image of what life should be for them in the face of the reality of what, for good reason, it in fact is. For this nun to face reality, to be in good faith, and to declare herself as she is seems more frightening because it could lead her to sense herself, her own freedom to be, and she chooses not to attend to this freedom.

Consider also the physician who stated in a group that the only way he knew he was worthy was through the approbation of others. When he was asked whether he ever got this kind of praise, he stated that he did. One group-member then replied that since he did get it, that should be over with now; he should now feel worthy. Another then asked whether "it worked"; whether, he in fact did feel worthy when he got the praise he wished. The man answered that there is never enough and that in the face of its complete bankruptcy, he still pursued his goal of winning praise from others. This man clearly wants to hold onto his mythology ("I am good when others say I am") based on a comparative, statistical maneuver that we term the *rating game*. He does not want to question its basic comparative-competitive structure. This is another good example of how persons *refuse to believe what they see.*

For the therapist, it is contradictory to at once accept a person as he is and, on the other hand, work for his change. By working for movement, change, actualization, or growth, the therapist affirms the self-deception of the person who comes to him for help. The therapist's goals imply that he, too, believes, covertly or overtly, that the person is somehow inhabited, bedevilled, or possessed—that he is somehow trapped by external forces in a position that he should not be in and does not want to be in, but cannot help. This is truly the demonology of modern psychotherapy.

I hold with Corey (1966) that a person is in precisely the state he should be in, and that if he truly believed he would be better off in some other state, he would be there. This is not such a radical thought as it sounds. There are intimations of this position in Jung (1966), Sullivan (1953), Fromm-Reichman (in Bullard, 1959), Maslow (1962) and Singer (1965). Further, I believe the person is where he is for the best of all possible reasons: as a result of his priorities, or more specifically, because he denies the negative consequences of his decisions and priorities. He would rather call himself deficient—and so still maintain control over basic ontological realities. Much as the medieval gnostics believed that if they were more pious, they would not fall ill with the ague, so modern man believes that if he were "adequate" or self-actualized or growing, he would escape the negative aspect, the price, the "coefficient of adversity," that must be embraced as part of life if life is to be lived in clarity.

Whether a client chooses to give up his denial of reality is up to him. Sometimes individuals will prefer their known pain to the unknown pain that changes will bring. As one person put it,

> Look, you bastard, I now have a beautiful relationship with him; I've made it. And it hurts so much when he rejects me. The good part is great, and the bad is awful. I guess the more aware you are, the more you feel everything. Who knows, maybe being alone as I was, depressed, not feeling much of anything, being safe, was better.

Perhaps! But this person chose to attend to the pain that being safe caused her. If she did not, she would never have sought help. She chose to risk opening herself to experiences that she had previously avoided. No one can say that there is some ideal, greater virtue in suffering the pain and joy of an intense relationship, as opposed to suffering living alone, experiencing the diminution of feeling generally but being tranquil (Dumont, 1968).

It is also not the therapist's task to point out alternatives, as many say, but merely to help the person become aware and to attend to the situation of his life as he structures and construes it.[12] The therapist's goal is to help the client see the meaning and integrity of his life, that he is doing what he wants, but chooses to ignore the negative consequences of these wants. A man who had difficulty attaining an erection with his girlfriend is an example here. The body does not lie; it tells the true nature of events that

---

[12]Such pointing out would imply that the person does not know the circumstances in *his* own life, that the therapist knows the patient's circumstances and options better.

persons do not wish to attend to on a cognitive level. A standard formulation of this man's lack of sexual potency might be,

> You don't become aroused with her because you have some unconscious conflict, some repressed wish that your impotency expresses in a twofold way by at once expressing the unconscious wish and punishing yourself for it. If you make the unconscious conflict conscious, if you discover why you don't get an erection with her, then you will attain genital primacy and be able to have satisfactory intercourse.

In contrast to this view, the HE might think about the man's "impotency" in this way,

> You're not turned on to her for good reasons. Your head is saying you should have sex with her, but your body doesn't lie. Let's look at the good reasons you may have for not being turned on. Under what conditions do you want to have sex? What are your values about making love?

If this person understood clearly why he does what he does (i.e. attempting intercourse when he really doesn't want to), the result might not be satisfactory intercourse, but rather that he would continue doing what he was doing beforehand with greater relish. This differs from the orthodox viewpoint, where the result of understanding would be considered to be the performance of satisfactory intercourse.

I find that the most effective comment is, "Are you really doing anything you don't want to do?" This sentence dignifies, affirms, and integrates the person's life. It is the basis for acceptance on the part of the therapist and implies that the person is following his own intentions for his own good reasons. The centripetal force in therapy is the assumption that persons act with integrity. This view is the framework that can lead to a reunification of the personality and is the authentic source of acceptance.

At this point, let us summarize the HE therapist's basic communication to the client: the way the client is, fully expresses who he is and what he has chosen; it denies (a) that he has chosen this way for the best of all possible reasons, (b) that there are negative and positive consequences of his or any choice, and (c) that he has denied the reality of his choices. The person has accomplished this by removing himself from the world into an uninvolved-with-the-world, omnipotent or decoupled position. Here he has denied the negative aspects of his choice or the world's or the other's independence through a project of self-controlling self-change. In this project of self-change, there is overt passivity, but secret or covert transcendent subjectivity.

The underlying assumption is that the person has been violated and has participated in (again, for good reasons) the violation of his experiential world (i.e., he has been evaluated, objectified, and disconfirmed). Consequently, he is fearful again, for good reasons, of knowing, uttering and declaring who he is, what he wants, what his project is, and the priorities that his basic choice orders. Prevented from direct self-expression by his fears, the person expresses who he is in devious ways, and permits himself little explicit self-awareness. His behavior seems to have only a distant relation to his appropriate, but unstated wants. Further, the person denies the reality that his feelings show him by tearing his feelings away from their objects. Instead, he prefers to see his feelings (or lack of feelings, as in apathy) as wholly intrapersonal and intrapsychic events. But feelings are *about* or *in terms of* a situation; they are between the person and the world.

The intention of the therapist's communication is to affirm the person *as he is*—to help him come into reality by helping him to utter, explicitly declare, and affirm the validity of his position as he sees it and experiences it now, and as his feelings inform him of it. *Always, always, it is a search for the truth and correctness of the client's position rather than pointing out the distortion of his vision.*[13] Affirmation helps the person reclaim what he *is* but has "lost" because he has sold out. The therapist also points out that the negative aspects of the client's choice *are real.* They exist in the world, and not necessarily within him as a function of his "neurosis." Further, and importantly, there are negative and positive aspects to (a) current choice; (b) his denial of that choice; (c) his choice to declare himself authentically; and (d) his accepting the good reasons for having chosen to be the way he now is, and to rechoosing a way of being.

Affirmation of the person's needs and wants, not his behavior, is a crucial element in therapy. The person's continuing self-affirmation, his ability to declare, "This is me; this is what I want," seems to be a function of his seeing the very good reasons for his behavior and how he denies the consequences of trying to achieve what he wants through the means that he has chosen. It is important to note the difference between confirming or

---

[13]Boileau (1958) has expressed a similar position:

It appears that the focus of most therapy is explanation and understanding behavior rather than the need, and in so doing, therapists expend great time and energy wending their way through symbol and defense to make order out of chaos, and conscious out of unconscious. This is calculated to effect in the patient an insight into the devious, symbolic, and distorted path between need and behavior. The emphasis is obviously placed on the unacceptable behavior and its developmental history. If, on the contrary, we should focus our attention, not on the complex, devious, and highly individual behavior, but on the more simple, universal and acceptable needs, we may be able to support the need with an ego-enhancing effect, *rather than interpret behavior and alienate the ego with what may be seen as criticism.* [emphasis supplied] In dealing, for example, with a problem involving a sexual fetish, one could focus his approach on discovering its origins, its fixating experiences, and possibly insightfully clarify for the patient certain oedipal facets of its emotional import. Our major communication would be directed toward separating the patient and his needs from his behavior, i.e., the symptom. If, on the other hand, we assume initially that the symptom is a devious way of getting love because a more direct method is blocked by fear, we can integrate the symptom into the need it expresses and deal with the total acting unit of the person. . . . Our communication is that the fetish equals love and love is acceptable, rather than that the fetish equals "wrong habit" and, therefore being unacceptable, must be understood and changed. . . . To reject the symtom by focusing interpretation on its process of development is *to repeat the provocative rejection* with which the parents previously blocked its normal direct expression [emphasis supplied].

Such approaches tend to suggest to the patient that the need is unacceptable because the expression is infantile (pp. 634-35).

supporting the person's behavior and affirming what the person wants, needs, and hopes for in a situation. A supportive statement might be:

Pt: I just don't want to hold my feeling back any longer.

Th: I think that's a good idea.

An affirming statement might be:

Th: Now you must have a good reason for feeling that way, for now choosing to declare yourself—not that there are no negative aspects to *that* choice.

The goal here is to affirm the person's *perception,* the good reasons for that perception, and the appreciation of the negative and positive aspects that come from that declaration.

Another goal, equally important, is to work towards the person's eventual independence from the therapist's affirmation, or anyone else's. An instance of this is given by Boileau (1958):

> All therapists are familiar with motivation problems expressed by patients in the form of complaints such as, "I don't know what I want to do," or, "I know what I should do but I procrastinate." Such patients usually regard their own accomplishments as worthless and insufficient. The therapist usually focuses his attention on the patient's deficiency and sets himself to uncover the conflicts which block the person from the attainment of his goals. He does not focus on what might be inappropriate, neurotically conceived goals. He does not conclude, as perhaps he should, that the patient is seeking love and acceptance through the pursuit of such goals, identifying his value, as perhaps his parents did, with achievement. When the therapist implies by looking at the patient's deficiency that the goals are legitimate and need no examination, he implies also that the patient is at fault. *He therefore repeats the original parental attitude which did not accept the person but criticized his lack of performance* [emphasis supplied]. A major conscious goal of the patient in therapy is to discover why he is unable to attain a certain criterion. He does not question the criterion; he questions himself. Often, an effort to adjust to an inappropriate criterion is hidden in an apparently legitimate complaint such as, an inability to study, concentrate, or get down to work. If the therapist accepts the problem at this level and attempts to aid the patient to understand why he cannot study, he is assuming the legitimacy of the goal and therefore becomes an exponent of the inappropriate criterion set by the patient. He again focuses on the symptom whether he intends to or not rather than on the simple need to feel of worth. If at all points of procrastination and lack of motivation, the therapist debunks the suggested goal with such statements as, "Why do you want to study?" or, "Why do you have to be anything at all?" two major reactions result: (a) the patient begins to evaluate these supposedly inviolate goals himself and begins to become his own criterion of what is worthy, (b) it becomes evident that he can feel of value and get acceptance even though he openly admits he doesn't care at all about writing the great American novel....

Pt: I seem to drop back in the same old rut. I messed around for four days. Didn't have any fun either because I should have been studying.

Th: What do you mean, "Should have been studying?"

Pt: Well, if I'm ever going to get that degree... if I get another "D" my old man will give me hell.

Th: What do you want the degree for?

Pt: Well, I can't be a bum all my life.

Th: Why not? Who says you can't?

Pt: You know sometimes I feel like just doing that ... lying around on some island.

Th: Is there anything wrong with that?

Pt: Well, no, I guess not, but I'd like to have some dough and do a few things.

Th: If it won't get you what you want, I see what you mean.

Pt: Yeah, I'll get that degree, and if I can use it I will, and if not, I'll tell people to go to hell and be a mechanic. I really like messing around with cars, but I could never afford one. If that degree can get me a car, it will be worth something.

By questioning the goal upon which he measured his degree of acceptance we can observe the beginning of motivation which makes the goal an avenue to reward rather than a criterion of his worth. We did not, on the other hand, make an effort to understand and explore the origins of his procrastination. Such a procedure would have placed us automatically in the position of the father attempting to discover why he did not measure up (pp. 612-13).

TRUSTING AND CARING

Often persons in therapy state that they do not wish to declare themselves because they don't trust the therapist, the others in their therapy group, or they are "not ready." But what is there to trust? In trusting, we wish to predict the future and control or limit the other's responsiveness to us. We do not want to be surprised. The need for trust as a precondition for self-declaration reveals precisely the decision that the person has made as to his position in the world.

The person who waits for trust declares that what is more important to him is not self-declaration, but how he will be received, how he will be responded to. "I trust you, therapist, wife, lover, friends, to respond to me without surprises, the way I want you to respond. In this way I can be safe from you and from a genuine encounter between us."[14] An authentic response would be, "Listen, I don't know how you will respond to me; you are not under my control. You are an independent entity. You are you and I am I, and since I can't predict how you will respond to my talking to you in this way, and anyway, I don't think I would want to since I respect your subjectivity, I'm merely going to say what I have to say in the face of the uncertainty of you." Indeed, the therapist who promises, as a precondition, to be kind, gentle, good, accepting, understanding, or supporting falls into bad faith himself since he will deny what he in fact feels and is. As Sartre

---

[14]See also Singer, 1965, pp. 220 *ff.*

(1956) points out, we may promise to make a rendezvous with ourselves to be a particular way when we enter into a particular situation, but we never know who shall show up to meet us there. Perhaps authentic promises are impossible between persons.

An unspoken promise or contract between persons to be kind rather than authentic leads to an obliviousness between persons and to an opacity within the self that eventually diminishes selfhood. If I deny my own feelings to others often enough, I soon begin to lose a clear sense of who I am and what is true for me. This is precisely the situation in which most persons find themselves when they come to therapy. They are so resigned to not paying attention to what is true for them, they so distort their selves by evaluating or judging what in fact they do feel, they so ignore the validity of their responses to a situation, that they find themselves terribly unsure and confused. They are so alienated that they do not know what to do. Usually alienated people have substituted an essentialistic, ideal world that exists "out there" for the truth of their own vision. A "serious" view of the world is used to distort, manipulate, control, and change what is true for that person. By placing himself under the aegis of an external reality, he can evade responsibility for his life, for the fact that each of us has, in fact, created the whole show.

I believe it is an error for the therapist to buy the trust paradigm as a precondition to authentic declaration, and thus permit the person to escape from his own and the therapist's freedom. By acknowledging the need for trust, the therapist reinforces the person's bad faith project of giving control of his responsiveness to someone else. On the other hand, a refusal to accept the need for trust (and the manipulating transaction it implies) runs right into the person's resistance because it is precisely the myth of external control that the person wants to maintain. His actions say, "Yeah, Doc, control over me is out there. I have nothing significant inside of me for which I need to be responsible, so condition me out of this state of mine. I don't have any control over it, nor over me. You do."

To put it another way, the project is for the person to make himself a complete subject to his biology, to his history, to his impulses, to Eros, to Thanatos, to conditioning sequences impinging upon him—in short, to abandon his subjectivity. And often the psychologist agrees, "No one owns his own personality . . . and society has the duty—and the means—to change it for the better" (McConnel, 1970, in the table of contents).[15]

Rather than support the client's need for trust, a more appropriate and honest response from the therapist might be, "You are right not to trust me. What you are saying by asking me for trust is in reality your wish to be safe of me and of others' free, spontaneous subjectivities." (Here, the thera-

---

[15]For an alternative point of view see Powers, 1973 a and b.

pist affirms both his own and the person's absolutely independent freedom). "The only thing that you can trust is that I shall respond as I respond, from me. But my response shall be to you."

Again, adopting the view that we are independent subjectivities does not evade the negative aspects of *that* position: it is risky, unsafe, felt as contingent, unpredictable. But it is the ground that may foster the growth of a genuine relationship, with its ecstasy and its despair. Much depends on how much ambiguity and discomfort a person can tolerate. If he has no set, narrow definition of life, he may be able to tolerate quite a bit; if his view of life is essentialistic and narrow, however, he may experience great discomfort. There is no a priori statement that HE can make about any one mode of life being better than another in some abstract, ideal way, just as long as the person is aware of what he is doing and authentically affirms it.

ON RESISTANCE AND TRANSFERENCE: AN HE VIEW

It would be helpful to discuss here two key factors in psychotherapeutic thinking—resistance and transference—in light of traditional counseling and psychotherapy and to compare them with an HE approach. My goal here is to elucidate a way of thinking about persons that permits the therapist to establish a more accepting and noncritical or affirming response to the person.

Resistance

Resistance has been defined by Freud as "anything that interferes with the course of analysis." It is the work of the unconscious Ego. Though recollection or the recovery of lost memories is still regarded as the goal of psychotherapy, it is believed that these will be recovered with less difficulty if attempt is made by the analyst at the same time to uncover and surmount the resistance. Freud has outlined recently five kinds of resistances: (a) Ego unwillingness to give up repressive counter-charge, (b) Ego reluctance to renounce symptom gain or relief, (c) Transference resistance (an Ego resistance)—an attempt to evade recollection through reenactment or repetition of infantile experience, (d) The Id repetition-compulsion urge . . . (e) The need for punishment arising out of the demands of the Super-Ego (Healy, Bronner, and Bowers, 1930, p. 466).[16]

It seems to be a major tenet in the psychotherapeutic literature that patients resist or even reject the communications offered by the therapist in his interventional comments, confrontations, or interpretations. Classically, this kind of resistance is thought of either as a part of the neurotic wish to sabotage the therapeutic process or a failure on the part of the therapist to intervene appropriately; the interpretation was "too deep," "given too early," or "too late" to be accepted. In any case, resistance on the patient's part is thought to be negative, something to be overcome or circumvented

---

[16]For an analogous modern view that is essentially similar cf., Strupp, 1968.

by the skill of the therapist or the healthful acquiescence of the patient.

Early formulations of resistance linked resistance to repression—both reflecting the more generalized *regressive* characteristics of people in general, and of patients in particular. As Healy et al. (1930) points out, resistance at first was thought to be a manifestation of the ego's machinery for keeping unacceptable id impulses under control and out of awareness. These impulses would otherwise disrupt the real world if permitted into consciousness. It is just this *partially* successful repressive force that was seen to be resistance in psychotherapy.

As I have commented earlier, new developments in psychodynamic therapy or depth psychology theory lend greater support to resistance as a function of the superego. Here, resistance is seen as a psychological masochism born of inevitable superego function and inherent intrapsychic conflict (Trilling, 1971). In this view, the patient must remain "ill" or neurotic in order to suffer and atone for the unatonable—for what he considers to be his essential and basic guilt. There are two important implications of this view: (a) The person will not get better or be cured because he feels he has not yet atoned for his guilt for incestuous impulses (in the case of the male) or penis envy (in the female); and (b) *He can never fully atone* because the superego is totally unreasonable: As Trilling clearly points out, "the more the Ego submits to the Superego, the more the Superego demands of it in the way of submission" (1971, p. 44).

It was thus that current psychodynamic thinking elevated psychic masochism as a central explanatory aspect of human and psychotherapeutic functioning. Man is a child of Thanatos, inexorably divided, and so he will and must resist all efforts at seeing reality. Resistance, therefore, is fully in line with the psychoanalytic image of what constitutes a person. Most theorists—and the HE as well—agree that denial of reality is at the core of human problems, but where the disagreement comes is on what man will see when he looks clearly. The psychoanalyst states that what will be seen by man is his inherently conflicted, regressive, violent, Thanatos-dominated nature. And most current theories are variations on that theme: the person (for unhealthy reasons) avoids looking at reality because seeing it clearly would bring an upsurge of anxiety. Resistance is but a sign of the "sickness" in man and must be overcome. This is true also for the neoanalytic schools that do not view resistance as a neurotic accommodation to the polarity represented by Eros, or the pleasure principle, and Thanatos.

The more proactive theorists such as Sullivan, Horney, and Fromm-Reichmann see resistance as a way in which the person courts survival. Here resistance is less a result of a regressive force than an expression of what the person sees as a basic necessity for ego-enhancement and self-esteem. In sum, it serves a personal integrity that would threaten the person's image of himself if he abandoned it.

In each system, however, the basic premise is that the person must change; he has to give up the neurotic foundation of his way of life for another—the therapist-theorist's view. In the therapist, the patient sees the model for which he must exchange his own experiential view. As Hans Strupp has written:

> The task of the therapist is to convince the patient of the irrationality, futility, and self-defeating aspects of his defense (resistive) maneuvers, thus encouraging their abandonment. As a substitute, he implicitly offers his own ego (attitudes, beliefs, values, etc.) as a new and better model for interpersonal collaboration (1968, pp. 309-10).

The presentation of this model as an alternative to his own view, the push to change, is the basis for resistance and anxiety in the person:

> The therapist cannot help but become anxiety-provoking because his behavior is a thorn in the side of the patient's orientation.... The analysis of resistance is, therefore, the therapist's expression of faith in an alternative in living, the patient's giving up resistance is his admission that he sees such a possibility (Singer, 1965, pp. 240-41).

But in HE terms, this *is precisely the violation* (i.e., the admonition to change) *that has caused the person to become a patient in the first place!* And now he is asked again, in subtle, covert, seemingly benevolent terms, to give up his view of reality for that of another—and for the therapist's reality yet! According to Singer, "It has often been said that the most depressed group of people in the world are psychiatrists and psychoanalysts. I think this is a correct observation and stems from good reasons ...and so I tend to be depressed about myself" (1972b, pp. 55-56).

How, then, to work with a person without placing *us* in the untenable position of at once accepting the patient as he is and at the very same time committing the implied violation of working for his change was the essential question to which we addressed ourselves before, and now again. In the HE view, what the person *resists* is:

1. The fact that he is free.
2. That he has chosen to be in the situation in which he now lives.
3. That he has done so for the best of all possible reasons.
4. That his situation, born of his project and personal myth, has negative as well as positive aspects—as does any situation.
5. That living with others has its negative and positive aspects, and is a difficult enterprise at best.
6. That he denies his being-in-the world via an omnipotent project— that there are other free subjectivities in that world: that there is facticity, and a coefficient of adversity that belongs to that world.
7. That his responses are his correct ones in terms of how he perceives others and the world, and
8. That each view of reality *and* his present position brings fear and

despair equally with joy and ecstasy. It is his choice to change or not. (See-ing clearly is change enough.) That even deadening or hardening one's heart against the world has its negative and positive aspects.

Thus, the HE therapist holds that resistance is *not* something to over-come but *is a valid position in the world.* The person has to accept himself as a resisting self, even embrace his resisting and defensive self. What tends to be denied is that *that* valid, resistive position has negative as well as pos-itive aspects, as does any other position. HE Affirmation Therapy and counseling neither hammers away at resistance through ever more pene-trating or arcane interpretations, nor ignores it. Instead, the HE therapist affirms resistance and the good reasons for it without implying (secretly) that the person would be better for its dissolution.

Rios and Ofman (1972) offer an instance of HE Affirmation Counseling with a Mexican-American youth:

Counselor:	Hi.
Jesus:	Nothing. (leans back in his chair, folds his arms, and places one leg upon the small table between the counselor's chair and his) Nothin' man, nothing to say.
Counselor:	O.K., that's fine.
Jesus:	Why you sayin' that?
Counselor:	Shoot, why not? You're saying that it's better if you talked rather than be silent?
Jesus:	Weeell, wouldn't it? Ain't that what it's supposed to be all about, talkin' is the thing, ain't it?
Counselor:	Hey no, man. I can't see that rapping is better than not talking. I dig that you don't want to talk today. You must have a valid reason for that or you wouldn't do it.
Jesus:	Yeah, I know, you're always sayin' that. You know there was somethin' I was thinkin' about rapping with you today about on the way over. But I don't know if I can trust you, I'm sorta scared. How you'd react, ya know?
Counselor:	Yeah, well, I understand that, why you want not to talk to me today. That seems right. It is scary to tell someone something you feel funny about. And you don't know if you can trust me—how could you know? You're right on about that you don't know how I would respond.
Jesus:	Yeah, you might think I'm a weirdo or something.
Counselor:	I think you're right, I might think that, but I don't know, and neither do you. Hell, I don't know how I'll be until I'm there. It's risky, scary.
Jesus:	Right on! (quietly but intently) But that's the way it is with me, I'm scared shit of chicks. That's why—that's why I hang around with the guys a lot. I mean in the john and all.

Counselor:	Yeah, I can understand that, I've felt it myself a lot. Being scared of people and chicks. But it's right, it seems, to be scared of people. You never really know about 'em, you can't psych 'em out, predict 'em. Like you said, you didn't know how I would react unless you confronted me and found out through that. Then you'd really know. And I might react altogether differently tomorrow. Sure, that's a heck of a good reason for hanging around the guys, you know, it keeps the fear down.
Jesus:	How . . . Yeah, but I can't hang around with those guys for the rest of my life.
Counselor:	Why not?
Jesus:	Well, it ain't much fun no more.
Counselor:	Yeah, I can see that. There are negative aspects to hanging around only with guys. You seem to feel you're missing something. But, on the other hand, it's safe.
Jesus:	Yeah, I don't like to go out and meet strange cats, chicks and all. But you know, I kinda feel that there is something weird with me because I feel like that, shy, you know. Hey, you mean there ain't nothing wrong with that?
Counselor:	I don't see any reason to change, do you? You seem to have chosen what you want (laughs), and for the best of reasons—like I keep saying.
Jesus:	Hey, I gotta split now, but what do you think, should I come in again Monday? Earlier than Friday, I mean.
Counselor:	That beats me. If you feel like this is good for you, sure, that's great (pp. 262-64).

Here, the counselor supports Jesus' silent position, even makes a good case for it, as he does with his preference for toying with homosexual activities. That leads us to an important point. After Jesus affirmed the legitimacy of his fear, he seems willing to come and talk more to the counselor "earlier than Friday"—not that talking to the counselor and relating has any greater ideal value than being shy and frightened. Relating has as a consequence its own fear and uncertainty. But it does seem to be a step for Jesus, who had been coming to the counselor sporadically. It should be pointed out that if Jesus had gone in another direction, that of not wanting to risk and relate, not even to deepen his relationships with the "guys," that would have been his responsible choice and, in that sense, perfectly legitmate.

At all points the counselor's purpose is to help the person face and affirm his reality and to see that the position the person takes has its associated coefficient of adversity. The goal here is not to make the counselee adopt a new position—that is up to him—but to help him face the reality of the negative aspects that are part of the position he has chosen for good reasons. His fears are not irrational. He is not sick or crazy. To intimate that is to play right into his defensive posture and cater to his lack of responsibility. Persons do what they do because it is all the anxiety they can tolerate. The issue, however, is joined when the counselee denies the negative aspects of the position he has chosen by choosing to feel inadequate, sick, inferior, or confused. The counselor chooses not to further that by joining with him in a project of change ("Yeah, you really are screwed up"), but rather addresses himself to the reality to which the client has chosen to attend and to the positive and negative aspects of his choices.

Corey (1966) gives an example of therapy that is quite in line with a HE Affirmation approach. In this example, he deals with the resistance of what he calls a "rigidly defensive impotent male" who sought help on the basis of his wife's threat to leave him:

Pt: I don't really have anything to talk about this evening. Maybe it's because I just left work and I'm thinking about that.

Th: I think that the reason you have nothing to talk about this evening, or really any of the other evenings you come in, is that there is nothing to talk about. There really is no problem to discuss. You've got it made, so to speak. Everything is going for you just the way you want it.

Pt: Well, if I have it made, as you say, why am I coming here and paying you all this money?

Th: Very simple. You don't really believe that you do have it made just the way you want it. The day you can see that that is true and understand why it is so, you won't need to see me any more. You insist upon seeing the situation as a great big neurotic problem for which there must be some big, unconscious pathological reason; and if you could only discover what that was, you could then approach your wife. Then you top it off with a big fantasy that that will happen in therapy some day, if you come long enough. The reason you don't have sex with your wife is because you don't want to; it's as simple as that.

Pt: Yes, but there must be some reason. It's not normal to not want to have sex with your wife.

Th: Who says you have to have sex with your wife, if you don't want to?

Pt: Yes, but that's why I'm coming to therapy—so I will want to. I'll admit you're right. I don't really want to. I think it's because if I try, I'll fail; and I don't want to fail.

Th: No. I think it's the opposite way. You fail because you don't really want to in the first place.

Pt: Yes, but again, that's why I'm coming to therapy—so I'll want to.

Th: I think you kid yourself. That's not why you are coming to therapy. You are coming to therapy to placate your wife, to get her off your back. What you do is kid yourself with this big delusion you are coming here to work on your problem, as you call it. In truth, you come here because you are afraid to go home and tell the wife to stop bugging you with this sex deal, and that you will have sex with her if you want and won't if you don't want to. Of course, it's understandable that you don't want to take the risk. You really have a good system for you here, at least while it lasts.

Pt: I guess you're right. I could certainly feel the anxiety in me while you were saying that. I wouldn't dare tell her I wasn't having sex with her just because I didn't want to. I fear she might leave me; this way she's very kind and patient because she knows I'm coming to therapy; and she realizes therapy takes a long time, particularly with a problem like mine (pp. 119-20).

In the final analysis, the HE sees resistance as the very appropriate effort of the person *not* to be violated by the other.

Transference

The basic, traditional psychodynamic viewpoint holds, as I have previously indicated, that man is basically conservative and thus is heir to a repetition-compulsion. This repetition-compulsion, because of the epigenesis of psychosexual development, tends to revolve around the basic problem of human development, the intrafamilial struggle, and especially the Oedipus Complex.

By transference we refer to a special kind of relationship toward a person; it is a distinctive type of object relationship. The main characteristic is the experience of feelings to a person which do not befit that person and which actually apply to another. Essentially, a person in the present is reacted to as though he were a person in the past. Transference is a repetition, a new edition of an old object-relationship.... It is an anachronism, an error in time. A displacement has taken place; impulses, feelings, and defenses pertaining to a person in the past have been shifted onto a person in the present. It is primarily an unconscious phenomenon, and the person reacting with transference feelings is in the main unaware of the distortion (Greenson, 1967, pp. 151-52).

Essentially, the transference is but one basic category of resistance, and its handling—the fostering of a transference neurosis—is the core of psychoanalytic treatment. As Fenichel (1945) says, "Understanding the contents of the patient's unconscious from his utterances is relatively, the simplest [!] part of the analyst's task. Handling the transference is the most difficult" (p. 29). Fenichel goes on to say that psychoanalytic treatment naturally produces powerful feelings such as joy, unendurable tension, happiness, and relaxation, as well as specific feelings towards the therapist—"an intense love, because the analyst is trying to help him, or bitter hatred because the analyst *forces* [emphasis supplied] him to undergo unpleasant experiences" (p. 29).

But, importantly, what complicates the problem is that the person experiences contradictory feelings such as hatred towards the analyst *for* the help he is offering the person, or the person loves him "for imposing an unpleasant restriction." Further complications obtain, states Fenichel, when the patient blatantly distorts or misconstrues the "real situation and loves or hates the analyst for something which, in the *judgement of the analyst,* is nonexistent" (emphasis supplied).

I will not comment on the fact that the situation in the analytic hour is so designed to bring about the "facts" that the analyst then "finds" in the patient (cf., Shepard and Lee, 1970). From the HE position, *little is absolutely misconstrued in the therapy hour*. It is true, in my experience, that troubled persons are often extraordinarily sensitive to the subtleties of human interaction and to the subtle violation inherent in roles, masks and games. They are experts in sniffing out violating transactions and respond to them even when the therapist deceives himself about them or is inattentive of them. In my experience, *each and every* time that a patient has committed a so-called transference distortion, the entity alluded to has been there but denied in me as a therapist. To deny missed feelings or ambivalence and to emphasize only one side of an emotional encounter is more comfortable for the therapist. When the person-who-is-now-a-patient sees behind the mask (which is denied) to the *totality* of the situation, and the therapist, because of threat or discomfort, denies that totality, the therapist commits the same kind of violating mystification that has made the person a patient. I can be certain that when a person sees ambivalence, hate, disdain, distance, fear, boredom, withholding, or indifference, *it is there*—even though it is there in minute degrees. He is essentially right, and it is up to the therapist to search out the part of the communication that holds the feelings that the person correctly senses. Conversely, when the therapist has blown up at a person or been angry, and the person responds with and to the seemingly opposite feelings as well ("You care for me"); that too is there!

Fenichel says, "Resistance (transference) distorts the true connection. The patient misunderstands the present in terms of the past" (1945, p. 29). The HE says that the patient understands and sees better than we are willing to admit because it forces us to face the totality of our feelings and the reality between us.

> Patients laugh and posture when they see through the doctor who says he will help but really won't or can't.... When you find people who will really help, you don't need to distract them. You can act in a normal way. I can sense if the doctor not only wants to help but can and will help."... This provides... striking confirmation... that the schizophrenic ceases to be schizophrenic when he meets someone by whom he feels understood (Laing, 1965, pp. 164-65).

Even though he is caught in the orthodox conception of transference phenomena as "distortions," Boileau (1958) sees that there is an implied violation in negating the reality to which the patient responds in his transference situation. Boileau points out that the common way of dealing with, let us say, a patient's reaction to his boss, seeing the boss as if he were the patient's father, was to "incur discrimination whereby the patient could know that feelings and attitudes relevant to his father were not relevant to his boss" (p. 636). This assumes that if the patient can discriminate adequately, he can then respond appropriately to both the father and the boss.

However, the hazard in such a therapeutic goal is primarily that in order to obtain this discrimination, the patient has to be shown that he is wrong—that the boss is all right but he, the patient, is misinterpreting the boss as father. This, in the HE view, is a violation, and the inevitable result of that violation is that the patient will feel misunderstood and criticized. The goal that Boileau wants to accomplish is short of the HE mark, but approximates it:

We all grant that a transferred reaction gives us, i.e., early reactions to the father in a present day form in the person of the boss. Emotionally for the patient the two people are equal. In making a therapeutic effort to get the patient to discriminate we not only deny the legitimacy of his father reaction, but we remove the boss as the father's present day equivalent against whom the patient directs his father conflict. If, instead of working for the patient's discrimination, we enable the patient for the first time to reject and direct his grievance against the father through the boss, we accomplish two major things. (a) We do not appear to criticize the patient by interpreting his transferred reaction but rather accept his anger against the father-boss as legitimate. (b) We enable the patient for the first time to attack and defend against the father, a thing impossible in his early dependent life....

Most important to our affirmation position:

Regardless of euphemistic defenses which a therapist may give that his interpretations are not criticisms, they can be felt in no other way by patients who in the case of transference interpretations are asking to discriminate between emotional identities, that is, parents and transferred parents (1958, p. 637).

Boileau correctly states that any interpretation is an implied violation and has to be dealt with as such. But the HE affirmation therapist addresses himself to the *correctness*[17] of the person's seeing—to that component that *is in fact* common to them both—the boss and the father, the father and the therapist—but the correctness of which is denied both by the person and by the therapist. The major focus *is not* upon the violating teaching of discrimination, but the opportunity for dealing with the problem of the person's attempt to encapsulate himself from a real relationship with the therapist by maintaining a decoupled, omnipotent position. The emphasis in therapy is on finding the person's correct perception and affirming it.

In the transference, the person experiences a want in terms of the therapist. It does not matter at all that the want is something the person may have wanted before, in childhood, in adolescence, or from someone else. We are what we are now because we have been. No one was born ready-made into the world as a youth or an adult. All of us have a history; it is us! While it is true that many attempt to "fix" their histories as if it were now, it really does not matter. It is *experienced* as we, now.

The major issue in therapy is that the person himself will not affirm the

---

[17]cf., Colm (1973).

legitimacy of his wants because doing so places him in the world of others with whom he will have to engage and deal. The person will not declare himself by stating "Hey, this is what I want from you" and permit the other to respond from his independent position, and thus remain in the engaged encounter. The person prefers to neutralize and diffuse the encounter by doing it all in his own head, by making it all pure interiority: "I will not permit him to reject me. I will reject him . . . or feel rejected before he has actually rejected me." Or the person asks without asking. Because of real violating circumstances in his past, the person correctly senses that asking is a risky business. One task of the HE therapist is to affirm the *correctness* of the person's perception of the risky business of (a) knowing what one wants, and (b) asking clearly what one wants. It needs only to be pointed out that there is an absolutely reciprocal relationship between these two operations.

Again, Corey (1966), gives an excellent example of this concept in the following brief interview:

Pt: I wish you would ask me to go out to dinner with you.

Th: You would like me to change the nature of our relationship?

Pt: Yes. Would you?

Th: I take it you would like to change the nature of our relationship, but you are asking me to make that change. What I am interested in is what changes *you* would like to make.

Pt: Well, I think it would be nice if we could go out to dinner together, and then maybe we could go over to my house for drinks afterwards.

Th: I haven't heard you ask *me* out to dinner.

Pt: Well, *would* you go out to dinner with me?

Th: From the way you say that I have the feeling that what you are really asking me is to state my position in this matter. Which, of course, is really quite a different thing than your really asking me for what you want, which then would be a statement of *your* position.

Pt: I can see what you mean. That would be frightening. I can feel the difference—but you wouldn't really go out to dinner with me. You'd feel it wasn't ethical for a therapist to take his patient out to dinner.

Th: How do you know if, in such a situation, I would be ethical or not?

Pt: Well, you know you would, wouldn't you?

Th: I wouldn't really know until I was asked. I would have to decide then. In certain ways it is similar to the situation that would exist if my colleague were to come to me and ask me to loan him a thousand dollars. I don't know if I would or wouldn't until he had asked me and I had heard him out. Now the point of all this is that one of the tricks you play upon yourself to control your anxiety is to create a fantasy that you know what the future holds and you know what's in the other person's mind. You see, if you already "know what my answer is, then you can tell yourself that you'd be a fool to ask. Of course, asking the other person for permission or agreement, or to state his wish are just techniques to avoid anxiety that true asking inevitably involves. You long for life and love, but close yourself off from it, too, and seek to approach life in safer ways. In past sessions you mentioned that you have become very demanding with your boy friend; this too, is another way of avoiding true asking. When we demand we are saying: "I don't want to know if your answer is yes or no; your answer must be of my choosing, because it creates too much anxiety in me to let myself be aware that I don't control you, my source of help and gratification.

If the patient should really ask the therapist for what was wanted, or at least the therapist thought so, the therapist would miss a fine, if not crucial, opportunity to provide the patient with a *no* experience. The transference brings this whole question into sharp focus for the patient. The criterion for real asking is the willingness to accept no for an answer. Usually a person says to himself: "The reason I asked was to find out what the real answer was, now I've got my answer, which is what I wanted." To the extent the person is demanding, he is still saying that he must have an answer of his own choosing (evidently the Biblical admonition, "Ask and ye shall receive," means that asking is what opens one up to receive the gifts of life). Again, the purpose is not to get patients to ask for what they want (though it may sound so) but to demonstrate that they don't and dare not ask, and that both advantages and disadvantages derive from their stance toward life that exposes them to the win/lose phenomena of reality: they are living in reality and are being "realistic" but don't know it (pp. 122-23).

In sum, the HE conception of the transference is that for good reasons, "*I* will not see *you* as a different, unique person in your own right. I have to make you, therapist, into a predictable, knowable, controllable object-person, who is *like* the people I knew."

In a very real sense, that speaks to all of us—to the way in which we choose to handle our projects in life—in either facing the hazard of being-in-the-world and engaging on a day-to-day, minute-by-minute basis with the unpredictable Other, or in remaining in a decoupled, encapsulated inner world where it is all in our own hands—where the Other and the world barely exist. The living in reality, in engaged reality, means giving up oneself to a responsible self and to a responsible world. Instead, many prefer the "You can't be you. You (world, Other) have to be as *I* want to be." Being in reality means giving up the paradigm: "I am God, but you are not, and I will not admit it." Living in reality means facing the most bafflingly real paradox in life: the living of life in all its immediacy where the question of how we can be two gods together is deeply engaged.

BEING THERAPEUTIC VS. THERAPEUTIC BEING

I have attempted, in brief terms, to sketch an HE approach to the therapeutic process. This approach is blatantly subjective, hominocentric, concrete and, in my view, occurs within the context of an engaged encounter. I have spoken of the HE position on some selected, standard, therapeutic practices, and emphasized that the relationship is the central core of the approach, the forge within which the person can come into reality. I have tried to touch upon some dimensions of the therapeutic relationship and want to conclude with the goals of HE counseling and psychotherapy.

Let me begin by referring to an amazing echo from the literary past: a 1917 review by D.H. Lawrence of Trigant Burrow's book, *The Social Basis of Consciousness* (Lawrence, 1963). Lawrence commends Burrow for being a truly honest man in that he is a truly *humanly* honest man. For example, he is honest about his own subjective experience which Lawrence says is rare among professionals. The cause of this rarity is the fact that men, "especially men with a theory, don't know anything about their own inward experiences" (Lawrence, 1963, p. 162).

Burrow was honest in that he saw that something was vitally wrong both in the theory and the practice of psychoanalysis, and his book was an answer to what was wrong. According to Lawrence, the following were Burrow's basic arguments:

1. In applying a theoretical structure to his patients he was, in our words, trading in the reality of that person "there" for a theory into which the person must fit. "But the mind could not be open, because the patient's neurosis, all the patient's experience, *had* to be fitted to the Freudian theory..." (p. 163). Burrow was dissatisfied with the mechanistic process of trying to fit the richness of life into a theory:

> In short [says Lawrence] the analyst is just as much fixed in his vicious unconscious as is his neurotic patient, and the will to apply a mechanical incest-theory to every neurotic experience is just as sure an evidence of neurosis in Freud, or in the practitioner, as any psychologist could ask (p. 163).

2. Instead of the conflict among impulses and instincts, the basic difficulty with man is his sense of isolation, alienation, or separateness that is born of his uniquely human consciousness. In man's ability to reflect upon his consciousness, man became split:

> Suddenly aware of himself, and of other selves over against him, man is a prey to the division inside himself. Helplessly he must strive for more consciousness, which means, also, a more intensified aloneness or individuality, and at the same time he has a horror of his aloneness, and a blind, dim yearning for the old togetherness of the far past, what Dr. Burrow calls the preconscious state [and for what we shall, in a moment, define as un-self-conscious, confident, being] (p. 164).

3. One of the contributing factors to this split is an egocentric absoluteness of the individual that is related to man's image building activity. With self-consciousness came man's building a picture of himself—an ideal image as it were, and then man began to live according to that picture. He began to believe in the press releases about himself—releases that he

created out of whole-cloth. Indeed,

> Mankind at large made a picture of itself, and every man had to conform to the picture, the ideal... and began to live from that picture: that is, from without inwards. This is truly the reversal of life. And this is how we live. We spend all our time over the picture. All our education is but the elaborating of the picture.... It is all the death of spontaneity. It is all, strictly automatic.... *The organic necessity of the human being should flow into spontaneous action and spontaneous awareness, consciousness* [emphasis supplied] (p. 165).
>
> Humanity, society, has a picture of itself, and lives accordingly. The individual likewise has a private picture of himself, which fits into the big picture. In this picture he is a little absolute and nobody could be better than he is. He must look after his own self-interest. And if he is a man, he must be very male. If she is a woman, she must be very female.
>
> Even sex, today, is only part of the picture. Men and women alike, when they are being sexual, are only acting up. They are living according to the picture. If there is any dynamic, it is that of self-interest. The man "seeketh his own" in sex, and the woman seeketh her own: in the bad, egoistic sense in which St. Paul used the words. That is, the man seeks himself, the woman seeks herself, always and inevitably. It is inevitable, when you live according to the picture, that you seek only yourself in sex. Because the picture is your own image of yourself: your *idea* of yourself. If you are quite normal, you don't have any true self, which "seeketh not her own, is not puffed up." The true self, in sex, would seek a *meeting,* would seek to meet the other. This would be the true flow; what Dr. Burrow calls the "Societal consciousness" and what I would call the human consciousness, in contrast to the social, or "image-consciousness."
>
> But today, all is image-consciousness. Sex does not exist, there is only sexuality. And sexuality is merely a greedy, blind self-seeking. Self-seeking is the real motive of sexuality. And therefore, since the thing sought is the same, the self, the mode of seeking is not very important. Heterosexual, homosexual, narcissistic, normal or incest, it is all the same thing. It is just sexuality, not sex. It is one of the universal forms of self-seeking. Every man, every woman just seeks his own self, her own self, in the sexual experience. It is the picture over again, whether in sexuality or self-sacrifice, greed or charity, the same thing, the self, the image, the idol: the image of me, and norm!
>
> *The true self is not aware that it is a self. A bird, as it sings, sings itself. But not according to a picture. It has no idea of itself* [emphasis supplied].
>
> And this is what the analyst must try to do: to liberate his patient from his own image, from his horror of his own isolation, and the horror of the "stoppage" of his real vital flow. To do it, it is no use rousing sex bogeys. A man is not neurasthenic or neurotic because he loves his mother. If he desires his mother, it is because he is neurotic, and the desire is merely a symptom. The cause of the neurosis is further to seek (p. 165).

I believe that the model for the therapeutic enterprise is not the distant, hierarchical relationship that exists in most of orthodox psychotherapy, but rather in an intimately engaged encounter between the therapist and the person. In such an encounter, the life of the violated person-now-patient is deeply engaged and reified in the microcosm that is the therapy situation. This kind of situation ought to be as natural, pedestrian, direct, and free from artifice as is possible in the paradox of a relationship lived within the constraints of a therapist's office.[18] It should be the very opposite of the isolation and loneliness of which Wheelis (1958) writes:

> What, then, is the experience of such an analyst in his chosen field? He directs toward his patients certain unconscious attitudes and impulses which, were they put into words, would sound somewhat as follows:
>
> "I am a technician of loneliness, but suffer from the malady I treat and spend my days alone, silent, listening. I am tormented by an ineludible yearning to lose myself in the inner life of another. And yet I never dare.
>
> But I am devious, I am clever. I find ways. My need lies unseen behind a mask of calm understanding. My synapses click briskly, indefatigably, with un-utterable dryness. I keep trying. I find ways. I have found a way to make others—others who suffer—come close to me.
>
> *Tell me your thoughts.*
>
> Speak to me . . . I want to be close to someone, want to lose for a moment the crushing burden of my insufferable and isolate identity. But I can't open my heart and come close to you. I am afraid. And deep down, because I am afraid, I hate. I don't dare come close to you. You come close to me. Tell me whatever crosses your mind.
>
> *Perhaps it is some thought of me that blocks you?"*

The HE engaged encounter is the converse of this very encapsulation. Stein, a modern Jungian analyst, offers an analogous view when he states that the new model for the therapeutic ritual must, above all, recognize that it is the genuine relationship (not the transference) between the therapist and person that is of central import in therapy. For him, the breaking of the encapsulated position and the cultivation of a human connection are the goals of the therapeutic process instead of self-knowledge or the expansion of one's consciousness. He recognizes, nevertheless, that these are inter-dependent goals:

> The goal of the relationship is to move from the initial archetypal Parent-Child constellation to one of equality and personal involvement. The goal of the process and the goal of the relationship go hand in hand, so that one can not be reached without the other. Thus, when the relationship becomes truly personal

---

[18]cf., Lomas:

In sum, what I am trying to show is that psychotherapy is primarily an ordinary interpersonal activity, and the special technical procedures to which psychotherapists resort are, at best, of secondary importance, and, at worst, inhibiting factors. The belief that it is primarily a technique is, to a large extent, a defensive maneuver—one that is subsumed by the contemporary scientific approach to human behavior—designed to avoid the pain, risk and uncertainty of emotional involvement. Many of the procedures which are characteristic of psychotherapy—understanding, interpreting, holding, and so on—may occur in ordinary life and would be taken for granted by a healthy society—one less schizoid-obsessional, more attuned to the recognition of human feelings, than our own. And even our society—so ready to apply the label "technique"—could hardly consider those qualities such as warmth, honesty, integrity without which a therapeutic endeavour is still-born, to be anything other than part of the ordinary business of creative living (1973, p. 149).

and individualized, [unique] this is an indication that the therapeutic ritual is nearing its goal (1973, p. 165).

To further illustrate the HE approach, the following pages present a therapy hour with a tyro therapist in the final stages of his therapeutic apprenticeship. It begins with discussion concerning a videotaped therapy session that this person conducted in a practicum setting and that was observed by the supervisor-therapist. The hour is at once an example of what is sought in therapy and a dealing with the usual issues in therapy.

One major point needs to be made. As therapist, I struggle along with the person coming to me to come into a genuine dialogue—an I-You relationship. Reality, responsibility, and radical authenticity are the issues that are engaged in this relationship and are the very fabric of the therapy. These are the subjects that I attempt to activate and realize in the work. Indeed, that *is* the work: the approximation and attainment of these goals, and the reaching for mutuality, which is the essentially healing act, the therapeutic happening. The mutual, engaged encounter cannot, must not be merely spoken *about* (though, at times, that cannot be helped, it seems); it must be incarnated in the hour. It must be real between us, not merely discussed.

Th: The basic idea which I want to expose to you is this: I want to talk to you about *response,* and what it really means to me—with most of us, Phil, and certainly in the way that you have been exposed to in Gestalt and your other therapy, you've been taught to be a therapist to you, to yourself, so that most of your respondingness to others has been in terms of how you have learned to respond to yourself, in terms of you. Your common position or common stance to the people whom you see is, "I am aware that you make me feel this way or that way." It is as if you, when you were doing therapy with Sue on the tape that I watched ...

Pt: Hm, hm ...

Th: Your gaze was down, into you, not at her. You were not looking at her. It was like this (therapist demonstrates Phil's body attitude as being bent over, with his head down, as if he were looking at his own knees).

Pt: Yeah, hm, hm. That's right. I can see that.

Th: So that what you were primarily aware of, Phil, is not of Sue but of you and your responses, inside of you. Phil, when I touch your hand, like this, technically, what I am aware of is that what I feel is my hand feeling yours. But phenomenologically—like if we were to ask a child what he feels—and existentially what I feel is your hand, I feel the roughness of your hand, a callous here, the separation of your fingers here, the cracks in your hand. It's like when you are inside your wife, when you are making love, that is, you don't feel your penis ...

Pt: (interrupts) I feel her vagina, yeah.

Th: That seems to be true.

Pt: Yeah, yeah (excitedly).

Th: You see that immediately! How come you can see that ...

Pt: That was . . . I believe that is my experience. I touch my wife, I don't sense myself touching her. I sense her. It's as if the feeling is there, not here.

Th: Here is what I want to share with you.

Pt: All right.

Th: When I concentrate on you, Phil, just as I am doing now, I am not here. The only reason that I know that I am here is because I am leaning forward and I see with my peripheral vision my hand waving in front of me. Phil, just look at me very carefully.

Pt: I am just . . . just thinking about that . . . that is very heavy.

Th: How?

Pt: Well, how, what makes it heavy is that, that in order . . . as I concentrate on you, as I am aware of you . . . in order to come back and be aware that you are doing this and this to me, I really have to leave you.

Th: You have to withdraw into yourself.

Pt: Yeah. I have to leave you.

Th: You have to withdraw into what you came into therapy for, into the controlling attitude. Control, Phil, means "I have to be aware not of you but of me—of my body, of my feelings."

Pt: Of your impact on me.

Th: Not only that. Kids never say, "I am aware that you are making me angry." They say, directly, "Get away from me." They don't inform the other of their inner process; they respond directly to the other by pushing him, shouting an epithet at him, but it is always a direct, nonmanipulative response, and it is immediate, and so when I am here looking and concentrating on you, interested in you, my responsiveness is full and in terms of you; it seems, I respond directly to you without the filtering process that is self-conscious of me. There is no self-consciousness at that moment, just a second ago.

Pt: Unless you do bring it back, and start looking around to see where you are at . . .

Th: . . . and then I leave you. Consequently, when I respond directly we can both un-self-consciously, spontaneously and confidently know that we are appropriately responding to each other. That I am not here, I am there, between us. Somehow when I directly attend to you, my attention feels over you, on you, all over you, that is how it feels. That is, by the way it occurs to me, the meaning of interest: "inter-esse."

Pt: Yeah, my attention is divided, my interest is divided when I choose to attend to both you and me as separate things.

Th: Now, and this is important because of what you call your sexual problem, you report to me that when you make love to your wife—or when you try to— when you are aware of your penis—whether you are hard or not—when you are aware of your condition, you are not turned on. When you say that you are paying attention to *her,* what your hand was feeling in her breast, in her face, in her hair, when you looked at her as you were caressing her, then you said that your penis was hard and full and throbbing.

Pt: My God, yeah . . . (quietly) yeah.

Th: You see, if I could lose my self-consciousness to let the normal organismic process of my body take over, I am a stud, and so are you. When a horse fucks, Phil, he does not look down at his penis to see whether it is hard, he just climbs on, and his body acts appropriately to the situation as he experiences it. His response is direct, and his attention is full.

Pt: (impressed) Hm. What I am thinking now, is how does this match up with my sex therapy[19] this idea of sensate focus on *me*. Maybe if I focused on her, not in doing things *for* her, but somehow on her—by God, that, it seems to me, is when things worked out the best, when we were into each other, not as you call it, paralleling, but just to go back to Sue for a moment, you feel that what I was doing, this thing with Sue, that I was concentrating on me rather than being with her. Where I was at...

Th: Rather than responding directly to her, it was as if you were responding to your responses—that's right! It's a second-order event. You were responding to your responses to her.

Pt: God! How does one, how do I respond directly? You know, I don't know how. How?

Th: With great difficulty! Because every bit of education and training, and especially therapeutic education...

Pt: ...has been what's going on with me.

Th: That's right. Has been to withdraw you to make that a...a...a withdrawn, therapeutic-theoretic distance between us. Where we substitute the person for the theory and, instead of immediately, Pow! like that to what the person presents, we substitute that for a studied "intervention."

Pt: Yes, yes, it has.

Th: That is, in a nutshell, I believe, what you say you are suffering from. Your loneliness—that you think, you deliberate, you withdraw—and for good reason—to sense the situation wholly within you instead of between us, between you and Sue, between you and your wife, between you and most everybody.

Pt: That's my stinginess, my control and my withholding, yeah, I really see it.

Th: Well, it would have to be that way, wouldn't it? That is why you come back next week and say you were angry last week.

Pt: Because I have to go back and think about it when I am alone.

Th: Yeah, that's the meaning of control.

Pt: (laughs, chuckles, in an embarrassed way) It's...sounds...it's such a thing. It's going to require some new...

Th: Look at me, you are looking out the window now. There it is, isn't it? You want to withdraw and work it out all within yourself.

Pt: My goodness, that requires a new way of being. No longer can I do my usual routines.

Th: Which are?

Pt: Which are, "You are angering me," or "I'm sensing...whatever," which is the usual thing that I do, or something, I know.

*   *   *

Last time with her, she was telling me that I wasn't telling her about my feelings. It hits me now, that I *was* my feelings, they were right out there, it is just that I wasn't verbalizing *about* them. The way I was acting *was* my feelings. It's like...

---

[19]The patient is concurrently conducting and in sex therapy.

Th: It's like the best way I would know that she was turned on was that she was wet. She doesn't have to tell me, "Oh, I am turned on, I am so excited, etc." That's the way I know. The body doesn't lie.

Pt: You mean the way she is acting.

Th: No, the way her body is.

Pt: O.K. But the wetness in her vagina, I mean, maybe she doesn't have a wet vagina when she is turned on. What I'm saying...

Th: Then she is not fully turned on...

Pt: You think that is the...

Th: Of course! Just look at it. What's more valid? "I am hungry," or "I want to eat and am preparing food?"

Pt: My point is a technical point. My point is that a woman does not necessarily have to be wet when she is turned on.

Th: Excuse me. My view is that the wet vagina is the turn-on. It is the sign and the signal that she wants sex. Unless there is some physiological pathology where she does not have those necessary glands, or something.

Pt: Oh. Hmm.

Th: Well, it is just like an erection. You don't, and I don't get turned on when you pay attention to you. You are, then, not with the woman, you are somewhere else. You don't permit *her* to turn *you* on. The situation between you is not a turn-on. And I can understand that desire to control. I want, you want to do it all by yourself. Can you see that? You are with your fantasy, or you're with you, but mostly you are with "How am I doing?" But you're not "there," you're (points to *Pt*) "here."

Pt: (says it simultaneously) Here. God, I've got to go home and listen to this tape.

Th: You are doing it right now. See that...

Pt: I've got to do that, to go home and listen to this.

Th: You're doing it right now. That is one of the reasons that I'm beginning to object to patients' taping of their sessions with their therapists.

Pt: I—O.K.—it's so difficult. Oh, I don't know how to do this. I am so used to being with people in this manner. I don't even know the language that goes with that.

Th: There is no language! You don't have to think about the language. Something will come.

Pt: What I want to do is go out and think about it, about this.

Th: Do you see how we withdraw?

Pt: I withdraw from everyone.

Th: I respect that. I mean, sure, you would have to according to the way in which you see things. I respect that. What is it? You seem itchy to me.

Pt: I...I'm...it's such a different way of being, it makes me sweaty and itchy.

                              *   *   *

Th: (later; *Pt* tells of an incident about last week) I am not interested in hearing about that.

Pt: (sarcastically mimicking the therapist) "I'm not interested in that, I'm not interested in that."

Th: You are reporting to me about you, and I'm not interested in that. It's dull.

Pt: Listen, when you say that you are not interested in that or something like that, it doesn't really bother me, well ...

Th: If it doesn't bother you, then you are not listening to me, you are erasing my importance and my significance here between us. You are not taking me seriously.

Pt: When you said it then, I said to myself, "Oh, fuck." It didn't faze me.

Th: But then you're saying that you are not paying attention to me. When I pay attention to you and I am really with you, "there," when you say to me that you are not interested in that, O.K. I am not going to go on unreeling myself in your presence; that is a rape.

Pt: Rape?

Th: When you are not interested in what I am saying, and I keep saying it anyway, I am raping you.

Pt: Well, I must rape you.

Th: It's like forcing a sexual act on someone who is not interested in that with you.

Pt: Yeah. I guess I rape you a lot. You say to me, "I am not interested in that," and my response is, "Well, I want to say it anyhow."

Th: Well, to whom are you speaking? You are, then, just speaking. You are not speaking to me.

Pt: Yeah, sometimes I talk just to hear myself talk ... sometimes.

Th: Well, no wonder you are lonely. That's withdrawal to which the loneliness is related.

Pt: I guess I don't want to wait around until you have decided you want to listen.

Th: Either you are interested in my being ... in what is happening here, interested in us and me, in what is happening in this relationship, in our having a relationship where we attend to each other, or you are interested in our being parallel witnesses one to the other.

Pt: Listen, I came in here very relaxed, and I feel very nervous now; it's a new idea. I can't be my old relaxed self like with the other therapists—tell them stories and report on me, what happened to me last week, last year, and so on or something. I am telling you ... sounds like the rules are different.

Th: The rules of therapy that you were used to with others are different here. Is that what you are saying, that you don't like that? You see, Phil, I am doing it now. I am withdrawing behind a withdrawn, self-conscious, reflective attitude now, where I am aware only of myself and very little of you. We've both done it. Even our physical postures are different. We've both sat back in our chairs. I feel my voice is much more controlled and even. Do you hear it?

Pt: Yeah. Reminds me of yesterday when I saw [X]. I think that is where I am now. I have too many goddamn things on my mind ... and ... and ... it seems like it's taking energy to stay here, to consider what we are talking about.

Th: What you're ... look, you don't want to pay attention to me.

Pt: I think that is what I am saying, yeah.

Th: All right. I can accept that. There must be a good reason for that.

Pt: Right now I don't want to relate to you. I do and I don't. It seems very significant to both of us ... and I don't want to spoil that opportunity because I don't want you to think badly of me—that I don't appreciate this.

Th: You are worried about me?

Pt: I am worried about your response to me or our relationship or something like that, yeah.

Th: Be clear with it so that I can really feel it and be with it.

Pt: O.K., you have really said something to me today. But when you, when we started our hour today, I thought you were going to say something critical of me, of my tape with Sue, or something like that. As though you had seen something in that tape.

Th: I did, I did!

Pt: I thought, God, what's gone on! Everyone there thought that tape was good, good work.

Th: Well, Phil, you are a perfect representative of that whole psychology department. That is what they teach people to do, don't they? To be self-consciously, intrapsychically reflective. But not to respond directly and immediately to the other person. To substitute the theory for the person, even authenticity for the person, but not to respond to that person who is there. You are a perfect example of what you have been taught.

Pt: (laughs) So, I've been doing very well.

Th: Magnificently! And that is what bothers me.

(*Pt* tells a story of what happened in one of his practice sessions and an argument he had with one of his supervisors.)

Th: I hate to admit this, Phil, but I was not with you at all. I thought you were not talking to me. I am somewhat ashamed of myself. But that's the truth.

Pt: I talk a lot for me. I say things a lot for me.

Th: Then it's no wonder that I drifted away. Goddamn, do you see that?

Pt: You sensed that I was not with you and . . .

Th: Yes, so I drifted off. How correct a response that is.[20] It kind of illuminated the reality of our situation at that moment. We were not engaged.

Pt: (sighs)

Th: What?

Pt: Eh. (laughs) You are presenting me with something new. I am really into that other mode of being of "I am feeling" and "I am sensing" and not really with you. I have never seen it so clearly, though, and in myself and in the other therapists that are in training with me.

Th: You were a perfect model of a therapist with Sue, the perfect model of an encapsulated man who responded to the response to the response to the response of what she presented to you.

Pt: Yeah, I responded to the response that she elicited in me. I agree.

Th: It is as if it were an echo from the other room.

Pt: Somehow, I must pay attention to you and not solely to me. Wow, that is hard!

Th: When you pay close attention to me, then you don't have to decide, to deliberate how you will respond. You *will* respond.

Pt: With whatever.

Th: Yes. That is how you begin to trust yourself and . . .

---

[20]That is a symmetrical response.

Pt: I can see why I would be afraid of that. I can see why I am afraid of it.

Th: Tell me.

Pt: Hell, I am afraid just to sit here and report, let alone look at you and pay attention to what is happening. I much prefer to kinda roll my eyeballs back into my head and just unroll what is in there. That is scary enough. But to talk to you or anyone who matters, directly—wow!

Th: You are afraid to be with me or anyone who matters.

Pt: Without an agenda or a script.

Th: Yeah, I know, without a "film" between us, without a structure where you can be the person who merely exposes himself to my mute, distant witnessing of your exposition.

Pt: Right on! I come in and just report on the contents of my head, or what happened.

Th: How well I know that. I used to do that with my shrink. I used to lie down on the couch for 4½ years and tell him *about* me. And he filtered the "about me" through his theory, his Freudian system, and occasionally—maybe 20 times during the 4½ years that I saw him, formulated me according to his theory. I knew absolutely nothing about him or about us. Except an intermittent clearing of his throat.

Pt: Hm. (shouts) I cannot concentrate! I leave all the time. But maybe I can watch you, look at you closely.

Th: Well, that is how lovers are, isn't it? They look at each other, hold each others' hand; they stay in contact.

Pt: Hm, hm. Maybe with my wife, I shouldn't think about whether I am turned on or whether I have a hard-on at all. Maybe I should just be with her, see how she is with me, like I'm being with you right now.

Th: How does that feel?

Pt: Oh, it's great, sweaty, and kinda scary. For once, if I can stay with it—I am really being with you, looking at you. It's O.K.

Th: You can sense it.

Pt: One thing is going on. I have a kinda total good feeling. Like you said, maybe I'm not a thermometer to myself. I'm not self-conscious. I am . . . almost, *you* feel good to me. It's like I'm . . . here.

Th: O.K. Our time is up for today.

CONCLUSION

In summary, the goals of HE therapy and counseling are the person's coming into reality and deep subjectivity (Poole, 1972). This means, in very simplified terms, a totally aware, accepting attitude toward *what is,* not what *should* be. It also entails the realization of how authentic being has been eroded by self-deception and by living in the serious world according to the picture of what man "should" be—by responding in the retroflective, preemptive mode (a mode, which, by delusion, *seems* to salvage man from the real insecurity, hazard, and contingency of immediate, lived life). Coming into reality implies embracing, in explicit awareness, the positive and negative consequences of each and every choice one makes. This embracing leads to the position where one can "pay attention" directly to the other, to others, and to what the situation is. Such attention and direct response put the person *in the world,* not inside himself. Attention to the other implies my momentarily becoming a "zero" and thus, permits me to respond. Because I have no room or time to go into myself and process the information through an ideal-image system, thus maintaining a distancing between me and you and between me and the world, I simply respond directly and immediately.

When I say I become a zero (see pps. 180ff), I do not mean to refer to certain mystic modes where I become one with the universe, cosmic consciousness or other such self-deceptive essentialistic structures. It does not mean that I become one with the other or that I lose my identity. It is the fear of such a loss that leads one further inside, deeper into an encapsulated, removed, totally intrapsychic position. In that position the person wills not to be affected and so his feelings are dampened or seem disconnected from others, from the situation.

The "cure" is the process of mutual responding, of engaged, responsibility, involved encounter; in my not being "here" (in myself) but rather being "there" (between us). I am totally responsive, totally attentive—attentive with my whole being.

All of me is activated and bears on that moment, on the essential we. In that way of being, in that mode, I am *un-self-conscious,* confident, totally accepting of you, fully aware. I am alive with and to you and we can each be—together.

References

Allers, R. *Existentialism and psychiatry.* Springfield, Ill.: Charles Thomas 1961.

Allport, G.W. *Becoming.* New Haven, Conn.: Yale University Press, 1955.

Allport, G. *Personality and social encounter.* Boston: Beacon Press, 1960.

Arbuckle, D. *Counseling: Philosophy, theory and practice.* Boston: Allyn and Bacon, 1970.

Arbuckle, D. *Counseling and psychotherapy.* Boston: Allyn & Bacon, 1975.

Arnold, M. *Emotion and personality.* New York: Columbia University Press, 1960.

Arnold, M. (Ed.). *Feelings and emotions.* New York: Academic Press, 1970.

Argyris, C. Essay review of *Beyond freedom and dignity. Harvard Educational Review.* 1971, *41,* 550-67.

Barnes, H. *Humanistic existentialism.* Lincoln: University of Nebraska Press, 1959.

Barnes, H. *An existentialist ethics.* New York: Alfred A. Knopf, 1967.

Bateson, G., Jackson, D., Haley, J., & Weakland, J. Toward a theory of schizophrenia. *Behavioral Science.* 1956, *1,* 251-64.

Becker, E. *The birth and death of meaning.* New York: Free Press, 1971.

Blanck, G. & Blanck, R. *Ego psychology.* New York: Columbia University Press, 1974.

Boileau, V. New techniques in brief psychotherapy. *Psychological Reports.* 1958, *4,* 627-45.

Bonner, H. *On being mindful of man.* Boston: Houghton-Mifflin, 1965.

Bordin, E. *Psychological counseling.* New York: Appleton-Century-Crofts, 1968.

Boss, M. *Psychoanalysis and daseinsanalysis,* New York: Basic Books, 1963.

Brown, N. *Life against death.* New York: Random House, 1959.

Bry, A. (Ed.). *Inside psychotherapy.* New York: Basic Books, 1972.

Buber, M. *I and thou.* New York: Charles Scribner's Sons, 1958.

Buber, M. *The knowledge of man.* New York: Harper Torchbooks, 1965.

Bugental, J. *The search for authenticity.* New York: Holt, Rinehart, and Winston, 1965.

Bugental, J. (Ed.). *Challenges of humanistic psychology.* New York: McGraw-Hill, 1967.

Buhler, C. & Allen, M. *Introduction to humanistic psychology.* Monterey, Calif.: Brooks/Cole, 1972.

Burgess, A. *A Clockwork orange.* New York: W.W. Norton, 1963.

Burton, A. (Ed.). *Case studies in counseling and psychotherapy.* Englewood Cliffs, N.J.: Prentice-Hall, 1959.

Burton, A. The long-term non-psychotic patient. *Voices.* 1969, *5,* 58-64.

Camus, A. *The stranger.* New York: Vintage Books, 1954.

Carkhuff, R. *Helping and human relations.* Vols. I and II. New York: Holt, Rinehart, and Winston, 1969.

Carkhuff, R. & Berenson, B. *Beyond counseling and therapy.* New York: Holt, Rinehart, and Winston, 1967.

Chein, I. *The science of behavior and the image of man.* New York: Basic Books, 1972.

Cioran, E.M. *The temptation to exist.* Chicago: Quadrangle Books, 1968.

Clive, G. (Ed.). *The philosophy of Nietzsche.* New York: Mentor Books, 1965.

Cohn, R. Therapy in groups: Psychoanalytic, experiential and Gestalt. In J. Fagan & I. Shepherd (Eds.). *Gestalt therapy now.* Palo Alto, Calif.: Science and Behavior Books, 1970.

Colm, H. *The existential approach to psychotherapy with adults and children.* New York: Grune & Stratton, 1966.

Colm, H. The therapeutic encounter. In H. Ruitenbeek (Ed.). *The analytic situation.* Chicago: Aldine-Atherton, 1973.

Combs, A. & Snygg, D. *Individual behavior* (Rev. ed.). New York: Harper & Row, 1959.

Conkling, M. Sartre's refutation of the Freudian unconscious. *Review of Existential Psychology and Psychiatry.* 1968, *8,* 86-101.

Cooper, D. *Psychiatry and anti-psychiatry.* New York: Ballantine Books, 1967.

Corey, D. The use of a reverse format in now psychotherapy. *Psychoanalytic Review.* 1966, *53,* 107-26.

Corsini, R. (Ed.). *Current psychotherapies.* Itasca, Ill.: F.E. Peacock, 1973.

Cronbach, L. *Essentials of psychological testing.* New York: Harper & Row, 1960.

de Beauvoir, S. *The ethics of ambiguity.* New York: Citadel Press, 1967.

Deese, J. Behavior and fact. *American Psychologist.* 1969, *24,* 515-22.

Dostoevsky, F. *The possessed.* New York: Macmillan, 1948.

Dulany, D. The place of hypotheses and intentions: An analysis of verbal control. In C.W. Eriksen (Ed.). *Behavior and awareness.* Durham, N.C.: Duke University Press, 1962.

Eliot, T.S. *The cocktail party.* New York: Harcourt Brace & World, 1950.

Esterson, A. *The leaves of spring.* Baltimore, Md.: Penguin Books, 1972.

Fagan, J. & Shepherd, I. (Eds.). *Gestalt therapy now.* Palo Alto, Calif.: Science and Behavior Books, 1970.

Farber, L. *The ways of the will.* New York: Basic Books, 1966.

Fenichel, O. *The psychoanalytic theory of neurosis.* New York: W.W. Norton, 1945.

Frankel, M. Morality in psychotherapy. In B. Henker (Ed.). *Readings in clinical psychology today.* Del Mar, Calif.: CRM Books, 1970.

Frankl, V. *Man's search for meaning.* New York: Washington Square Press, 1963.

Freud, S. *Beyond the pleasure principle.* New York: W.W. Norton, 1961.

Freud, S. One of the difficulties of psycho-analysis. In S. Freud. *Collected papers.* London: Hogarth Press, 1925.

Freud, S. *An outline of psychoanalysis.* New York: W.W. Norton, 1949.

Freud, S. Wild psychoanalysis. In S. Freud. *Standard Edition.* London: Hogarth Press, 1953.

Freud, S. *The complete introductory lectures on psychoanalysis.* New York: W.W. Norton, 1966.

Fromm, E. An interview with Eric Fromm. *McCalls.* October, 1965.

Gendlin, E. Existentialism and experiential psychotherapy. In J. Hart & T. Tomlinson (Eds.). *New directions in client-centered therapy.* Boston: Houghton-Mifflin, 1970.

Gide, A. *The counterfeiters.* New York: Modern Library, 1955.

Giovacchini, P. *Tactics and techniques in psychoanalytic therapy.* New York: Jason Aronson, 1975.

Glad, D. *Operational values in psychotherapy.* New York: Oxford University Press, 1959.

Greene, M. *The knower and the known.* New York: Basic Books, 1966.

Greenson, R. *The technique and practice of psychoanalysis.* New York: International Universities Press, 1967.

Grings, W. Verbal-perceptual factors in the conditioning of autonomic responses. In W.F. Prokasy (Ed.). *Classical conditioning.* New York: Appleton-Century-Crofts, 1965, 71-89.

Hall, C. *A primer of Freudian psychology.* New York: World, 1954.

Halleck, S. *The politics of therapy.* New York: Science House, 1971.

Healy, W., Bronner, A., & Bowers, A. *The structure and meaning of psychoanalysis.* New York: Alfred A. Knopf, 1930.

Hitt, W. Two models of man. *American Psychologist.* 1969, *24,* 651-58.

Hobbs, N. Sources of gain in psychotherapy. *American Psychologist.* 1962, *17,* 741-47.

Hoch, P. *Differential diagnosis in clinical psychiatry.* New York: Science House, 1972.

Hora, T. The process of existential psychotherapy. *Psychiatric Quarterly.* 1960, *34,* 495-504.

Horney, K. Culture and neurosis. *American Sociological Review.* 1936, *1,* 221-30.

Horney, K. *New ways in psychoanalysis.* New York: W.W. Norton, 1939.

Horney, K. *Neurosis and human growth.* New York: W.W. Norton, 1950.

Hospers, J. *An introduction to philosophical analysis.* Englewood Cliffs, N.J.: Prentice-Hall, 1967.

Huxley, A. *Island.* New York: Harper and Row, 1962.

Jacobson, E. *The self and the object world.* New York: International Universities Press, 1964.

Jong, E. *Fear of flying.* New York: New American Library, 1973.

Jourard, S. *Disclosing man to himself.* New York: Van Nostrand-Reinhold, 1968.

Jourard, S. The therapist as guru. *Voices.* Summer/Fall, 1969, 49-51.

Jourard, S. *The transparent self.* New York: Van Nostrand-Reinhold, 1971.

Jourard, S. *Healthy personality.* New York: Macmillan, 1974.

Jung, C. *The practice of psychotherapy.* Princeton University Press, 1966.

Kaiser, H. *Effective psychotherapy.* New York: The Free Press, 1965.

Kaplan, A. *The new world of philosophy.* New York: Random House, 1961.

Kaplan, A. *The self and its identity.* Mimeograph, 1970.

Kaufmann, W. *Existentialism from Dostoevsky to Sartre.* Cleveland, Ohio: Meridian, 1956.

Keen, E. *Three faces of being.* New York: Appleton-Century-Crofts, 1970.

Kelman, H. *A time to speak.* San Francisco: Jossey-Bass, 1968.

Kempler, W. The therapist's merchandise. *Voices.* Winter/Spring, 1969-1970, 57-60.

Kempler, W. Experiential psychotherapy with families. In J. Fagan & I. Shepherd (Eds.). *Gestalt therapy now.* Palo Alto, Calif.: Science and Behavior Books, 1970.

Kiesler, C. & Kiesler, S. *Conformity.* Reading, Mass.: Addison-Wesley, 1969.

Krasner, L. Behavior therapy. *Annual Review of Psychology.* 1971, *22,* 483-532.

Laing, R. Mystification, confusion, and conflict. In I. Boszormenyi-Nagy & J. Framo (Eds.). *Intensive family therapy.* New York: Hoeber, 1965.

Laing, R. *The politics of experience.* New York: Pantheon, 1967.

Laing, R. *The politics of the family and other essays.* New York: Pantheon, 1971.

Laing, R. & Cooper, D. *Reason and violence.* New York: Vintage Books, 1971.

Laing, R. & Esterson, A. *Sanity, madness, and the family.* New York: Basic Books, 1965.

Langer, S. *Philosophy in a new key.* New York: Mentor, 1942.

Laszlo, E. *Introduction to systems philosophy.* New York: Harper & Row, 1972.

Lawrence, D.H. A new theory of neuroses. In M. Rosenbaum & M. Berger (Eds.). *Group therapy and group function.* New York: Basic Books, 1963.

Leary, T. The diagnosis of behavior and experience. In A. Mahrer (Ed.). *New approaches to personality classification.* New York: Columbia University Press, 1970.

Leeper, R. The motivational and perceptual properties of emotions as indicating their fundamental character and role. In M. Arnold (Ed.). *Feelings and emotions.* New York: Academic Press, 1970.

Leonard, G. *Education and ecstacy.* New York: Dell, 1968.

Lewin, K. *Brief encounters.* St. Louis, Mo.: Warren H. Green, 1970.

Lewis, E. *The psychology of counseling.* New York: Holt, Rinehart and Winston, 1970.

Lomas, P. *True and false experience.* New York: Taplinger, 1973.

London, P. *The modes and morals of psychotherapy.* New York: Holt, Rinehart, and Winston, 1964.

London, P. *Behavior control.* New York: Harper & Row, 1969.

Lowe, C. *Value orientations in counseling and psychotherapy.* San Francisco: Chandler, 1969.

Lyons, J. *Experience.* New York: Harper & Row, 1973.

Maslow, A. Existential psychology; what's in it for us. In May, R. (Ed.). *Existential psychology.* New York: Random House, 1960.

Maslow, A. *Eupsychian management.* Homewood, Ill.: Irwin-Dorsey, 1965.

Maslow, A. *Toward a psychology of being.* Princeton, N.J.: Van Nostrand-Reinhold, 1968.

Masserman, J. *Behavior and neurosis.* University of Chicago Press, 1943.

Masserman, J. The biodynamic roots of psychoanalysis. In J. Marmor (Ed.). *Modern psychoanalysis.* New York: Basic Books, 1968.

Matarazzo, J., Saslow, G., & Pareis, E. Verbal conditioning of two response classes. *Journal of Abnormal Social Psychology.* 1960, *61,* 190-206.

Matson, F.W. *The broken image.* Garden City, New York: Doubleday, 1966.

Matson, F.W. *Being, becoming and behavior.* New York: George Braziller, 1967.

Matson, F.W. (Ed.) *Without/within.* Monterey, Calif.: Brooks/Cole, 1973.

May, R. *Existence.* New York: Basic Books, 1958.

May, R. (Ed.) *Existential psychology.* New York: Random House, 1960.

May, R. On the phenomenological process of psychotherapy. In E. Strauss (Ed.). *Phenomenology pure and applied.* Pittsburgh, Pa.: Duquesne University Press, 1964.

May, R. *Psychology and the human dilemma.* Princeton, N.J.: Van Nostrand-Reinhold, 1967.

May, R. Existential psychology. In *International encyclopedia of the social sciences.* Vol. 13. New York: Free Press, 1968.

May, R. *Love and will.* New York: W.W. Norton, 1969a.

May, R. Humanism and the problem of will. In R. MacLeod (Ed.). *William James: Unfinished business.* Washington, D.C.: American Psychological Association, 1969b.

May, R. *Power and innocence.* New York: W.W. Norton, 1972.

McConnel, J. Criminals can be brainwashed now. *Psychology Today.* 1970, *11,* 14*ff.*

Merleau-Ponty, M. *Phenomenology of perception.* London: Routledge and Keegan Paul, 1962.

Miller, A. *The price.* New York: Bantam Books, 1968.

Moustakas, C. (Ed.). *The self.* New York: Harper & Row, 1956.

Mowrer, O.H. Learning theory and the neurotic paradox. *American Journal of Orthopsychiatry.* 1948, *18,* 571-610.

Mowrer, O. H. Learning theory and behavior therapy. In B. Wolman (Ed.). *Handbook of clinical psychology.* New York: McGraw-Hill, 1965.

Muller, J. *The children of Frankenstein.* Bloomington: Indiana University Press, 1970.

Murray, E. & Jacobson, L. The nature of learning in traditional and behavioral psychotherapy. In A. Bergin & S. Garfield (Eds.). *Handbook of psychotherapy and behavior change.* New York: John Wiley & Sons, 1971.

Murphy, G. *Outgrowing self-deception.* New York: Basic Books, 1975.

Naranjo, C. Contributions of Gestalt therapy. In H. Otto & J. Mann (Eds.). *Ways of growth.* New York: Viking, 1968.

Needleman, J. (Ed.). *Being-in-the-world.* New York: Harper & Row, 1968.

Ofman, W. The counselor who is: A critique and a modest proposal. *Personnel and Guidance Journal.* 1967, *45,* 932-37.

Ofman, W. *Psychotherapy as an humanistic existentialist encounter.* Los Angeles: Psychological Affiliates Press, 1970.

Oppenheimer, J. Analogy in science. *American Psychologist.* 1956, *11,* 127-35.

Pande, S. The mystique of "Western" psychotherapy. *Journal of Nervous and Mental Disease.* 1968, *6,* 425-32.

Patterson, C. *Theories of counseling and psychotherapy.* New York: Harper & Row, 1966.

Patterson, C. *Theories of counseling and psychotherapy (2nd ed.).* New York: Harper & Row, 1973.

Paul, G. Outcomes of systematic desensitization. In C. Franks (Ed.). *Behavior therapy.* New York: McGraw-Hill, 1969.

Perls, F. *Ego hunger and aggression.* San Francisco: Orbit Graphic Arts, 1966.

Perls, F. *Gestalt therapy verbatim.* Lafayette, Ind.: Real People Press, 1969.

Perls, F. *The Gestalt approach and eye-witness to therapy.* Ben Lomond, Calif.: Science and Behavior Books, 1973.

Perls, F., Hefferline, R., & Goodman, P. *Gestalt therapy.* New York: Julian Press, 1951.

Peters, R. *The concept of motivation.* London: Routledge and Keegan Paul, 1958.

Pirandello, L. *Naked masks.* New York: E.P. Dutton, 1952.

Planck, M. *Scientific autobiography and other essays.* New York: Philosophical Library, 1949.

Polanyi, M. *The study of man.* University of Chicago Press, 1963.

Polanyi, M. *Personal knowledge.* New York: Harper & Row, 1964.

Poole, R. *Towards deep subjectivity.* New York: Harper Torchbooks, 1972.

Powers, W. Feedback: Beyond behaviorism. *Science.* 1973a, *179,* 351-56.

Powers, W. *Behavior: The control of perception.* Chicago: Aldine-Atherton, 1973b.

Prokasy, W. (Ed.). *Classical conditioning.* New York: Appleton-Century-Crofts, 1965.

Pursglove, P. *Recognitions in Gestalt therapy.* New York: Harper & Row, 1968.

Raimy, V. *Misunderstandings of the self.* San Francisco: Jossey-Bass, 1975.

Rappaport, D. The structure of psychoanalytic theory. In S. Koch (Ed.). *Psychology: A study of a science.* Vol. 3. New York: McGraw-Hill, 1959.

Reisman, J. *Toward the integration of psychotherapy.* New York: John Wiley & Sons, 1971.

Rhinehart, L. *The dice man.* New York: William Morrow, 1971.

Rios, R. & Ofman, W. The Chicano, counseling and reality. In D. Brown & D. Srebalus (Eds.). *Contemporary guidance concepts and practices.* Dubuque, Iowa: William C. Brown, 1972.

Rogers, C. & Skinner, B. Some issues concerning the control of human behavior. *Science.* 1956, *124,* 1057-66.

Rosenbaum, M. Controversies in group psychotherapy. In L. Eron & R. Callahan (Eds.). *The relation of theory to practice in psychotherapy.* Chicago: Aldine-Atherton, 1969.

Rosenhan, D. On being sane in insane places. *Science.* 1973, 250-57.

Rotter, J. *Social learning and psychotherapy.* New York: Prentice-Hall, 1954.

Ryan, V. & Gizynski, M. Behavior therapy in retrospect. *Journal of Consulting & Clinical Psychology.* 1971, *37,* 1-9.

Rychlak, J. *A philosophy of science for personality theory.* Boston: Houghton-Mifflin, 1968.

Rychlak, J. Lockean vs. Kantian theoretical models and the "causes" of therapeutic change. *Psychotherapy.* 1969, *6,* 214-22.

Rycroft, C. *A critical dictionary of psycho-analysis.* New York: Basic Books, 1968.

Sadler, W. *Existence and love.* New York: Charles Scribner's Sons, 1969.

Sartre, J-P. *The emotions: An outline of a theory.* New York: Philosophical Library, 1948.

Sartre, J-P. *Being and nothingness.* New York: Philosophical Library, 1956.

Sartre, J-P. The humanism of existentialism. In J-P. Sartre. *Essays in existentialism.* New York: Citadel Press, 1967.

Sartre, J-P. Foreword to R. Laing & D. Cooper. *Reason and violence.* New York.: Vintage Books, 1971.

Schachter, S. Cognitive effects on bodily functioning. In D. Glass (Ed.). *Biology and behavior: Neurophysiology and emotion.* New York: Rockefeller University Press, 1967.

Shepard, M. & Lee, M. *Games analysts play.* New York: G.P. Putnam's Sons, 1970.

Simkin, J. Mary: A session with a passive patient. In J. Fagan & I. Shepherd (Eds.). *Gestalt therapy now.* Palo Alto, Calif.: Science and Behavior Books, 1970.

Singer, E. *Key concepts in psychotherapy.* New York: Random House, 1965.

Singer, E. The patient aids the analyst. In B. Landis & E. Tauber (Eds.). *In the name of life.* New York: Holt, Rinehart, & Winston, 1971.

Singer, E. Frommian therapy. In A. Bry (Ed.). *Inside psychotherapy.* New York: Basic Books, 1972.

Skinner, B.F. *Science and human behavior.* New York: Macmillan, 1953.

Skinner, B.F. *Beyond freedom and dignity.* New York: Alfred A. Knopf, 1971.

Skinner, B.F. *About behaviorism.* New York: Alfred A. Knopf, 1974.

Snow, C.P. *Variety of men.* New York: Charles Scribner's Sons, 1967.

Spiegelman, J. *Transference, individuation, mutual process.* Paper presented for the C.G. Jung Club of San Diego, Calif., April 14, 1972.

Spielberger, C. & DeNike, L. Descriptive behaviorism versus cognitive theory in verbal operant conditioning. *Psychological Review.* 1966, *73,* 306-26.

Stein, R. *Incest and human love: The betrayal of the soul in psychotherapy.* New York: The Third Press, 1973.

Steinzor, B. *The healing partnership.* New York: Harper & Row, 1967.

Stent, G. Limits to the scientific understanding of man. *Science.* 1975, *187,* 1052-57.

Storr, A. The concept of cure. In C. Rycroft (Ed.). *Psychoanalysis observed.* Baltimore, Md.: Penguin Books, 1968.

Strupp, H. Psychoanalytic therapy of the individual. In J. Marmor (Ed.). *Modern psychoanalysis.* New York: Basic Books, 1968.

Sullivan, H.S. *Conceptions of modern psychiatry.* New York: W.W. Norton, 1941.

Szasz, T. *The myth of mental illness.* New York: Hoeber, 1961.

Tillich, P. Existentialism and psychotherapy. *Review of Existential Psychology and Psychiatry.* 1961, *1,* 8-16.

Toulmin, S. *The philosophy of science.* New York: Harper & Row, 1953.

Trilling, L. Authenticity and the modern unconscious. *Commentary.* 1971, *52,* 39-50.

Truax, C. & Carkhuff, R. *Toward effective counseling and psychotherapy.* Chicago: Aldine-Atherton, 1967.

Underwood, B. The representativeness of rote verbal learning. In A. Melton (Ed.). *Categories of human learning.* New York: Academic Press, 1964, 47-78.

van den Berg, J. *The changing nature of man.* New York: W.W. Norton, 1961.

van den Berg, J. *A different existence.* Pittsburgh, Pa.: Duquesne University Press, 1972.

Walker, E. & Heyns, R. *An anatomy for conformity.* Belmont, Calif.: Brooks/Cole, 1962.

Watzlawick, P., Beavin, J., & Jackson, D. *Pragmatics of human communication.* New York: W.W. Norton, 1967.

Weisskopf-Joelson, E. The present crisis in psychotherapy. *Journal of Psychology.* 1968, *69,* 107-15.

Wheelis, A. *The quest for identity.* New York: W.W. Norton, 1958.

Wheelis, A. How people change. *Commentary.* 1969, *47,* 56-66.

Wheelis, A. *The desert.* New York: Basic Books, 1970.

Wheelis, A. *The end of the modern age.* New York: Basic Books, 1971.

Whitehead, A.N. *Science and the modern world.* New York: Macmillan, 1925.

Whitehead, A.N. *Modes of thought.* New York: Macmillan, 1938.

Wild, J. *Existence and the world of freedom.* Englewood Cliffs, N.J.: Prentice-Hall, 1963.

Wolman, B. (Ed.). *Handbook of general psychology.* Englewood Cliffs, N.J.: Prentice-Hall, 1973.

Yankelovich, D. & Barrett, W. *Ego and instinct.* New York: Random House, 1970.

Yates, A. *Behavior therapy.* New York: John Wiley & Sons, 1970.

Yontef, G. *A review of the practice of Gestalt therapy.* Los Angeles: Trident Shop, 1971.

Zimbardo, P. *The cognitive control of motivation.* Glenview, Ill.: Scott, Foresman, 1969a.

Zimbardo, P. The human choice. In W. Arnold & D. Levine (Eds.). *Nebraska symposium on motivation.* Lincoln: University of Nebraska Press, 1969b.

Zimbardo, P., Cohen, A., Weisenberg, M., Dworkin, L., & Firestone, I. Control of pain motivation by cognitive dissonance. *Science.* 1966, *151,* 217-19.

Zimbardo, P. & Ebbesen, E. *Influencing attitudes and changing behavior.* Reading, Mass.: Addison-Wesley, 1969.

Zimbardo, P. & Montgomery, K. The relative strengths of consummatory responses in hunger, thirst, and exploratory drives. *Journal of Comparative Physiological Psychology.* 1957, *50,* 504-8.

Ziskin, J. *Coping with psychiatric and psychological testimony.* Los Angeles: Law and Psychology Press, 1975.

Appendix
Two Issues: Therapy and Counseling;
Diagnosis and Treatment

There are two issues upon which the HE psychotherapist takes a very definite and different stand from his contemporary colleague in the field: the difference between counseling and psychotherapy, and the use of diagnostic labels and the assessment procedures underlying them. As with most other things, I believe that these issues bear upon the central way in which persons are viewed, and thus must be considered in a manner that transcends mere utility or facility of intraprofessional communication. They are, ultimately, issues in the philosophy that underlies one's conception of what man is, what psychopathology is, and what therapy is.

In their monumental book, Yankelovich and Barrett (1970) clearly state that the basic problem in psychological therapeutics is a philosophical one (and I recall that Bugental, 1967, agrees). They further allude to the issue in psychology that calls for more adequate scientific means—better tests, better experiments, better methods:

> The problem is not a matter of inadequate means. That is to say, more of the same will not solve it. . . . [More adequate means] would only heighten the contrast between data and truth, information and understanding. *The problem is ultimately philosophical and lies in our basic ideas and grasp of the material* [emphasis supplied]. Science, where it touches upon the human world, is not at all points congruent with the latter, and at some points may be violently out of touch. The scientific study of man does not yet draw close to ordinary human experience (Yankelovich and Barrett, 1970, p. 8).

The philosophical underlay of the issues raised in the following pages probes the manner in which attempts to make a science (i.e., a quantifiable measurable or well-defined event) out of the interhuman, existential events born of human experience may contribute to a bifurcated view of nature[1] and, more importantly and immediately, to a bifurcated or divided view of the self on the part of the person who is presenting a human plea to another human whom he has chosen as his therapist.

---

[1]This is a phrase noted by Whitehead (1925, 1938) when he spoke of the gulf between personal experience (as of warmth, for instance) and the causal explanation (agitation of molecules of matter) of that experience—essentially that view of appearance and reality that assigns secondary qualities such as warmth and color to subjective experience and assigns primary qualities to the sphere of the physical.

THERAPY AND COUNSELING

It should be stated at the outset that I do not believe there is a serious distinction to be made between counseling and psychotherapy. I agree with Patterson (1966), and Arbuckle (1970, 1975) who conclude that there are no significant differences between counseling and psychotherapy as they are viewed along traditionally addressed dimensions: the quality or nature of the relationship between the helper and the person who comes to him; the nature of the process, the methods, and the techniques used; the goals or outcomes sought; and the classification of persons who seek counseling or therapeutic help.

Yet there does seem to be a subtle difference between the work of the counselor and the work of the psychotherapist. I believe that the difference is a function of the way in which we have been accustomed to categorize, label, and think about persons in terms of their psychological processes. One example here is the concept of depth. Much of current psychiatric and analytic thinking is based on the medical model that employs a hydraulic view of man in which some processes are "deeper" (that is, deeper in the unconscious) than others. In a Jungian context for example, the personal unconscious, symbolic meanings and the person's psychological complexes would not be considered as deep as the collective unconscious with its origin in total human evolutionary experience. Consequently, material interpreted by the therapist as being archetypal or suprapersonal would be deeper than complexes alone.

Similarly, primary process material arrived at by analysis of person's resistance within psychoanalysis would be considered deep, while ego or character analysis may not be considered as deep. In the Freudian sense, a deep interpretation is one that addresses itself to unconscious infantile conflicts. A less deep approach (as in Freudian-based counseling) would be:

> ... concerned rather with the way in which these conflicts appear in conscious or preconscious actions. Psychological counseling [as opposed to psycho-therapy or analysis] attempts to bring to awareness those aspects of infantile conflicts which are already close to awareness and are not deeply threatening to the ego.... Although the counselor makes use of transference elements in his client's reactions, unlike the analyst, he does not encourage an intense, con-suming transference reaction. He may make use of positive transference, but does relatively little interpreting of it (Bordin, 1968, p. 120).

The concept of depth, of course, is intimately entwined with the image of man held by a psychological theory. For instance, the HE therapist (thera-pist being the generic term for how the HE engages the person who comes to him for help) does not think of persons in hydraulic terms. He does not divide psychological functioning into various portions such as conscious and unconscious or ego, id, and superego. For the HE, man is unity and there are no parts of him that are not immediately or proximally available for inspection. Consequently, the term depth may not exist or has a very different meaning in the HE framework. In a sense, dealing with deep material in an HE frame may be thought of as dealing with those very basic ways in which the person engages and structures his world. But the *evidence* of a person's projects is everywhere. He expresses the projects in everything he does, although mainly the evidence is in how he conceives of his relation to freedom and his authentic position in explicitly knowing (uttering-and-facing) the way that he in fact *is* (there is no fixity intended here) and how he may live in bad faith by denying his intentions and the positive and negative consequences of the acts that are based on his intentions. In short, it is not so much that there is a difference between counseling and psychotherapy, as there are differences among psychotherapeutic schools, approaches, theories, and philosophies.

Arbuckle aptly summarizes the position that I hold:

> While there may be a logical difference between intellectual guidance with a person whose stresses and strains do not control his actions, and counseling with an individual whose actions are dominated by and subject to his emotional stresses, there is no such differentiation between counseling and psychotherapy (1970, pp. 260-61).

THE MEDICAL MODEL, DIAGNOSIS AND ASSESSMENT

Closely related to the difference between counseling and therapy is the question of psychological diagnosis and assessment. Testing, measuring, assessing, and diagnosis have been traditional activities of counselors and therapists and are central to the psychiatric profession where differential diagnosis (whether meaningful or valid) may lead to specific differences in treatment strategies (Hoch, 1972).[2] Many therapists have generally adopted the medical, disease-model and have unquestionably accepted the need for diagnosis or evaluation (often called assessment). These therapists operate upon the assumption that effective therapeutic intervention cannot occur without such diagnosis or without the testing to support a diagnosis.

For the HE therapist, testing or assessment violates the person's deep subjectivity in that he becomes an object both to himself and to another. The person who is a client or a patient is rarely without his own judge or self-evaluator present with him in all relationships and activities. Such self-observation robs the person's spontaneity, self-trust, genuine awareness, and action. In fact, persons often come to therapists just because they

---

[2]There is no need here to burden the argument with the concept of diagnosis in medicine. The physician simply has to know which bone is broken in order to set it, or whether there is fever in connection with a sore throat in order to know whether there is bacterial or viral infection and then, upon inspection, tests, thermometer readings, etc., whether to prescribe antibiotics or not.

cannot "let themselves be." The image of who one "should" be and the constant comparison or rating game between oneself and others, between oneself and the ideal image of what one should be constitutes an ongoing self-objectification.[3] By participating in the objectification process, the diagnostician-assessor-evaluator-therapist does two things at once: (a) he infuses the ensickening act with value by the metacommunication that people, and particularly the patient, are appropriate objects for evaluation or assessment;[4] and (b) joins with the person's ongoing self-objectification that has brought that person to the consulting room in the first place.

In discussing the philosophical basis for the enterprise of classification, Leary (1970) reminds us that the whole process has its roots in a dynamic psychology built upon a scientific philosophy that is outdated, "ineffective, one-sided, and in terms of human values—dangerous." This outmoded philosophy is nondialectic in conception. It is "impersonal, abstract, static, externalized, control-oriented [and based upon] a conception of nineteenth-century physics that led man to classify the elements and processes of a depersonalized subject matter and to determine the general laws which governed these elements and processes" (p. 211).

The HE prefers to see the question of diagnosis and assessment in this way: what is it that the person thinks he needs to know that he already does not know or cannot know by careful attention to his life; and secondly, what does it signify that the person *asks another* for knowledge about his own psychological functioning?[5] When a client asks, "How sick am I?" what does that imply? The HE looks at the question being asked in the first place and begins to interact immediately with the questioner. On what basis does he see himself as "sick," and what does it mean about the degree of his sickness (as if there were really a scale somewhere). Of central interest is the way in which that person sees human reality and his reality in particular, and how that leads him to think in such categories about himself:

> Whether the therapist knows it or not, through his behavior he constantly defines and redefines himself to the patient, whether by acts of commission or of omission. What the therapist pays attention to and what he seems less interested in; what questions he asks and what questions he does not ask; whether he asks any questions at all are only some of the indicators which are

---

[3]This is what Karen Horney (1936, 1950) called the "Tyranny of the Should."

[4]Here we are following a model of man and of the scientific enterprise as it applies to man that is essentially nondialectic (Cooper, 1967; Chein, 1972; and Esterson, 1972).

[5]We put aside, for the moment, the issue of what an *institution* may wish to know about a person—a prediction as to his performance in that institution, and whether that is an appropriate task for a therapist or counselor. "Evaluation, however, is a legitimate activity for the counselor as long as he does not attempt to evaluate the person with whom he has had a counseling relationship," says Lewis (1970, p. 133). In this mode, the person is not acting as a therapist or counselor, but as an evaluating agent of the institution of which he is a representative; he is not an agent of the person. I question that use of counselors or therapists.

communicated and make for the therapist's definition in the eyes of the patient.... From the very beginning the patient's statements and his reactions to the therapist's responses to him have diagnostic and therefore...therapeutic value. Inevitably, and for better or worse, therapy starts from the earliest moments of the patient-therapist encounter (Singer, 1965, p. 135).

ABOUT TESTS

I have already commented on the general concept of evaluation or assessment in the therapeutic process. However, the ideal of a nonjudgmental or nonevaluative, nonobjectifying position in therapy—as in life—is difficult or perhaps impossible to achieve. The HE strives for equality, reciprocity, and symmetry by the very process of addressing himself constantly to the issue and dilemma of a nonviolating exchange between the persons involved—to the issue of power, influence, and objectification. The therapist focuses primarily on establishing a mutual process and a symmetrical encounter with the client. He strives for a way of being with another that minimizes a critical, or even subtly superior, "more knowing" position. Indeed, that issue may be the central concern of therapy because the essentially ensickening acts are seen in terms of interpersonal violations against which the person defends himself by various maneuvers, holding on to images and hopes that, despite massive disconfirmations, will help him regain and retain a semblance of integrity and authenticity. The person who is disturbed does the best he can, in light of violating circumstances, to maintain his selfhood.

The first and most common argument in support of the use of testing instruments in the therapeutic process or the counseling process is that the therapist needs to have certain information about the client in order to treat him—information that the client does not have and cannot have (since it may be unconscious). I have already addressed that question in the preceding section.

Another argument in support of testing is that the client lacks and must have certain information about himself in order to promote self-understanding. But if tests promote self-understanding at all, they do so only by comparing a person to others.

The HE therapist's goal is for the person to confront the essential projects and his personal myth in a responsible manner—responsible within the context of his own (and owned) willingness to achieve, let us say, or not achieve. Within limits, academic achievement, for example, is dependent not on IQ alone, but on the so-called "nonintellective factors," such as what the person is willing to do. What is central is how he sees studying, intellectual achievement, work or a profession in relation to his basic commitments and personal myth.

The concept of under- or overachievement is empty for the HE since he

believes that a person essentially does only what he wants or is willing to
do. Consequently, to say that a person is not achieving at his potential is
nonsense—who knows of what we are capable under the right conditions?
Who works "at his peak" and, indeed, what is "peak?"

The following excerpt addresses this issue:

Juanita: They (the school vice-principal) said I had to come here and talk to
             you or I'd get kicked out or suspended or something.

Clor: Does that sound so bad to you?

Juanita: Yeah, man, I don't want that, all my friends are here. Oh, yeah. I
             see, the reason you're here is to get Mr. B. off your back so that you
             can stay with your friends. Hey, that sounds like as good a reason as
             any for coming here, what would you like to do with the time? I've
             got quite a bit of it left yet. You could just stay in that chair, read
             your book, or walk around, or whatever.

Juanita: I don't know, I guess you're supposed to talk to us kids about our
             problems.

Clor: I don't know about what I'm *supposed* to do; but as for you, you
             don't sound as if there is any problem.

Juanita: Shoot. (silence) Cheez. (quietly and hesitantly) I'm not doing so hot
             in classes. My home-room teacher always tells me I'm not doing
             what I could do.

Clor: Is that true?

Juanita: Yeah.

Clor: Well, all that means to me is that you could, if you wanted to, do
             better. Evidently for some good reason you don't seem to want to,
             so I don't see any problem there. Look, if you wanted to make better
             grades you would, wouldn't you?

Juanita: But the teacher's always saying you should work up to your ca-
             pacity, to do the best you could.

Clor: Wow! Who works up to his full capacity? I don't. I don't even know
             what that is.

Juanita: Well, I do want to graduate and go to J.C., and if I don't make the
             grades, I can't go.

Clor: Well, what I hear there is that there are some advantages to your
             making good grades, but if you don't elect to study and really dig
             in school, you must have some very good reasons for that. Doing
             something else, not studying, seems more important to you than
             getting the advantages of studying and getting grades. Hey, what are
             those advantages—I mean of not studying. If you're interested, we
             could talk about that (Rios and Ofman, 1972, pp. 260-61).

The HE therapist holds no necessary brief for socially utilitarian and col-
lectively accepted goals. He is not necessarily an agent of the institutional
process (Wheelis, 1958; Ofman, 1967). Rather, the therapist stands for the
process based on the assumption of individual responsibility and authentic
interpersonal relating.

While there are numerous exceptions, too many of the counselors and of the teachers who send students to them still cling to the idea that successful adjustment to the established order is the desired goal.... If, as so often happens these days, the student's problem... stems from bewilderment at what seems to be our human condition and from hostility toward contemporary society, he will rightly resent being told that adjustment to what he has rejected is the only solution. In the eyes of those who are rebellious as well as unhappy, the counselor is often the epitome of the flat mediocrity against which they are revolting. The [therapist]... who has never seriously questioned either the authenticity or the philosophical foundations of his own life is ill equipped to meet this new kind of challenge. He is tempted to see it as merely a surface symptom of the "deeper," more familiar conflicts which he is used to treating, e.g., resistance against parental authority or sibling rivalry, or an Oedipus complex... God is dead, but don't worry. The psychiatrist is in charge and will see you at eleven (Barnes, 1967, pp. 313-14).

Arbuckle (1970, 1975) points out that a serious distinction might be made between the person who seeks further information about himself in the way of test data so that he can compare himself with others as to IQ, interests, or aptitudes (though I question that activity as its base) and the student who feels a modicum of self-ambiguity, or stress and who sees tests and their results as the answer to his problem. The former student, Arbuckle states, needs guidance (though I question even that position) while the second student seeks counseling, and rarely does information, even valid information presented in a cognitive mode, help the person come into authentic existence.

We have enough difficulty in therapy addressing ourselves to only whatever aspect of a person is represented in *that hour* (though in a deeper sense, all of him *is* represented there) without doing further violence to the interaction by partialing the person into test scores or scales, into ego, adult, intellective, or conative functions. That partialing and categorizing of the already divided self-view that most clients have is merely a continuation of the violence from which the person suffers. That violence consists in objectifying the person by labeling him. When we elect to parcel man into components for testing, measuring, and study, we ignore the totally interdependent aspect of a person. That is, his commitment to ever transcending and mutually modifying long-range projects that have immediate positive and negative implications. Nor are the modern testers immune from our criticism.

In general, the use of tests brings with it overwhelmingly negative aspects. Basically, testing interferes with the genuine encounter with the person "there," it places the therapist in a superior position; it reinforces a view of man that is antithetical to an existential view; it increases and reinforces the message that only a scientist Other can know the person; and it abets the "segmented man" view redolent in therapeutic circles and held by the person who is a client (Bannister and Fransella, 1971). Perhaps the most serious constraint is the price paid for not facing the issue of man's ambiguous, uncertain condition. The HE believes it does violence to help people hope that answers to life exist, but that we keep them secret.

> The patient or subject should be seen and treated not as a passive thing to be done to, but as the equal of the psychologist in the collaborative research. The patient, after all, is the world's leading authority on the issue at hand—his own life and the transactions in which he is involved. Here I am urging *phenomenological equality....* I now come to the inevitable and unmistakable criterion of unreality and depersonalization on the part of the psychologist: *secrecy.* Although psychologists regularly claim to hold no secrets, although we are committed to the open society, although we say that the patient must help himself and work out his own solutions—in reality, we act as though there are secrets. Most of our psychometric, clinical and institutional machinery is set up on the basis of secrecy. Our professional identity is tied to the mysterious, based on the practice of keeping information from the subject. But let us look at this secrecy in the cold light of the following reality. We are, after all, dealing with human beings. We cannot treat human beings objectively, i.e., as objects, without eliciting exactly the same reactions. If we depersonalize patients, rest assured, they will depersonalize us back. If we keep secrets from them, rest assured they will keep secrets from us (Leary, 1970, p. 213).

I end this discussion of tests, assessment, information, and evaluation with a corollary to the issue of secrecy, and this has to do with a concern of HE therapists: that of duplicity. And in this context, let us extend the dialogue that has taken place in psychology about the use (or misuse) of persons in psychological experiments where persons are lied to with malice aforethought about the nature of the investigative or experimental process. Without going into the ethical problem involved in such a use of persons, I believe that persons ought to have freedom of choice in terms of responding to psychological instruments—that freedom is possible only when the person knows what the instrument is asking of him or testing him about. But as Raymond Cattell (in *Psychology Today,* July 1973) implies, the modern psychological test is difficult to fake or to see through because it is a subtle test. And Cronbach (1960) states that "any test is an invasion of privacy for the subject who does not wish to reveal himself to the psychologist" (p. 459). Yet what is it that the person is going to reveal (or not reveal) if he or she does not know to what the questions on the test refer? Typically, when a person takes an MMPI, he does not know—indeed, cannot know—that certain items are related to a particular diagnostic category. It is equally so with such innocuous tests as the Strong Vocational Interest Blank:

> The empirically scored test can be used for purposes the subject never suspects. The Strong ostensibly assesses vocational interests, but one scoring key combines those items which men answer differently from women into a "masculinity-femininity" score. It is presumably possible to distinguish communists from noncommunists, or girls who are likely to marry and stop working from

those who are likely to remain in an occupation. The inventory could likewise be keyed to distinguish juvenile delinquents from nondelinquents, or potential suicides from nonsuicides. The basic principle is that any group which differs on one psychological quality differs on other qualities. Reports on some of these qualities are likely to be falsified to gain social approval. The remaining qualities, which carry no connotation of approval or disapproval, permit valid indirect measurements. Actuarial scoring is by no means certain to eliminate distortions, as the faking studies on the Strong blank show. Basing the scoring weights on empirical connections makes it more difficult for the subject to guess what significance will be attached to his statement that, for example, he likes to read the *Geographic* (Cronbach, 1960, pp. 457-58).

This kind of situation is certainly cause for suspicion and resistance on the part of the person. In my view, a person has an absolute right—for any purposes whatever—to dissemble or not choose to reveal himself to an unknown evaluator or psychological worker.

Aside from the fact that many psychological tests or instruments are of tenuous validity, my basic objection is to the very factor of which Cronbach and Cattell are proud: to their subtle, covert, and duplicitous nature of tests. When a person is asked to take the IPAT Humor test, for instance, or the IPAT Music Preference Test of Personality, he sees relatively benign tasks such as rating jokes as funny or not, or evaluating certain piano excerpts. But taken together, these two tests yield many personality scores which, to the test-taker, *seem* unrelated to the task of the test.

It becomes increasingly clear, then, that insofar as "objective" personality tests that are factorially or actuarily scored are concerned, the person's freedom is truncated through deception or, at best, subtlety. The person who takes the test is deceived into revealing more of himself than he may choose to reveal were he only to know what is involved. Such a deception is, in HE terms, a clear violation.